FAITHFULLY
SEEKING
FRANZ

ESSENTIAL ESSAYS 82

Canada Council **Conseil des Arts**
for the Arts **du Canada**

ONTARIO ARTS COUNCIL
CONSEIL DES ARTS DE L'ONTARIO

an Ontario government agency
un organisme du gouvernement de l'Ont

Canadä

Guernica Editions Inc. acknowledges the support of the Canada Council
for the Arts and the Ontario Arts Council. The Ontario Arts Council
is an agency of the Government of Ontario.

We acknowledge the financial support of the Government of Canada.

ELANA WOLFF

FAITHFULLY SEEKING FRANZ

GUERNICA
EDITIONS

TORONTO—CHICAGO—BUFFALO—LANCASTER (U.K.)

2023

Guernica Founder: Antonio D'Alfonso

Michael Mirolla, general editor
Julie Roorda, editor
Interior and cover design: Errol F. Richardson
Interior photos: Elana Wolff

Guernica Editions Inc.
287 Templemead Drive, Hamilton, ON L8W 2W4
2250 Military Road, Tonawanda, N.Y. 14150-6000 U.S.A.
www.guernicaeditions.com

Distributors:
Independent Publishers Group (IPG)
600 North Pulaski Road, Chicago IL 60624
University of Toronto Press Distribution (UTP)
5201 Dufferin Street, Toronto (ON), Canada M3H 5T8

First edition.
Printed in Canada.

Legal Deposit—Third Quarter
Library of Congress Catalog Card Number: 2023937046
Library and Archives Canada Cataloguing in Publication
Title: Faithfully seeking Franz / Elana Wolff.
Names: Wolff, Elana, author.
Series: Essential essays series ; 82.
Description: 1st edition. | Series statement: Essential essays ; 82 | Includes bibliographical references.
Identifiers: Canadiana (print) 2023023741X | Canadiana (ebook) 20230237428 | ISBN 9781771838207 (softcover) | ISBN 9781771838214 (EPUB)
Subjects: LCGFT: Essays.
Classification: LCC PS8595.O5924 F35 2023 | DDC C814/.54—dc23

To the Readers

Itinerary

1. Before the Door
2. Kafka's Death House
3. At the Cemetery
4. Paging Kafka's Elegist
5. Kafka-in-Between
6. Resurrecting Frank's Foot
7. Two Short Talks
8. Weisser Hirsch
9. What More Is There to Say of Hearts
10. Back at the Office
11. In Berlin
12. K.
13. At Marienbad
14. So Good at This
15. Mary Lou Paints the Little House on Her iPad
16. Franz Among the Animals
17. Ottla
18. Surfacing Behaviour Váňovský Pond, Třešt, Czech Republic
19. The Mammoth Village & Gmünd
20. Snapshots from Pension Stüdl
21. Sanatorium Hartungen, Riva del Garda
22. Merano, 1920 / 2019

23. Concatenations: Hotel Gabrielli-Sandwirth, 1913 / 2019
24. Tacitly / Translating
25. Franz of the Magic
26. At Planá
27. Graal-Müritz
28. A Circle
29. Trumpeldor Cemetery, Tel Aviv
30. Rereading "Conversation with the Supplicant" in the Pandemic
31. Notes on Questing
32. On Translation
33. K. Under Erasure
34. Later
35. On Falster
36. Josef K.'s Mother Submits Her Report on the Trial
37. Concern for Soul Consumes Me

Notes
Key Dates in Franz Kafka's Life
Acknowledgements
Sources
About the Author

"I believe in the power of places ... perhaps I'm not allowed to remain too long in one place. There are people who can acquire a sense of home only when they are travelling."
—**Franz Kafka,** *Letter to Robert Klopstock*
from Müritz, Germany, July 24, 1923

"... since our apparitions, the part of us which appears, are so momentary compared with the other, the unseen part of us, which spreads wide, the unseen might survive, be recovered somehow attached to this person or that, or even haunting certain places, after death. Perhaps."
—**Virginia Woolf,** *Mrs. Dalloway*

"His books are amazing. He himself is far more amazing."
—**Milena Jesenská,** *Letter to Max Brod, August 1920*

"A thing in motion will always be better than a thing at rest."
—**Olga Tokarczuk,** *Flights*

Before the Door

In a story of parameters, a man from the country
comes to a door that's guarded by a keeper.

The keeper is a cog in the wheel, the countryman—
let's say—is free. The keeper has a furry-collared

coat, a set of rules: He can't permit the man
to enter now, though maybe later.

(Isn't "later" the rub …)
Mindset or anticipation bring the man to wait for days,

until the days are years.
Had he had imagination—just a smidgen's whit—

he might have walked away.
Had he been a fighting man,

he might have dared the keeper to a duel.
Had the keeper not had rules,

he wouldn't have known the power to retain.
As it is, he gets to keep his watch, the furry-

collared coat. Even as the fleas in it increase,
the keeper doesn't flinch; he doesn't have to stoop

at all to conquer. The free man
wearies over time, his sight and hearing

fail. Still, he waits before the door, until his end
is nearing. Finally, the keeper slaps the onus

reach our destination, so to speak, once we arrived. I hadn't found information regarding contacts, opening hours, tours, etc., and was counting on momentum.

The bus ride ended at Klosterneuburg where the spires of the medieval abbey rose into a misty void over the town—summoning images of the castle of Count Westwest in Kafka's unfinished, posthumously published third and last novel, *The Castle* (*Das Schloss*). We walked across the street to *Buchhandlung John Doran* where I figured someone would be able to direct us to the *Sterbehaus* in Kierling.

The woman at the counter spoke a clear, clipped English. "We don't often get people coming into the bookstore asking about the Kafka Museum. You are only about the third and fourth in twenty years," she said quite seriously. "The person you want is Herr Winkler, Secretary of the Kafka Society." She happened to have Herr Winkler's phone number in her Rolodex, and called him for us on the spot. "There are two people here from Canada who have come to visit the Kafka Memorial Room (*Gedenkraum*)," she announced into the receiver. It was midmorning and we'd apparently disturbed Herr Winkler's sleep. But he agreed to meet us—in front of the Hofer. "He will be there in twenty minutes," the woman told us. We browsed the bookstore quickly, purchased two books by way of appreciation, hailed a cab to Kierling, and arrived at the Hofer in under twenty.

The Hofer is a supermarket next to the former Hoffmann Sanatorium—now a residential building. A man in a red and black jacket pulled in to the car park a few minutes after we arrived, sprang out of his car, hastened toward us extinguishing his cigarette, and introduced himself as Winkler, Norbert—no longer Secretary of the Kafka Society of Austria, but still on call for tours at the Kafka Memorial Room. He led us next door to the staid three-storey building—its narrow entrance located oddly at the far right. A plaque to the left of the entrance identified the building as the *Sterbehaus* of Franz Kafka, and on the intercom panel: the names of the present residents. Barghouty, a prominent Palestinian surname, I noticed, appeared twice.

We followed Herr Winkler up the stairs. He unlocked the door to apartment 6—the Kafka Memorial Room. "This is not the room where Kafka stayed," Herr Winkler informed us. "Tenants occupy that space now. But the balcony where Kafka sat can be viewed from the Hofer car park."

Kafka spent seven weeks at the Hoffmann Sanatorium—from April 19, 1924 till his death. Sunshine was prescribed for TB patients and, weather permitting, he would sit shirtless on the balcony, gazing at the garden below and into the firs and pines of the Vienna Woods—the *Wiener Wald*—beyond.

He was in the countryside, attended to around-the-clock by Robert Klopstock and Dora Diamant—whose hand he'd asked in marriage, probably at the end of April, when hope of remission was buoyed by spring weather, country quiet, fresh fruit, and the scent of cut flowers. Lilacs, peonies and columbine are named on the 'conversation slips'. "Can't laburnum be found?" he wrote on one of the slips. Laburnum is a flowering shrub with bright yellow flowers. One wonders if he was aware that all parts of the plant are poisonous.

The Memorial Room was stark: medical records and death registers displayed in glass cases, alongside instruments once used in treating TB; copies of Kafka's last letters to his parents, a family tree, photos of Kafka, Klopstock, Dora and others mounted on the high walls, historical photos of the sanatorium, a few chairs, a table, a guest book—which I signed—and a bookcase of books by and about the author. No original furnishings, nothing personal. I suppose I'd vaguely expected to see the actual room Kafka had slept in, preserved as it had been when he took his last breath; to feel something there of his presence.

Herr Winkler showed us down the hall—to the original elevator, no longer in operation, which Kafka would have used on arrival and departure. The old apparatus reportedly made a huge racket and drained the village's electrical reserves, so that flickering lights in the surrounding houses announced every use of the elevator on arrivals and departures at the Hoffmann Sanatorium. We walked back down the stairs and out, to view the rear of the building and the balcony on the second floor where Kafka sat and viewed the *Wiener Wald* trees—evergreens in the distance.

Herr Winkler offered us a lift back to Klosterneuburg, apologizing for the state of his car; he'd been transporting his girlfriend's dogs. We thanked him for his generosity, but neglected to give him a tip, which struck me as soon as we boarded the bus back to Heiligenstadt Station. This oversight—which needles me whenever I think of it—can only be explained, though not excused, by our absorption in the day's extraordinary unfolding: how we'd been carried by some fortuitous momentum to entering the place where Kafka had languished and passed.

There's no scoop to offer on Franz Kafka. He died at noon on June 3 after begging morphine from Robert Klopstock. "Kill me," he's said to have commanded his friend, "or you're a murderer." Klopstock administered the morphine. He'd sent Dora on an errand so that she wouldn't be present at the time of the final ministrations. She returned with flowers, and Franz, it's told, inhaled their scent as he succumbed in her arms.

What happened between that hour and the hour of his burial on June 11 at the New Jewish Cemetery in Prague-Strašnice is only sketchily on record. Jewish funerals are normally held as soon after death as possible—within a day or two at most. Kafka was buried eight days after his death, and one wonders, why the delay? He'd lived much of his life resisting life and a certain recalcitrance seems to have attended his last passage as well. The great astronomical clock in Prague's Old Town Square is said to have stopped still on June 11 at 4 p.m.—precisely at the time of his interment.

At the Cemetery

I'VE BEEN TRACKING Franz Kafka—in places he lived, worked, sojourned, and convalesced. Hoping to locate traces.

The spark was kindled outside the walls of a Toronto high school (Kafka wasn't in the curriculum), in the pages of his quasi-Gothic novella, *The Metamorphosis*. It was the creaturely protagonist Gregor Samsa who first brought me to question what it means to be human. So unsettled was I by the story—dire for me from the first inimitable sentence—that reading would not be the same again.

In that well-worn Schocken edition (now held together with elastic bands), the opening sentence is translated: "As Gregor Samsa awoke one morning from uneasy dreams he found himself transformed in his bed into a gigantic insect." The physical metamorphosis (*Die Verwandlung*), from human being into bug has begun, and is announced, matter-of-factly off the top. But the narrative actually begins in *media res*. At the beginning of the story Gregor Samsa is not yet fully transformed. His form continues to alter, and the story unfolds his unhappy fate. The backstory—what led up to the initial transformation—is never more than slightly alluded to.

A vagueness is also maintained as to the kind of creature Gregor turns into. The family charwoman calls him "dung beetle," and he's often been depicted as a giant cockroach, but Kafka gave clear instructions to his publisher, Kurt Wolff, that the "ungeheueres Ungeziefer"—the enormous bug—not be shown in any way. Kafka evidently wanted readers to take up the task of imagining for themselves.

Some translators have rendered Kafka's term for the creature "monstrous vermin." "Monstrous," in the sense of grotesque and inhuman, is one of the meanings of "ungeheuer." It can also mean "tremendous," "immense," "huge," "formidable," colossal," and "dreadful." Kafka, a deliberate wordsmith, no doubt chose a descriptor that permits nuanced readings. Yet with hindsight on the deadliest of centuries, his choice has been read as signally prophetic. Reduced to the label "vermin" by the Nazi state, human beings were exterminated as pests, Kafka's three sisters among the millions.

Kafka had no lens on the extremities of World War Two, but he was intimately familiar with the rigidities and absurdities of the Austro-Hungarian legal, administrative, and educational systems. He was also prescient. He deeply understood that anyone perceived or labelled as different was a target for discrimination, or worse: dehumanization, expulsion, dis/solution. Gregor Samsa attempts desperately to contend with his difference from inside his carapace, to remain in the realm of the human family, until his physical transformation is complete. Inevitably, as vermin, he's jettisoned, even by those closest to him: his parents and his sister.

Franz Kafka, it might be said, reinvented Gothic horror as social sur/realism. Fear as a presence in itself becomes fear of being excised by society, even by one's own family. The Gothic paranormal becomes the terrifyingly real; the natural, stranger than the supernatural. Fear, dread, gloom and death—Gothic topics—are skewed and acquire anti-Romantic gravity in Kafka's cool, precise, implacable writing. The tyrannical father-figure (Kafka had lifelong father issues) appears in *The Metamorphosis* as a caricature—a blustering martinet who "refused to take off his uniform … with its many, many stains and its gold buttons radiant from constant polishing." Gregor assumes the dual role of tragic anti-hero and damsel-in-distress. 'De-formed', debased and emasculated, there's no one to save him, and he can't save himself.

Most of the action in *The Metamorphosis* takes place in the close quarters of the Samsa family apartment, not under a Gothic moon on a dark and stormy night. Yet the castle and the abbey—the architectural edifices from which Gothic literature takes its name—cast their shadows on the story's streets.

Kafka wrote *The Metamorphosis* in 1912. He was twenty-nine at the time, living with his family in the House "Zum Schiff" ("Of the Ship") at what was then 36 Niklas Street in Old Town Prague. This was one of the grand apartment buildings built in the razed area of the Jewish ghetto and the Kafkas rented a corner apartment on the fifth floor. The family had a panoramic view of the Moldau (Vltava) River and the Castle Quarter on Laurenziberg Hill (Petřín) on the other side of the river. The layout of the rooms in *The Metamorphosis*—as scholar Hartmut Binder has mapped—faithfully reproduces the layout of the Kafka apartment.

The "House of the Ship" was destroyed in 1945 at the end of the War, and the InterContinental Prague Hotel erected in its place in the 1970s, at what is now 30 Parížská Street. Outside and in, the hotel is a modernist block that preserves nothing of Old Town Prague. M. and I stayed in a corner room on the fifth floor of the hotel for one night in August 2017; I wanted to take in the same (or similar) view as Kafka and Samsa had, to gauge impressions.

***

Upon entering the room, I go straight to the window. The day is rainy. There's a gloomy pall over Castle Hill: over St. Vitus Cathedral and the Royal Gardens by Chotek Park (Chotkovy Sady)—Prague's first public park and one of Kafka's favourite walking spots; over the former Civilian Swimming Pool building—now a Thai restaurant—where Kafka spent hours swimming and rowing. I feel a ripple of sympathy— in seeing the grey river from this angle, and am reminded of a letter Kafka wrote to Felice Bauer in June 1913, describing this same vantage point: "As I look out of the window … I can see, just opposite, outside the swimming baths, a strange youth rowing around in my boat. (As a matter fact this is something I've seen almost every day for the past three weeks, since I cannot get myself to replace the missing chain.)"
This is the view that Kafka had, yes, and it's something to see. But I can't say that I feel anything of his presence at the InterContinental Hotel. It would seem that the apartment at the "House of the Ship" is adumbrated only in pages now—the spectre of the author perched somewhere above, like his grey-black avian namesake: 'kavka' in Czech means jackdaw—the smallest member of the crow family.

***

Crows and creatures of all kinds populate Kafka's work: dogs, horses, jackals, apes, mice, moles, goats, vermin … Creatures singing, shrieking, speaking, whistling, burrowing into themes key to their maker: the nature of power, alienation, the strange absurdities of modern life, disappointment, guilt, shame and death. Death as a major theme of the Gothic novel takes diverse forms. Death of a loved one, death of the unloved. Death as deterioration: broken buildings, ruined landscapes, rotting bones … the dried-up corpse of a "snuffed," "thin," "flat" protagonist—Gregor Samsa. Anything unknown. Death as the undead: the living dead.

In his enigmatic fragmentary story, "The Huntsman Gracchus" ("Der Jäger Gracchus"), Kafka takes up the trope of the living dead, the ever-wandering soul. After a fatal accident while pursuing a mountain goat on a hunt—centuries prior to events in the story—the huntsman still sails the earthly seas in his death-vessel. Something went awry in the post-death passage and he's permanently caught in transit, unable to sail away from the world of the living and unable to pass fully into the beyond.

"The Huntsman Gracchus" is one of only a few Kafka stories that names actual geographic settings: The Black Forest—where the fall occurs—and the port city of Riva on Lake Garda in northern Italy. This story has been taken to be self-referential—not only because Kafka vacationed in Riva in 1909 and 1913, and had there in 1913, a mysterious romantic encounter, but also because in Italian 'gracchio' (Gracchus) means grackle or jackdaw, like 'kavka' in Czech.

In a second, even more enigmatic fragment of the story, the wandering Gracchus tells the Mayor of Riva—that he (Gracchus) is "dead, dead, dead," yet remains a "guardian spirit … who receives prayers." "Don't laugh," Gracchus entreats the Mayor, and the latter replies, "Laugh? No, truly not."

***

The spectre of "The Huntsman Gracchus" returned to me with Gothic resonance on an earlier visit to Prague, in 2015. On an overcast Friday afternoon in November, M. and I ventured out to Kafka's resting place in the New Jewish Cemetery in Prague-Strašnice. We took the subway, for the experience; entered at Můstek Station, purchased two 90-minute tickets, descended the long escalator deep beneath the city, boarded the eastbound train and rode out to Želivského Station. The stone wall surrounding cemetery and the gilded Hebrew inscription above the entrance arch came into view as we ascended the stairs to the street: *Dust you are and to dust you return* (in Hebrew).

We entered at the main gate and stood before a Neo-Renaissance chapel, administrative buildings to our left and a rectangular, immaculately maintained bed of red roses to our right. The roses—oddly still in bloom in gloomy November—stood out against the backdrop of stone and foliage. There wasn't a soul in sight.

A sign on a pole by the roses directed us to Dr. Franz Kafka ➜ 250 M. (Dr. in recognition of Kafka's doctor of laws degree.) We followed the arrow along the gravel path parallel to the outside wall and came to a second sign: Dr. Franz Kafka ➜ 100 M.

Kafka's tombstone came into view as we approached it— photographs don't fully capture its grace: a tall grey hexagonal column, tapering to a pyramidal point. The inscription, obfuscated slightly by lichen, translated from the Hebrew, reads:

Dr. Franz Kafka
1883 - 1924
Tuesday, June 3, 1924, First day of Sivan, 5684 on the
Hebrew calendar
The glorious young man, Anschel, peace be upon him,
passed on
Son of the respected Mr. Hennich Kafka
And the name of his mother, Yettl
May his soul be bound up in eternal life

Kafka's parents, who outlived their son, are buried in the same plot. A memorial plaque for Franz's three younger sisters, Gabriele, Valerie, and Ottilie, all murdered in the death camps, rests at the base of the monument. Kafka's Jewish name, Anschel, from Asher in Hebrew — meaning happy—was after his maternal grandfather. Interestingly, Anschel (also written Amschel) is similar to Amsel, the German word for blackbird, which is similar to crow.

The gravestone stands in a square enclosure filled with pebbles and sundry offerings: wreaths, bouquets, small pots of hot-coloured fake flowers, votive candles and folded notes. It is Jewish custom to recite a prayer at the graveside and place stones on the gravestone to mark one's visit. But Kafka's monument is smooth and comes to a point at the top; it has no place for stones. M. recited the memorial prayer. I submitted my own silent request: *Franz, please give a sign.* I wanted to feel a personalized connection, to have a sense of his presence for us in this place. I also wanted to place a stone on the gravestone. I found a tiny pebble and managed to balance it at the top of the pyramidal point.

We left the plot—Area 21: Row: 14 Number: 21— and returned to the entrance. I admired the Neo-Renaissance chapel. It was locked so there was no viewing the interior. It would soon be dusk and we had to head back. As we turned to go, I heard something like a little laugh from above. I looked up. On top of one of the gate columns sat a compact black and grey bird.

"Look," I called out to M., pointing.

"I think it's a jackdaw!" he said. "A 'kavka'."

"It is a jackdaw," I exclaimed. "How amazing is that! I wasn't going to mention it, but I asked for a sign at the graveside, and here he is!"

M. knows something of the way my mind works: I'm sensitive to resemblances, synchronicities. Signs. They're confirmation of seeing, affirmation of meaning. Antonyms of randomness. Evidence of the outer world and one's inner world connecting. Sometimes the connections I perceive are weak, I have to admit. But in this case, the timing and likeness were just too right. The sudden appearance of this 'kavka' felt to me like a bona fide sign. A visitation.

The bird fluttered above us and landed in a leafless tree by the gate, sidled down to the end of a branch, close to where we were standing— his gaze fixed clearly on us. He tottered nearer and nearer, as if waiting to be engaged, deliberate as day. M. reached into his pocket.

"Look what I've got," he announced. "Peanuts!" (He just happened to have peanuts in his pocket from our side-trip to Marienbad a few days prior.) He tossed three nuts to the ground. The 'kavka' swooped down, gobbled two of them on the spot and ferried the third back up to the tree. He gave us the knowing eye, didn't utter another thing. For my part, the interaction was complete. I felt answered.

"That was pretty comical," M. said on the subway back into town.

"Comical," I replied, "*and* amazing. An actual acknowledgement from Franz."

We were silent for a while, then M. piped up:

"But what if that wasn't a jackdaw? What do we know what a 'kavka' actually looks like? Maybe that was a magpie ..."

"What does it matter," I said, annoyed at the literalness. And then, unwilling to surrender the revenant's presence: "They're all in the family: jackdaws, magpies, crows ... *grackles*."

Paging Kafka's Elegist

I FIRST MET Kafka's elegist in the pages of Kafka's diary: the entry for March 25, 1915. He was not then an elegist. He appeared, compressed to initials, as "L. the western Jew who assimilated to the Hasidim"—a branch of Judaism that holds mysticism and simple piety as fundamental to the faith. In the same entry, a few lines forward, he appeared again—as "G. in a caftan"; that is, G. in the long cloak of Hasidic garb. In Kafka's entry for March 25, he is both L. and G.—L. for Langer and G. for Georg. His full name, reflecting a complexity of identity, was Georg (Jiří) Mordechai (Dov) Langer: Georg for George in German; Jiří, the same in Czech; Mordechai in Hebrew; Dov, his second Hebrew name; and Langer—the family name. He used all five, depending on context.

Georg Mordechai Langer (1894-1943) is not a household name and I would not have known it, if not for my reading of Kafka. I was drawn to Kafka as a teen. First to *The Metamorphosis* (*Die Verwandlung*), then to *The Trial* (*Der Prozess*), both of which link to the year Kafka and Langer met and became friends. 1915 was the year *The Metamorphosis* was published. It was also the year *The Trial* was abandoned, unfinished—only to be released posthumously at the initiative of Kafka's and Langer's mutual friend, Max Brod (1884-1968). But this was not known to me at the time of my initial reading. I read Kafka uninitiated, on my own—without background information or the guidance of a teacher, mentor, classroom, or syllabus. Somehow, I was brought to Kafka, and became wrapped in his wry, maddening, precise yet parabolical world. His fictions were irresistible. They've proven to be inexhaustible also. One returns to Kafka, and reads him through the works of others. Though largely unknown at the time of his death, he has come to suffuse literature and art of the twentieth, and now the early twenty-first century as well.

A hundred years ago, when Kafka and Langer met, Kafka was not yet KAFKA. He was not yet thirty-one. His publication credits were few, his writing known only to a small group of discerning readers. But "there was no need of his works," wrote Max Brod in his 1937 volume,

Franz Kafka: A Biography, "the man produced his own effect, simply by virtue of his personality, his occasional remarks and his conversation. Despite all the shyness of his behaviour, he was always recognized by men of worth as someone out of the ordinary"—though his résumé outlines a man typical of his station and time. He achieved his law degree at Prague's Charles University and was employed for most of his working life as an insurance lawyer at the semi-governmental Worker's Accident Insurance Institute near Prague's Old Town—a few streets away from the Town Square where he was born, raised and schooled, and where his parents owned and ran a successful fancy goods store.

The literary fruit of Kafka's short life—lived for the most part within a taut two-mile radius—rankled me. I couldn't quite love it and couldn't give it up. I've dwelled in many places, let go of many books, but I still have the $5.95, 1976 Schocken paperback edition of *Kafka, The Complete Stories*—now bound with elastic bands—that I took on my first trip to Israel and read and reread during my gap year. Kafka—who never wrote the word Jew in his fiction—became part of my Jewish awakening. I felt the Jewishness in his catholic writing before I knew the fullness of it.

In 2010 I chose Franz Kafka as my subject for a final presentation-assignment in the Biography as Art course I was taking; Kafka was a natural choice. Throughout fall and winter and into spring of 2011, I pored over his oeuvre anew—the stories and novels; diaries, letters, and biographies—in search of threads and motifs in his lifeline, their metamorphoses through cycles and crises, a picture of how his life intentions were or were not met.

A key theme in Kafka's biography is the centrality of friendship to his literary development and posthumous acclaim. Particularly the uncommon friendship of Max Brod. The two came from the same assimilated German-Jewish, middle-class Prague background and met at Charles University—both aspiring writers, both studying law. They connected quickly over love of literature and argument. Early in their friendship Brod introduced Kafka to others who would also have an impact on his life and writing, including his muse and two-time fiancée Felice Bauer (1887-1960), whom he never married, his publisher Kurt Wolff (1887-1963); also Georg Mordechai Langer.

Brod encouraged and promoted Kafka throughout his lifetime and as his literary executor famously saved his friend's unpublished work from incineration, disavowing Kafka's will that everything—apart from the few published works—be burned unread. Instead, Brod negotiated and prepared for publication Kafka's three unfinished novels: *The Trial* (*Der Prozess*) in 1925, *The Castle* (*Das Schloss*) in 1926, and *Amerika* (*Der Verschollene*) in 1927. He secured his friend's manuscripts and advocated on behalf of his literary legacy. He edited and arranged publication of much of his private writing: the diaries, the great body of correspondence; also stories, sketches, reflections and meditations. No doubt, without the intercession and dedication of Max Brod, Kafka would not be known as he is today.

Brod was Georg Mordechai Langer's literary executor too. Max Brod had a life and post-death impact on both of his Prague friends. Georg Langer is threaded into a half-page of Brod's biography of Kafka: "I used to spend a lot of time, together with my cabalistic friend Georg Langer, at the house of a miracle-working rabbi, a refugee from Galicia who lived in dark, unfriendly, crowded rooms in the Prague suburb Žižkov. Unusual circumstances of life had brought me near to a kind of religious fanaticism … It is worthy of note that Franz, whom I took with me to a 'Third Meal' at the close of the Sabbath … remained, I must admit, very cool. He was undoubtedly moved by the age-old sounds of an ancient folk life, but … Franz had his own personal mysticism, he couldn't take over from others a ready-made ritual." This passage, likely drawn from Brod's own diary, parallels Kafka's diary entry recording the same Sabbath visit. Brod might have said more about Langer, more about Kafka and Langer … about the three-way friendship. He had what to say. But his slant on his Kafka's legacy was so specific, his focus on his best friend so close, that anything outside the aura of that aperture was not admitted. Brod's biography of Kafka has been criticized for crossing into hagiography.

Franz himself saw his own character as deeply, irredeemably flawed. He sought perfection in writing, but was harassed by intermittent self-loathing and lifelong hypochondria. He may have suffered from an anxiety disorder, perhaps clinical depression. Writing was a necessity, essential to his sense of being. And while providing a measure of pleasure, release, and consolation, his writing also records the struggle out of which it emerged. In this respect, he and Georg Langer were not unalike.

***

I did not include Langer in my June 2011 biography presentation of Kafka. The information I had at the time was insufficient. But a short entry I came across in *A Franz Kafka Encyclopedia*, stating that Langer's "importance in Kafka's life was largely overlooked," intrigued me. As did the reference in the *Encyclopedia* (and elsewhere) to an elegy for Kafka, written by Langer in Hebrew and published in a small collection at the Prague Jewish printing works in 1929. I was eager to find the book, and to know more about the Kafka-Langer connection. I began with a more thorough reading of Kafka's *Diaries and Letters*.

There are five references to Langer in the *Diaries*—four in 1915, one in 1920. The 1915 entries all cover Jewish topics: Langer the Hasid; the Sabbath visit with Langer and Max to the home of the Žižkov Rabbi; and excerpts of Langer's Hasidic stories. A one-line entry on October 1920 records a visit to Kafka at his parents' home—"first Langer, then Max." Kafka had been diagnosed with tuberculosis in the fall of 1917 and by fall of 1920 his health was in decline. Only close friends were admitted to the family home for visits.

There are also five references to Langer in Kafka's *Letters*—two from Marienbad in July, 1916. Kafka spent ten days at the Bohemian resort with Felice Bauer (in adjacent rooms). Langer happened to be there at the same time, together with the entourage of the ailing Rabbi of Belz. After Felice's departure, the two friends met up for evening walks. A long letter to Max details the walks and time spent with Langer; a shorter letter to another mutual friend, Felix Weltsch (1884-1964), also dwells on the walks. Langer next appears in a postcard sent to Max in November 1917, from Zürau in the west Bohemian countryside. Kafka was then taking his first medical leave from work, resting in the care of his youngest sister Ottla on their brother-in-law's farm. The note addresses the possibility of Franz securing work for Langer in the Kafka family business; nothing came of it. In spring of 1920 Kafka was convalescing in Meran in northern Italy. In a reply to Felix Weltsch, he writes of a "childish giddy gladness" that he is "shamelessly given to" with respect to something Langer had conveyed about him to Weltsch. Whatever it was, is not spelled out. The last mention of Langer appears in a letter to Max, written from Villa Tatra sanatorium in the Tatra Mountains of Slovakia in December 1920. The reference is to Langer's having formed a *Mizrachi* group in Prague, indicating by this time his commitment to the religious Zionist movement.

The ten references to Langer in Kafka's *Diaries* and *Letters* point to a friendly connection over a span of years; they do not seem to indicate a particularly intimate bond—at least not from Kafka's perspective. The one letter that stands out for ambiguousness of tone and message is the note about Langer sent to Weltsch in spring of 1920. The "childish giddy gladness" juxtaposed to "shamelessness" is curiously coy; it's hard to know what to make of it.

From Kafka's writing alone one would not know that Langer was also a writer. In fact, Langer began publishing articles in Czech and German in 1919, published his first poems in Hebrew in 1923, and that same year—the year before Kafka's death—published with Diederichs of Munich a book-length study titled *Die Erotik der Kabbala* (*The Eroticism of Kabbala*). In 1937 he published with Elk of Prague, *Devět bran* (*Nine Gates*), a collection of Hasidic tales of wonder-working rabbis, the likes of which Kafka had heard from Langer and recounted in his diary in 1915. In July 2011 I located *Nine Gates*—first published in English translation by James Clark of London in 1961—at the York University Library in Toronto, and read it with keen interest. The stories not only provide a fascinating window into a devout Eastern European Jewish world, now vanished; the Foreword to the collection, titled "My Brother Jiří," written by Langer's older brother František Langer (1888-1965) for the English edition, also contains the most extensive biography available on Langer. Though, like Max Brod's biography of Kafka, František's Foreword (as would become clear), is slanted.

Jiří (Georg Mordechai) was born in the Prague suburb of Královské Vinohrady, the youngest of three sons. The Langers, like the Kafkas and Brods, were westernized, middle-class Jews. Langer senior was a shopkeeper, a practical man, minimally observant. (Langer's mother, "poor thing" František writes, "was deaf.") "Father," as he is referred to, favoured Czech over German (the predominant language of Prague Jewry), belonged to the patriotic Sokol sport movement, and unlike Kafka's and Brod's fathers, sent his sons to Czech schools. František, the eldest, followed the trajectory of his father's assimilation, becoming a chief physician in the Czech army during World War One, and later an acclaimed Czech-nationalist playwright. Josef, the middle brother, went into the family business. Jiří, described as a lonely boy who was reading Czech mystical poetry by age fifteen, became "infected" with enthusiasm for mysticism by way of his friend Alfred Fuchs. The two learned Hebrew and read Jewish literature together. Fuchs converted to Catholicism and the friendship ended. Jiří immersed himself in the study of Torah, Talmud, and Hebrew (for which he had a gift), quit school, and at the age of nineteen, in 1913, set out for Belz in Eastern Galicia and the Hasidic court of Rabbi Yissachar Dov Rokeach (1851-1926).

Apart from a few breaks, Langer lived for five years in the Hasidic community and became thoroughly versed and immersed in its ways. Kafka and Langer met in March 1915 when Langer was back in Prague. He'd been drafted into the Austrian army, then discharged for refusing to obey orders that contravened his religious observance. Kafka and Brod were both exempted from military duty—Brod for medical reasons and Kafka on grounds that he was indispensable to the Worker's Accident Insurance Institute. The Langer family, by František's account, were deeply distressed by Jiří's Hasidic conversion and "exhibitionism" upon his first return from Belz. František likens the Langer family situation to that of the Samsa family in *The Metamorphosis*. In both cases—the real and the fictional—the cozy family nest is upended by a 'monstrosity'. The Samsas ultimately dispose of their son and brother, once he's fully dehumanized and deceased. At least, says František, the Langers were "practical," and sought the help of a sensitive local rabbi to persuade Jiří to modify his ways. František writes that he himself never met Franz Kafka, but that his brother and Franz became friends during the War: "Kafka evidently found in Jiří a kindred spirit and the two used to go for walks together in Prague."

What was the kindredness? What did Kafka find in Jiří; Jiří in Kafka? No doubt part of the attraction was mutual interest in an authentic non-Western Jewish experience. Both were contemptuous of the "insufficient scrap" of Judaism, as Kafka put it, practised by Western Jewry. Langer found authenticity in Galicia, within the strictures of the Yiddish-speaking Hasidic court. Kafka found his version of Jewish authenticity in Prague, by way of a Yiddish theatre troupe from Galicia. The *Diaries* include some thirty entries on the troupe that performed in Prague from 1911 to 1913—descriptions of the actors, synopses of the plays, critiques of the performances. Kafka saw in the passion of the actors and their melodramatic plays a living, breathing Judaism, and he connected with it. Aspects of the mystical, the folkloric, and the parabolic were common to both men's quests from the pre-War period forward, though Kafka remained cool to religious study until his later years. Both were also interested in Yiddish and Langer became fluent during his stay at Belz. Langer, gifted at languages, knew Hebrew prior to the War; Kafka did not. It's quite possible that Langer's knowledge and great love of Hebrew spurred in Kafka the will to learn the old-new tongue as well.

Langer left the Belz community for good at the War's end and went to Vienna to study at the Hebrew Pedagogic Academy. When he returned to Prague, he supported himself by teaching Hebrew and Jewish studies and working in a clerical capacity for Zionist organizations. To František's relief, he'd given up his Hasidic garb and assumed a more "normal attitude" toward the family. But he remained observant and to František's new chagrin, he'd taken up study of Freud and his disciples in Vienna and had begun to use psychoanalytic methods in analyzing sources of Jewish ritual, mysticism, and the religious idea. (This interest resulted in the publication of *Die Erotik der Kabbala* in 1923.)

As for Kafka, he surreptitiously began learning Hebrew on his own during the War. It came as a revelation to Max that, by December 1917, Kafka had worked his way through forty-five lessons of the formidable textbook of the time, *Hebrew Grammar and Reader for Schools and Self-Instruction*, by Moses Rath. In a rare instance of censure, Brod writes of his friend: "So he was trying me out when he asked me some time ago, with every appearance of innocence, how do you count in Hebrew. This making a big secret of everything. There is something very great about it, but also something evil." Yes, Kafka was secretive. He was also evidently serious about his study of Hebrew and in the spring of 1918 asked Langer to give him private lessons. A note in Max Brod's collection of Kafka's *Letters to Friends, Family and Editors* records that in the fall of 1921 Brod and Kafka took Hebrew lessons from Langer together as well. The rejuvenation of Hebrew as a living language was one of the important steps towards the revival of a Jewish State in the historical homeland, and, as such, fundamentally tied to Zionism. Did Kafka's diligence in learning Hebrew mean that he, like Brod and Langer, became an avowed Zionist? In active terms; that is, in terms of immigrating to Eretz Israel, no. But he planned to immigrate, and if health had permitted, he likely would have. By the end of his life, his sympathies were with Zionism.

František closes his Foreword to *Nine Gates* by relating how he escaped Prague in 1939, first to France then to England, where he settled. Brother Josef chose suicide over deportation to the death camps. (Like Kafka's parents, though not his sisters, František's parents died before the War.) In 1939 Jiří escaped Prague for Palestine along the Danube-to-Istanbul route. (Max Brod also escaped Prague for Palestine—on the last train before the borders were closed—carrying Kafka's manuscripts in his suitcase.) Jiří contracted nephritis during the tortuous passage; it became chronic and led to his premature death in Tel Aviv in 1943. During his last years, living his Zionist dream, he was frequently too ill to work. He received a small grant for refugees and some financial assistance from František—"once difficulties from the war had been overcome." He turned to translating his Hasidic tales into Hebrew and resumed writing Hebrew poetry. Max Brod and Jiří were friends to the end, František relates, and as his brother lay dying, Max brought him the proof-sheets of his second book of poems—"written in Palestine." Brod also arranged Langer's funeral, attended to his literary estate, and oversaw the posthumous publication of his second small Hebrew collection, titled *Me'at Tsori (A Little Balsam)*.

I was unable to locate Langer's poetry in Toronto or online. In August 2011 M. and I were visiting in Israel. I was hoping to find a copy of Langer's first book of poetry—cited by František as *Piyyutim ve-Shirei Yedidut (Poems and Songs of Friendship)*—in one of the secondhand- or rare-book stores. We searched and came up empty-handed. We did find the title in the National Library system—at the Givat Ram campus of The Hebrew University in Jerusalem—but the book was in storage and we were told it would take several days to locate, if it could be located at all. The day before our departure, I received email notification that the book had been retrieved and was on hold at the Judaica Reading Room.

I did not know that a book could make me so emotional. Standing under the high light of the dry and quiet room, I held the little volume in my hands like a first-time mother, stroked the simple cardboard cover. The author's name, printed in thin square Hebrew letters above the title—*Piyyutim ve-Shirei Yedidot*—different, I noticed, by one letter, from how František had cited the title in his Foreword to *Nine Gates*. The contents—sixteen poems listed in triangular configuration. The place of publication—Prague. Year—1929, in Hebrew letters, not numerals. Publisher—Dr. Josef Fläsch. I was holding one of a limited-edition that Langer had surely brought with him on his long escape from Prague in 1939 and bequeathed to the library. There was not a single due-date stamped on the sign-out form pasted to the right-hand side of the next page. A wave welled up inside me. I turned each page carefully and stopped when I came to the twelfth poem, "On the Death of the Poet—after Franz Kafka," the name printed plainly under the title. The elegy. I had found what I'd come for and knew in the moment that I would read these pieces closely, and together with M., translate them faithfully.

M. was a hesitant partner in the search for Langer's poems, until then. Once we found the book and started to read the pieces, he too was captivated. The poems that opened out to us were the work of a gift-ed Hebraist—well-versed in grammar, syntax, and diction; poems rich-ly informed by Biblical and Kabbalistic sources. Liturgical in style and craft, modern in theme and reach. It soon became plain that these were intensely personal pieces. Poems of passion, spirituality, longing, lone-liness, and unreciprocated homo-romantic love; written male to male.

Franz Kafka is the only person named in the collection, which does not mean that Kafka is the subject or addressee of all the poems. But it seemed to me that he was implicit in more than one—based on descriptions, allusions, and juxtaposition. The elegy itself is an expression of exalted and impassioned love beyond death: "The water-fire-air, the animate-plant-inanimate / join with me together, who were estranged from me till now; with every expression of kindness they lend me a hand, caressing me genteelly and behold you are among them! ... Place between my breasts the weight of your shadowed soul / and the dream of your bones, lay down on my pillow's softness." And the elegy is followed by the poem "Alone," in which "I did not press you to my breast, / my arms did not envelop you, / and that my heart was all aflame / I did not tell you / with my mouth, I could not. / And now you are gone, / and nothing is left / but the remembering / and regret." The poem "Like the Dying Inside" speaks of "tremours of a secret love / you dare not / love / to the end." "The Strength in Splendour" announces "my belovèd" ... "his comely face" ... the "pearls shower from his mouth," then "grief: a tear ... and trembling." There is no way of knowing who Langer addressed in more than one of his love poems, and whether Franz Kafka was the great love among other male loves, but it seemed possible that he was.

What is certain: Georg Mordechai Langer's disclosure of his homo-romantic passion with the publication of his poems was a daring act of self-expression. Given that he was religious throughout his life, he would have been living with immense inner pressure—that of making meaning of his sexual identity in light of his commitment to orthodox Judaism, which proscribes same-sex relations. If the repeat expression of unfulfilled love in his poems is an indication, however, Langer did not act on his desires. The poems were an earnest channel for his feelings of both ecstasy and rejection; a release, a haven, a consolation. In one of his most agitated and unshielded pieces he writes, "Only my poetry is an escape, my lamentation, my refuge."

Once our translation was underway, I began to see František's Fore-word to *Nine Gates* with different eyes. The family "horror" narrative over Jiří's religious "ostentation" and the condescension over Jiří's "in-nocent" yet "blasphemous" Freudian turn, could have been František's masking of a deeper, more shameful family secret. Anyone who was close to Langer and anyone who read his poems with understanding would have known his homoerotic truth, including Franz Kafka.

***

In the fall of 2011, I pitched the idea of a bilingual edition of Langer's collection to my publisher. Guernica Editions is known for its translations, but a bilingual Hebrew / English work had never been done, and it would present challenges. Fortunately, publisher and editor-in-chief Michael Mirolla, himself a Kafka enthusiast, was keen on having the first English translation of an elegy to Kafka published with Guernica. So much has been published on Kafka, yet somehow the elegy remained obscured. It was like a piece out of the ethers. And the back story to the project had added appeal. Then came a stroke of synchronicity. My Langer-pitch coincided with a manuscript submission to Guernica: a new translation by American author Thor Polson of two of Kafka's late story collections, *A Country Doctor* (1919) and *A Hunger Artist* (1924). Langer and Kafka arrived at Guernica together. What were the chances of that? As it turned out, the two books were released under one cover in 2014—in an inventive flipside format. Given the Kafka / Langer connection, the two-in-one flipside solution was brilliant. But I'm getting ahead of myself.

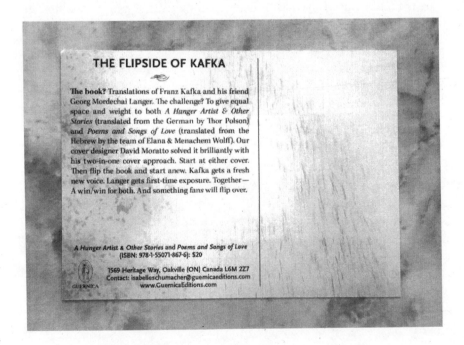

THE FLIPSIDE OF KAFKA

The book? Translations of Franz Kafka and his friend Georg Mordechai Langer. The challenge? To give equal space and weight to both *A Hunger Artist & Other Stories* (translated from the German by Thor Polson) and *Poems and Songs of Love* (translated from the Hebrew by the team of Elana & Menachem Wolff). Our cover designer David Moratto solved it brilliantly with his two-in-one cover approach. Start at either cover. Then flip the book and start anew. Kafka gets a fresh new voice. Langer gets first-time exposure. Together— A win/win for both. And something fans will flip over.

A Hunger Artist & Other Stories and *Poems and Songs of Love* (ISBN: 978-1-55071-867-6): $20

1569 Heritage Way, Oakville (ON) Canada L6M 2Z7
Contact: isabelleschumacher@guernicaeditions.com
www.GuernicaEditions.com
GUERNICA

During the course of reading, researching, drafting, discussing, writing and rewriting our translations, M. and I, I felt, were coming into a new nearness. We hadn't done this kind of work together before and it brought out qualities in our individualities that had not previously met in the open. One day M. set his pen on the kitchen table—beside the pile of papers, notebooks, dictionaries and tea cups—and said that he felt we were doing the work of *ilui neshama*—elevation of the soul. By reading and translating the poems of Georg Mordechai Langer we were giving them new life, we were acknowledging the impact of Langer's life and work in the world, we were elevating his soul—together. M. had not spoken this way of poetry and soul before.

We'd been living with the intimacy of Langer's poems for a year and a half when we next returned to Israel. We made a point of fitting into our schedule a visit to Langer's grave at the Nachalat Yitzhak Cemetery in Givatayim, just east of Tel Aviv. Founded in 1932, the cemetery contains more than 30,000 graves, including mass graves for unidentified soldiers, graves of children, graves of cultural and political figures, graves of Rebbes of Hasidic dynasties, memorials to communities lost in the Holocaust, and reinterred ashes. We had no idea where to find Langer in this dense and sprawling resting place. We entered the low white office building inside the main gate to ask for assistance. It was a bright, clear, chilly day at the end of February, 2013.

The custodian, a pale man with a large black yarmulka, reddish beard, and long curly sidelocks, could have fit František's description of Jiří himself when he first returned from Belz. The man was amiable, eager to help. We spoke in Hebrew. We told him we were looking for the grave of Georg Mordechai Langer. He tapped the name into his computer and came up with the information: Area 41: Row: 24 Number: 21. "Where are you from?" he asked us. "From Canada, we told him." "You must have come for the *yahrzeit*," he said. (*Yahrzeit* is the Yiddish word for the anniversary of a person's death.) "It was just his *yahrzeit* … Are you family?" he asked. "No, we're not, and we didn't realize it was his *yahrzeit*. We just wanted to visit his grave, to pay our respects," we told him. "I'll take you there," he said. "You won't easily find it on your own."

He led us along the narrow lanes, the tightly crowded tracts. When we arrived at Area 41: Row: 24 Number: 21, we were silent in seeing the simple inscription: *Ha-Meshorer* (The Poet) Mordechai Langer, and below his Hebrew name the date of his death. There were several stones on the grave. People had visited and placed them there—as is the way. "You're not family?" the custodian asked us again quizzically. "No," M. said, "we're admirers." (The description sounded odd in Hebrew.) "He was a poet, a friend of Franz Kafka," M. continued. "You know … Kafka." "No," said the custodian, "never heard of him."

The three of us stood there. The custodian then asked us if we would like him to recite a psalm. We could have done this ourselves but since he asked, we said yes. He recited "Psalm 130, A Song of Ascents." Afterwards he returned us to the cemetery entrance. We thanked him, tipped him for his service, and left. We hardly knew what to say to one another. We'd been so nonplussed by the experience that we'd forgotten to place stones on the grave to mark our visit.

***

M. had the painstaking work of resetting the Hebrew poems—with their complex vowel notations. We wanted the original poems to correspond line-by-line with the translations, too, on facing pages. This required a combined effort of precision, as did composing the notes on the individual pieces. I wrote the Introduction, including the back story to the project, and a Note on Translation. Nothing was quick. And we were grappling with puzzles, hunches, and corrections along the way.

The matter of the title was resistant. František cited it as *Piyyutim ve-Shirei Yedidut* in his *Nine Gates* Foreword, which translates as *Poems and Songs of Friendship*. This is what I'd seen in other references to the collection as well. But I immediately noticed, as soon as I set eyes on the original book, that the last word of the title was actually *Yedidōt*, not *Yedidut*. At first I didn't attribute much significance to this. In Hebrew, this is a difference of one small vowel-dot, and the more common word is *yedidut*—meaning "friendship." However, the less common word—*yedidōt*, together with *shirei*—meaning "songs", translates as "love songs." The term *shirei yedidōt* appears in the liturgical song, "Shir Ha-Kavōd"—"Song of Glory," attributed to Rabbi Judah the Hasid (1150-1217). Langer was a Hebraist and he knew his liturgy. He had surely chosen his source and worded his title carefully to say exactly what he meant. For months M. and I proceeded under the working title *Poems and Songs of Friendship*. But the more we lived with Langer's language and sources and the content of his poems, the more we understood that he really had not written poems of friendship—a non-romantic relationship that connotes mutuality of feeling. He had written poems of romantic desire, longing, dejection and loneliness: unrequited love songs.

I closed my Note on Translation with a gloss on our decision to title our English translation *Poems and Songs of Love*. But another point in František's Foreword continued to needle me. František wrote that, as Jiří lay dying, Max Brod brought him the proof-sheets of the book containing the Hebrew poems he'd written in Palestine: *Meʾat Tsori* (*A Little Balsam*), published posthumously in 1943. František relates that in these poems Jiří writes fondly of Prague and the Old-New Synagogue, and with "rapturous adoration" about the "beauty of the

Palestinian countryside," but "not a great deal about people." It struck me that František should have this much to say about the content of Jiří's second collection when he'd said next to nothing about the first, which was in fact a great deal about people.

Initially I'd been drawn to the first collection only—primarily because of the elegy for Kafka. But entering into Langer's life as we had, through translating his poems, altered things, including something between M. and me. And I knew we would be remiss if we didn't seek and read the second collection. I had questions as well. I was interested to see if, in addition to paeans to the Land and reminiscences on Prague, there were new romantic poems among the few "about people" that František alluded to. More so, I was curious to see if any of the pieces from the first collection had been reprinted in the second. František made no mention of this, but I had a hunch that Langer might have decided to bring his dearest pieces forward—from the first to the second collection—to make them part of his last legacy in a book published in the Land of his dreams.

Michael Mirolla wanted our final materials submitted by the end of February 2014 at the very latest—to allow for a fall release of the book. The translations of the poems were ready. The Introduction, Notes on the poems, and the Note on Translation were also written. But I was still living with puzzles and hunches when M. and I visited Israel in January 2014, a month before our submission deadline. This time I was hoping to find an original copy of Langer's second book—at the historic Beit Ariela Library in Tel Aviv. We were thrilled to hear that *Me'at Tsori* (*A Little Balsam*) was in the stacks and available to us to peruse as non-members. What we found was not a copy of Langer's little original, however. Instead, a 286-page volume of Mordechai (Dov) Langer's *Asupat Ketavav* (*Collected Writings*)—a 1984 edition compiled by Israeli poet / scholar Miriam Dror, including a biographical preface by Professor Dov Sadan (1902-1989), photos, letters, Hasidic tales, Langer's two collections of poems, prose pieces, and Dror's MA thesis on Langer's poetry.

There was so much to surprise and delight in the volume—most exciting of all a short essay by Langer titled "Something About Kafka," originally published in the Tel Aviv journal *Hegeh* (*Voice / Rudder*) in February 1941 at the request of then-editor, Dov Sadan. Nowhere in anything I'd read on Kafka or Langer had I seen reference to this astonishing short piece. We read it word for word on the spot and I knew it had to be included in our translation. "Something About Kafka" establishes a deeper, closer Kafka-Langer connection than is portrayed in other published sources. It confirms that the two spent regular quotidian time together "for a full medley of years"—walking, talking, learning, riding the city rails together and speaking in Hebrew. "Unlike the other Prague Zionists," Langer indicates, Kafka "spoke a fluent Hebrew"; they spoke Hebrew to one another, and Kafka took "heartfelt pride" in his knowledge of the language. "Though Kafka maintained he was not a Zionist," Langer says, "he deeply envied those who fulfilled the great principle of Zionism, bodily; that is, the principle of immigrating to the Land of Israel." Langer also confirms what I could not know from what is available in Kafka's *Diaries, Letters* and other sources, but could only infer from context and hint; namely, that Kafka did know that Langer wrote Hebrew poetry, and in fact read it and understood it.

Langer refers to the publication of his first poems that appeared in the Warsaw literary journal *Kolōt* (*Voices*) in 1923: "Kafka said to me that they resemble, a little, Chinese poetry. So I went and purchased for myself a collection of Chinese poetry in French translation ... and from then on this delightful book never left my table." This reference affirmed what I had surmised all along: that there was a Kafka-connection to Langer's poem "On the Poems of Li-Tai-Pei," which appears immediately before the elegy in *Poems and Songs of Love*. Langer was evidently inspired, by Kafka's indication, to write the Chinese poem and he placed it next to the elegy because of the connection. I had also been struck by the inverse symmetry of the two poems. In both pieces Langer waxes exultant then woeful to evoke union / disunion. In the Chinese piece he opens with exultation—"a heavenly voice from the depths," the "intoxicating scents of summer"—and closes on a note of remorse, thwarted in understanding and "bitter as the world and everything in it." In the elegy he begins with "the bond is at an end, / a bond made of waves of the sea of the world." There is "wailing and ululation," due to the "turn" (Kafka's decease), but true union does not end with the disunion of death; for Langer, incorporeal Franz remains present in the very elements. If there is to be "jubilant" joining of "free men," however, it will be "in the bosom of the universe. / On the fount from which together life and death as brothers spring." Not in this life, not in this existence.

In tone, content, and allusion, "Something About Kafka" affirms Langer's awe of Kafka. Kafka is the "great and wondrous personality" in whose "shadow" he, Langer, "dwelled." Langer does not paint the relationship as equal, in the way of usual friendship. The statement: "Hardly a day goes by that I do not call up his memory before me" indicates greater intensity of feeling than that which attends usual friendship. And while his memories of Kafka may be clear and acute, Langer maintains restraint. Not everything that can be said, is said. Langer acknowledges Kafka's secrecy, his furtiveness, and his will and right to conceal, even in revealing. With Kafka there is always enigma, paradox. In "Something about Kafka," there's also shielding. There's nothing categorical in Langer's piece to confirm that Kafka was his one great love. Neither is there anything to rule it out, and there's enough to suggest that, at least from Langer's perspective, the attraction exceeded feelings of mere friendship.

My other hunch was validated as well. Langer had indeed included in his second book of poems, *Me'at Tsori / A Little Balsam*, pieces from the first book, *Piyyutim ve-Shirei Yedidot / Poems and Songs of Love*, published fourteen years earlier. Significantly, the five poems he chose to reissue were: "On the Poems of Li-Tai-Pei" and "On the Death of the Poet—after Franz Kafka," juxtaposed, as in the first collection; the two poems that were first published in the Warsaw journal *Kolot* in 1923—that Kafka told Langer reminded him of Chinese poetry; both of which expound Langer's sadness in being thwarted in his deepest romantic leanings and longings; and the piece titled "Like the Dying Inside," set to the Eastern European tune for reading aloud the Biblical Book of *Lamentations* that ends with "tremours of a secret love / you dare not / love / to the end."

The theme of the secret also comes up in one of the poems "about people" in *Me'at Tsori / A Little Balsam* that František alluded to in his *Nine Gates* Foreword. True to report, the pieces in Langer's second collection are mostly patriotic panegyrics. There are only a few "about people" (which might have been František's mask for homo-romantic poems), and the short lament from which the title of the second collection is drawn recalls lines written on the margins of a song to a male companion. The last line of the adjacent poem, titled "Hidat Lila" ("Night Riddle"), contains the line: "A secret I will not reveal," which corresponds to what Langer says about Kafka in "Something About Kafka," written in the same period as the poem: "He simply did not want to be revealed. He wanted to, but did not want to. He reached out and didn't reach. And he succeeded in both objectives."

Langer, like Kafka, lived with concealment. He, too, wanted to reveal and be revealed for who he was in his deepest being, and he was able to do this, to an extent, in his Hebrew poems. But he also concealed. And this concealment, we found, extended to Miriam Dror's MA thesis on Langer's work as well. Dror cites as Langer's themes: man and his place in the world, the lyrical religious experience, life and death, and, predominantly, loneliness. She holds that Langer's loneliness stemmed from his inability to conform to societal norms, which is reminiscent of František's couched language. It was striking to us that an academic study should distinguish itself by gingerly skirting one of the most essential and certainly the most profoundly daring aspect of the subject's work. To us this seemed akin to not acknowledging that the emperor has no clothes: the obvious deliberately not admitted.

***

M. and I returned to the Nachalat Yitzhak Cemetery during our January 2014 visit. This time we knew how to reach Langer's resting place. We made our way through the narrow lanes and crowded rows and tracts and stood again before the grave. Again, we gazed at the simple inscription: *Ha-Meshorer*—the Poet Mordechai Langer. This, evidently, is how he wished to be remembered—as a poet. He'd written perhaps thousands of pages of prose and criticism and journalism; he'd published fewer than forty poems. Yet these he considered his definitive, most meaningful work: His poems were where his heart lay. Of these pieces, five were dear enough to be chosen twice, and among these, at least two can be connected with certainty to Franz Kafka. I looked up from my thoughts, and who should be standing there in the next row of graves but the pale custodian with the large black yarmulka, reddish beard, and long curly sidelocks. He looked at us and we looked at him. "It's the Canadians," he announced. "Yes," we said, "you remember us!" We were sincerely surprised. There are 30,000 graves at Nachalat Yitzhak and the man must see hundreds of people pass through the cemetery each day. What were the chances he'd be standing behind Langer's grave precisely when we arrived, and that he would remember us. "We brought our prayerbook this time," we told him. He nodded, we smiled, he went back to his business, M. recited the designated psalms, and this time we placed stones on the grave to mark our visit.

***

Locating Miriam Dror's book *Me'at Tsori: Collected Writings* of Georg Mordechai Langer precisely when we did was a boon. It provided a number of answers, and fodder for further investigation. I included an Afterword along with our translation of "Something About Kafka" in my February 2014 submission to Michael Mirolla. The two-in-one flipside book—*A Hunger Artist and Other Stories / Poems and Songs of Love*—was launched in Toronto in September 2014. It went into a second printing in 2015: a new translation of Kafka's late stories, a first Hebrew / English bilingual translation of Georg Mordechai Langer's love poems; the two together, Kafka and Langer; a fragment of a backstory.

Kafka-in-Between

THE TWENTIETH CENTURY claimed Franz Kafka as one of its darkest / brightest modernist lights, yet Kafka lived more than a third of his short life in the long nineteenth and drew deeply, by his own account, from that well—on naturalist masters Grillparzer, Kleist, Flaubert, Dostoevsky, and Dickens—even as he broke their modes. Kafka's feet, as it were, were in the long nineteenth, his trunk in the early twentieth, his head in prescient depths, and his aura: with us still.

I walk the streets of his hometown, Prague, take routes he knew, view views he viewed, enter spaces he worked, lived and dreamt in. Wondering, can I filch a glimpse inside the man inside the writing, tap the veiled "tremendous world" he said he had in his head. And when I'm not wondering, I start wondering again. I'm not put off from wondering and wandering, questing after Kafka—

Some might call it stalking …

In Prague I've seen commodification: Kafka's grave aesthetic face on walls and stacks of books and *tchotchkes*. Kafka—'kitsched'—on coffee mugs, Franz (like Amadeus) stamped on plates, T-shirts, pencils, boxes of chocolate. The remnant of his birth-house on the edge of the former Jewish ghetto, advertised in letters cribbing his signature. Franz Kafka Café, Franz Kafka Bookstore, The Kafka Museum Shop—copies of the author's 'best' in high demand translations.

I'm surprised I haven't found, in a hotel lobby, a walking-tour map—lines connecting dots to all the Kafka spots in the city. Kafka, if he knew, would be aggrieved: "I can believe that."

M. photographs me standing with my hand on the full-metal jacket of sculptor Jaroslav Róna's belated tribute to Prague's unsettled son. A bronze colossus, unveiled in 2003—3.75 metres high, 800 kilos—set on the spot where Old Town meets New: Dušní Street, the corner of Vezenská—Church of the Holy Spirit on one side, the Spanish (Sephardic) Synagogue on the other. Kafka-in-between.

The statue shows a hatted dandy balanced on the shoulders of a heavy, empty suit. Róna found his inspiration in Kafka's earliest extant work, "Description of a Struggle" ("Beschreibung eines Kampfes")—a story richly liminal, the only work in the oeuvre set explicitly in Prague. City streets and landmarks are named in the German of Kafka's tongue and time: Ferdinandstrasse, Laurenziberg, Franzenquai and Schüzeninsel, Mühlenturm and Karlsbrücke, Karlsgasse, Seminarkirche, Kreuzherrenplatz, the Ringplatz.

Kafka laboured longer on "Description of a Struggle" than on any other work. The first version probably dates to 1904 when he was a law student at Charles University. He persevered at the novella, as he termed it, on and off for several years before finally abandoning it in fragments. But he didn't destroy it, as he did with so much of his writing, and he was satisfied enough (at least temporarily) with parts of it, to extract a few for publication.

Biographer Rainer Stach has deemed the work "no more than a footnote in literary history." Yet "Description of a Struggle" can be seen as a valuable testing ground, important to the unfolding of Kafka's creative process. One sees in it the poetics of the later work in gestation, recurring themes and techniques: the dubiousness of the double, the competition of opposing drives and pulls, the dreamy and fantastical juxtaposed to the real and often cruel, the city as site of disorientation, the gap or non sequitur as tactic to surprise and destabilize. Physical, emotional and discursive struggle. Overall ambivalence.

I'm thinking that Jaroslav Róna was probably drawn as much to the imagery of duality in "Description of a Struggle" as he was to the Prague setting of the story. And the episode he chose to represent is one of the most evocative: the section titled "A Ride," in which one young man—the narrator 'I'—leaps onto the shoulders of another young man—the acquaintance—and "rides" him through the city in a dreamy yet hyperreal sequence punctuated with casual acts of violence. In the Schocken edition translation the stark part (here compressed) goes like this:

> "I leapt onto the shoulders of my acquaintance, and by digging my fists into his back I urged him into a trot. But since he stumped forward rather reluctantly ... I kicked him in the belly several times with my boots, to make him more lively ...

As soon as my acquaintance stumbled I pulled him up by the collar and … boxed his head … pressed my hands together and … made [him] choke … Then my acquaintance collapsed and … I discovered that he was badly wounded in the knee. Since he could no longer be of any use to me, I left him there on the stones without much regret and whistled down a few vultures with serious beaks …"

Róna invested his statue with the surreality of Kafka's "ride," while rendering it more civically friendly than the text. There's no digging-in of fists, no belly-kicking, head-boxing or choking. No wounding or gesture of abandonment of one man by the other, and no whistling down of vultures. Róna's sculpture represents the alert realism of Kafka's writing style while invoking a lighter take on the gritty aspects of the story. The figure on top—who bears a striking likeness to Franz—is smartly dressed in suit, vest and fedora (Kafka was a hat man, especially in his student years), perched firmly on the shoulders of a much larger figure—a headless, handless, footless suit. The Kafka figure on top is a miniaturized man, almost like a child in adult attire. One wonders what he's doing up there, riding the big man suit. And why is the little man pointing—right forefinger extended in gunslinger position? The Róna sculpture, like the Kafka text, is enigmatic and invites interpretation.

There's an English-speaking student group standing by the statue when M. and I arrive. The students take turns posing with the statue for their cameras. The guide gives his spiel, noting that the sculptor based his creation on Kafka's earliest, yet last-to-be-published and little-known work, "Description of a Struggle." In closing, he asks the students which of the figures they think is meant to be Kafka. "The one in the hat," several chime in. "Obviously," another responds, "the other is a suit, a nobody." The guide smiles and says: "Perhaps both figures are meant to be Kafka—in the way that players in a dream are all aspects of the dreamer." The students nod in apparent approval and the group moves on.

Two-in-oneness is perhaps what Jaroslav Róna did mean to convey in inscribing his work, at its base, with the title *Franz Kafka*: the duality of Franz, the dreamy doubling of rider and ridden. In the text, the episode does in fact situate "the ride" on the screen of the author's mind—in the "interior of a vast but as yet unfinished landscape," where things are let "grow along the road." The "nobody" (no body?) that one of the students saw in the empty suit also makes an appearance in the text: "... nobody among a pack of nobodies ... everyone in frock coats."

I step up, get close to the statue; touch it, as have so many others before me. The bronze is lighter and shinier where it's been touched the most: on the coattails, pant legs and crotch of the huge suit. Also where the suit legs meet the bronze base, feet nowhere to be seen—sunk somewhere below, chopped off. I touch the big suit jacket. The little man on top is too high to touch, except for his boots, and they are the lightest and shiniest of all. It's the feet that people have most wanted to feel. I too want to feel the feet, to have that vicarious connection with the part of the sculptor's art that's most recognizably Franz.

In one of the photographs that M. snaps, my back is to the camera, my arms upraised; I'm holding the little bronze boots. It's an odd image. I'm wearing a black coat and my hands—extending from the sleeves, wrists to fingertips—cover the boots, giving them the appearance of skin. My hands look like Franz's feet—exposed below his pant legs. Abnormally long, bare, white feet. Not quite human. Not bronze statue-feet. More like frog-feet of an amphibious man-figure dressed for cruising.

Resurrecting Frank's Foot

I'VE BEEN LEARNING to play a card game that I'll never learn to play. I could have known this from the get-go by its name: *Franzefuss*. Frank's foot. That's how I first read it: *Franz*—German for Frank, and *fuss*—meaning foot. It turned out not to be so straightforward. It hardly ever is with translations, or with games. Or with Franz, who drew me to the card game that contains his name, and to which he was curiously (dis)connected.

My attraction to Kafka—not cards—began in my teens, first in *The Metamorphosis*, then in *The Trial*, the inexhaustible novel that made me ask: What is just? What is punishment? What is self-destruction? Also, what is the work of humour in a work of spiritual fiction? For *The Trial* felt seriously spiritual to me, even though the theatrics in it instilled humour. I was a mystified teen. Kafka's story of a man arrested and prosecuted by an inaccessible court authority—the nature of his crime disclosed neither to him nor to the reader—and in the end sacrificially killed in a stone quarry by two pale strangers in frock coats and top hats, struck me as both deeply Biblical and eminently contemporary. I was infuriated by it, and enticed.

It was during my gap year, lying on a patch of kibbutz grass in the Jezreel Valley, reading *The Trial* in my time away from picking citrus and stomping on cotton, that I became a Kafka convert. I read avidly and eclectically that year—Philip Roth, Anaïs Nin, Lawrence Durrell, Ursula LeGuin, Mordecai Richler, Herman Wouk, Natan Alterman, Camus, Hesse, and Mann. But nothing struck like Kafka, and I returned to him—reading his sentences aloud to the goats and the grass and the valley.

Gradually I read and reread everything by Kafka I could get my hands on. By biographer Reiner Stach's account, Kafka left to posterity about forty stories—amounting to about 350 pages. In addition to the prose texts, he generated about 3,400 pages of diary entries and fragments, including his three unfinished novels—*The Trial*, *The Castle*, and *Amerika* (a.k.a. *The Man Who Disappeared* and *The Missing Person*)—originally prepared for posthumous publication by his best friend and literary executor, Max Brod. Overriding Kafka's will that all his writings be destroyed, Brod had secured—by the time of his death in Tel Aviv in 1968—publication of everything in Kafka's literary estate he deemed publishable, including some 1,500 letters. (Work on German critical editions of all of Kafka's works—the restoration of the fictions, letters and diaries to their original form—was begun by an international team of experts in 1978. Published by S. Fischer Verlag with financial support of the German government, these editions are nearing completion. Mark Harman's translation of *Das Schloss / The Castle*, based on the restored text, was published by Schocken Books in 1998; Breon Mitchell's translation of *Der Prozess / The Trial*, based on the restored text was also published in 1998 by Schocken; Harman's translation of *Der Verschollene / Amerika: The Missing Person* was published by Schocken in 2008.)

Brod defended his decision to defy Kafka's final wish and made clear his determination to preserve and publish all his friend's work—including the private writings—as gifts to humanity. Kafka would no doubt have been deeply disturbed at the thought of the publication of his letters, especially, even though he himself was an enthusiastic reader of the letters of some of his own favourite authors, Flaubert and Kleist among them. Brod has been criticized for many of his decisions regarding Kafka, not least for his resolve to publish the letters. Yet he wasn't wrong in assessing the value and appeal of his friend's entire oeuvre. According to Kafka scholar Julian Preece, "the letters complete the oeuvre, like a map makes the world complete." But one can't help but feel a little transgressive in reading them—since letters are primarily personal, and there are things written in them that are meant for the writer's and recipient's eyes only. Even so, the most intimate form of writing is always an act of potential communication, and as Kafka rose to posthumous fame and acclaim, his 'private writing', no less than his fiction, came to be seen as essential work of a singular creative mind.

Diaries, which Kafka kept on and off from age twenty-seven in 1910 until a year before his death in 1924, feel less private than the letters. Diaries provided Kafka an outlet for expressing feelings, ideas, and dreams (recorded in inordinate detail), as well as a repository for sketches of stories—many of which he shared with friends. With a few notable exceptions, the diaries may not contribute greatly to an understanding of the fictions, but since Kafka dramatized himself to such extent and effect, they are nonetheless captivating, if fragmentary reading; also useful as sources of information on his everyday life. Even more so the letters. In terms of volume, letters, which constituted the bulk of Kafka's daily writing, amount to almost double the collected fiction, and are three times the size of the diaries. He wrote to male friends—most extensively to Max Brod; to editors and publishers, to family members—especially his favourite, youngest sister, Ottla; to love interests—principally his fiancée Felice Bauer, but also to Felice's friend Grete Bloch, to Czech journalist and first translator of some of his works, Milena Jesenská, and to other women as well. Then there is the long, mordant and self-revelatory *Letter to His Father* (first published in 1953) that Kafka wrote in wake of a quarrel with his father over engagement to Julie Woryzhek. According to Max Brod, Kafka gave the letter to his mother to read and she handed it back, refusing to pass it on to his father. Later he gave the manuscript to Milena Jesenská—as their attempts at romance broke down—that she might better understand him.

What makes the letters unique is not only Kafka's talent for writing them, but the overall effect of their readability. The five-year correspondence with two-time fiancée Felice Bauer is the pre-eminent example—comprising over 500 letters, postcards and fragments, and amounting to nearly 700 printed pages. The collection of letters Franz sent to Felice is almost complete; she secretly preserved most of them and late in her life, pressed by economic straits, sold them to Schocken Books for publication. Franz, for his part, did not keep Felice's letters, and kept only a small portion of the letters he received from his many other correspondents. Thus, all the collections of the Kafka letters— like the three novels, diaries, and collections of unpublished short fiction—are fragments and fractures. Fracture, it would seem, is one of the components of Kafkaesqueness. Nevertheless, even one-sided, the letters to Felice are fascinating and can be read as an old-fashioned epistolary novel in which Franz and Felice are the main players, and the plotline a twisted track of the course of Franz's tormented marriage fantasies.

Kafka could not have imagined that within a century of his death the full body of his retrievable work would be published, and that the acclaim accruing to his oeuvre would expose his ghost to an extraordinary, obsessive kind of scrutiny. Every aspect of Franz Kafka's work and life apparently has the power to captivate; I include myself among the captivated. In recent years, I've been spurred in particular by the idea that small peculiarities in his life might shed light on the broader picture, holographically as it were, and bring me closer to the man inside the writer. This is where the cards come in.

***

Cards and card playing do not feature prominently in Kafka's fiction. There's a reference to card play—*Kartenspiel*—in "A Hunger Artist" ("Ein Hungerkünstler"), written in 1922 when he was seriously ill with the tuberculosis that would take his life within two years. The protagonist is a circus performer who earns his living by public performances of fasting. Fasting is both art and life for the hunger artist—something the circus-going public cannot understand. The hunger artist would not, even under compulsion, have taken any food during the fasting period—limited to periods of forty days. The honour of his art forbids this, as any insider (author and close reader) knows. As a formality, however, and to appease the spectators in the story, watchmen are charged with the duty of keeping an eye on the hunger artist around the clock, lest he sneak a morsel. Card play is the device by which the watchmen divert their attention from the hunger artist in order to allow him some small form of sustenance on the sly. Nothing was more excruciating to the hunger artist than watchmen like these, writes Kafka. They made him feel dejected—for their suspicions assailed his personal integrity and the integrity of his art.

"A Hunger Artist" is a mind-bending story. The artist's longing to perform his starvation art, purely, to perfection, and to achieve admiration for it, is doubly damned: In the end his perfectionism wins him neither admiration nor fulfillment. He fasts himself to death in the isolation of his performance cage after his act ceases to appeal (the panther in the next cage becomes more of a draw), and his deepest longing—to find the right sustenance—read: the higher food of absolution—remains unfulfilled. In a bitter real-life twist, Kafka himself—unable to take food or drink due to the spread of pulmonary tuberculosis to his larynx—died the day after he finished correcting the proofs of the book titled for the story.

"A Hunger Artist," first published in 1922 and released in book form as the title piece of a four-story collection in October 1924, four months after his death, is one of a small number of works that Kafka considered fit to publish, and it stands among his final artistic manifestos. Card play—*Kartenspiel*—is mentioned only once in the story, yet it plainly represents degradation and dishonour. It's striking to me now how many times I read the story without attending to the crucial significance of the cards. Only after many rereadings of the *Letters* and *Diaries*—in which cards and card play are mentioned a number of times—did the import of *Karten* and *Kartenspiel* dawn on me; their importance both in and beyond the context of the story.

Cards are mentioned at least four times in Kafka's letters to Felice; three times in the diaries, and once, very signally, in Kafka's *Letter to His Father*. The earliest mention comes in a letter to Felice, written on November 12, 1912, three months after they first met: "I ... would be unable to sleep, for as soon as they (the parents) get together next door and start playing cards (perhaps the only thing in which I couldn't force myself to participate in, even for father's sake, except on the rarest occasions), there is no more peace for me." Kafka was perennially sensitive to noise and the clatter of card play seems to be the major complaint here, yet this mention is also a comment on Kafka's insularity—his resistance to participating in his family's social ritual, "even" in consideration of his father. Father is part of the card-quotient from first mention.

In a letter written on January 19, 1913, Kafka complains again to Felice about the racket in the apartment: "... my brother-in-law and the cousin's husband are playing cards; amidst the laughter, jeering, screams, and slamming of cards, my father occasionally interrupts to imitate his grandson, while high above them all sings the canary." Father, for whom card playing was a daily form of decompressing after a long day's work at the family shop, is singled out here—not only for his loud card-play behaviour, but also for the way he mocks his grandson.

On March 3, 1913, he writes Felice: "My sisters and their husbands have gone; it is already 10:30 (p.m.); but my father has sat down again and ordered my mother to play cards. Owing to my recent cold-catching tendencies, I am obliged to share the living room, and so am writing to the sounds of the card game." Here he bemoans the noise and admonishes his father for ordering his mother to play cards, and at such a late hour. On April 14, he again complains of "having to write in the presence of [his] card-playing parents ..." Card playing disrupts the quiet required for writing and Franz has no patience for family play and games, especially where father is involved.

In a revealing entry on May 27, 1914, he writes: "Mother and sister are in Berlin. I shall be alone with Father in the evening ... Should I play cards (*Karten*) with him? I find the letter K offensive, almost disgusting and yet I use it; it must be very characteristic of me." The initial K, common to both *Karten* and Kafka, is not merely a letter for Franz; it is a consonant infused with contempt. The K name he shares with his father and associates with cards, is triangulated with disgust. The cards can be avoided, but the name remains—a permanent mark of loathing.

The triangle of father-son-cards contempt is most plainly spelled out in Kafka's *Letter to His Father*—written in November 1919, when he was thirty-six and convalescing in Schelesen (Želízy) north of Prague. At over 100 pages, it reads more as a short autobiographical book than a letter, and of all Kafka's private writing is the most personally explicit—a calculated and scathing portrayal of a son's lifelong struggle with a father depicted as coarse and tyrannical.

In the immediate sense, the letter was prompted by Father's rejection of Franz's plan to marry Julie Wohryzek, the daughter of a synagogue beadle; in other words, to marry down. But the broken engagement let go a tidal wave of hurt and blame that had been building and bottled for years. Not only did Franz feel he could not measure up to his father the successful paterfamilias—an achievement he considered "the utmost a man can accomplish"—but he felt dismissed by his father for his own chosen path as a writer: "My vanity, my ambition certainly suffered from your acknowledgement of my books, which became legendary among us: 'Put it on the table by my bed!' (Mostly you were playing cards when a book arrived)." Here, embedded in the *parent*hetical aside is the deep parental connection between *Karten* and Kafka. As Franz saw it, and it was likely so, his father would rather have played cards than read a book by his son, even if the book was dedicated to him, as was the story collection *A Country Doctor*.

Father, a business-minded family man, had no interest in, regard for, or understanding of his son's literary artistry and the solitude he required for writing. And Franz, for his part, felt he could not meet his father on the grounds of marriage, family, and business. These were the domain of Kafka senior from which he, the son, was excluded. And the cards—*Karten* and *Kartenspiel*—became the emblem of division and antipathy, in real life and in writing.

The final diary-mention of cards comes in October 1921, a few months before "A Hunger Artist" was written. On October 25: "My parents were playing cards. I sat apart, a perfect stranger." (It is Franz who excludes himself, feels alien, even with his parents, in his own home.) "My father asked me to take a hand, or at least to look on." (It isn't father who is exclusionary here.) "I made some sort of excuse." (It's Franz who's aloof.) "What is the meaning of these refusals, oft repeated since my childhood?" (He acknowledges his history of resistance.) "And I could have availed myself of invitations to take part in social, even, to an extent, public life." (He recognizes that he's had many opportunities to be socially involved.) "Everything required of me I should have done, if not well, at least in middling fashion." (He allows that skill was never an issue.) "Even card playing would not have bored me overmuch—yet I refused." (Even the derided *Kartenspiel* might have been enjoyable, had he permitted himself to engage.) "Judging by this, I am wrong when I complain that I have never been caught up in the current of life, that I never made my escape from Prague, was never made to learn a sport or trade, and so forth—I should probably have refused every offer, just as I refused the invitation to play cards … I always refused …" (And here Kafka indicts himself for his general intractability, not only where cards are concerned, though cards are the targeted symbol of his social self-contempt.)

On October 29, he resumes the thread: "A few evenings later I did actually join in, to the extent of keeping score for my mother. (It's telling that when he does join in, it's on the periphery—keeping score, not playing—and on the side of mother, not father, who would remain his chief life-rival.) "But it begot no intimacy, or whatever trace there was of it was smothered under weariness, boredom, and regret for the wasted time. It would always have been thus. I have seldom, very seldom crossed this borderland between loneliness and fellowship." The "borderland" was Franz's main dwelling place, by his own designation, and intimacy a lifelong bogey.

Kafka frequently complained of outer isolation and inner abyss. Yet given his many male friendships—several longstanding and close, his allegiance to his youngest sister Ottla especially, his high standing and popularity among colleagues at the office, and his several relationships with women, some of whom loved him—Kafka's self-portrayal seems overly punitive, and disjunctive.

***

It frustrated me that nowhere in the *Kartenspiel* entries in Kafka's *Diaries* or in the *Letters* could I find the name of the game his family played. I searched and came up with nothing. Maybe it was Rummy … This was the game my in-laws brought with them from Transylvania and continued to enjoy playing, up until my mother-in-law's passing in 2004. Or maybe it was Tarock … a gambling version of Tarot mentioned in a novel by Irvin Yalom, set in Austria, and popular in central Europe during Kafka's era …

I asked around in Prague during a visit to the city in November 2015, but no one I spoke to was familiar with either Tarock or Rummy. I did get a few other suggestions—a game called *Prší*, which translates "Raining," and is similar to the American "shedding" game Crazy Eights, but this game, I was told, was more for children. Also *Mariáš*, which, I read online, is part of the King-Queen set of card games with many variations throughout Europe and beyond—like Pinochle, Whist, and Bezique. I read that an elaborate form of *Mariáš*, called *Klaberjass*, was especially popular in Jewish communities. This seemed to be a good lead, but there was no confirmation from Kafka himself, so I remained stumped—

Until I read the translated second volume of German biographer, Reiner Stach's, formidable three-volume biography of Kafka. Titled, *The Decisive Years*, volume two covers the years 1910—when Kafka started keeping diaries—to 1915, when he was thirty-three. In chapter one of the book, Stach names the card game the Kafka family regularly played: *Franzefuss*! Though the source is not cited.

Mist lifted when I came upon that word: *Franzefuss*, which I instinctively translated as "Frank's foot." How comedic, I thought, how Franzesque—a card game containing the name of the person who couldn't stand it.

Once I found the name of the game, I was determined to try to acquire an original *Franzefuss* deck, and despite my own disinterest in card play, learn how to play the game that Franz himself abhorred.

I couldn't find anything under *Franzefuss* online, except for reference to Stach's book in a review by Rivka Galchen. I did, however, find a site—TaroBear's Lair—billed as "your one-stop shop for European regional playing card decks of all kinds." The site showed a wide assortment of contemporary and historical-looking decks, though none designated as *Franzefuss* decks. I decided to give the proprietor, Gary Brunger of Cleveland, Ohio, a call: mid-December, 2015.

Gary Brunger—card importer, avid player, instructor, card club organizer, and affable phone-interlocutor—had never heard of *Franzefuss*. But as an aficionado he was up for helping me out with my project; he told me he'd look into it. By month's end he emailed to report that "all indications point to a German-suited deck used in Prague at that time, the style of card deck commonly known as the Bohemian, or Prague pattern!" This deck, he wrote, "is currently used in Bohemia, and virtually nowhere else! The rest of the Czech Republic, as well as the rest of Central Europe (former Austro-Hungary), uses a different style German-suited deck. Unfortunately, I won't have any of these in until mid-January." I wanted to have the deck shipped to my mom's place in the States in December—to save on shipping. I was taking a trip out west and hoped to pick up the deck while there, maybe even try playing the game with my mom, who happens to be something of a card sharp. He did have a demo deck on hand, which he offered at half the regular cover price of $4.50—if I wasn't prepared to wait till mid-January for a new deck, then added that he "still plans to research some more."

I was open to taking the demo deck for the bargain price of $2.25, but later the same day Gary emailed to say he'd made a call to a local customer, now a collector, who'd bought three of the Bohemian decks and "has one or two that he never opened! I've also sent an email to John McLeod, owner of the pagat.com website (a site that features card games from around the world), to see what he might know about the game and which cards were used." John McLeod was reportedly in England at the time and Gary didn't expect a quick reply. But within a day John McLeod verified that Gary had "indeed deduced the correct card deck!" "Doing the happy dance here, lol," Gary wrote. John McLeod also forwarded a summary of the game in English, sent to him by another enthusiast in the network, one Tomás Svoboda of the Czech Republic:

1. Cards: German deck, 32c
2. Rank of cards, Point value
2.1. Trumps: hearts 10 („Šanta") =40p, clubs S („Pamfl") =30p, Q („Jass") =20p, 9 („Minela") =14p, A=11p, 10=10p, K=4p, J=2p, 8, 7,
2.2 Other suits: A=11p, 10=10p, K=4p, Q=3p, J=2p, 9, 8, 7
3. Players: 2
4. Object of the Game: to score 500 points before opponent (in one or more games) for melds and taking tricks which contain cards with point value (or to score more points in a single game than one's opponent)
5. Melds
5.1. Sequence: 3 cards („darda") =20p, 4 cards („kvarta") =50p, 5 cards („fuss") =100p
5.2. „Bella" (trump K+Q) = 20p
5.3. „Figura" (Four of a Kind): 4xQ=200p, 4x10 or J or K or E=100p
6. Pot: Each player antes agreed money, forming the pot („labeta").

7. Trump suit: is determined by cut by nondealer, by taking out any card and turning it up on table. If he does not cut, trump is determined by last card of pack.

8. Deal: 3x3 cards (9 cards each), rest of cards are placed on the table as stock pile („talon")

9. Play

9.1. Both players draw from stock pile after every trick until the stock is exhausted. Winner of previous trick draws first in following round.

9.2. After stock is exhausted, there is an obligation to follow suit or to use trump. The obligation to trump is not valid for hearts 10 („šanta")

9.3. The player holding the 7 of trump may exchange it for turned-up card while stock pile is not exhausted.9.4. Melds may be declared only before stock pile is exhausted.

9.5. Only one meld may be declared each trick. The player holding, for example, „fuss", may declare, in six separate tricks, „darda" three times, „padesátka" two times and „fuss" one time. There is obligation to declare melds from lower to higher.

9.7. A meld with higher ranking cards takes precedence over a meld with lower ranking cards. It is possible to declare the lower ranking meld in subsequent tricks. If both players declare same meld, the player who plays his trick first prevails.

9.8 „Bella" is declared with playing first of both cards.

10. Calculation

10.1. After each game, points are added up and then summed together with points from previous games.

10.2. Player who first reaches 500p and announces „enough" wins the pot.

"The above seems a little cryptic to me," Gary said, "probably due to the translation, but I'm trying to figure it out!" If it was a "little cryptic" to him—the expert—to me it was completely opaque. I printed it out anyway, to take out west to my mom's, with little hope that she'd be able to make any sense of it either. Nonetheless, I now had confirmation of the game and deck, and a set of rules, which came prefaced with the blurb: "*Franzefuss was a popular game in the Czech Lands, played until the Second World War, especially in the Jewish community. The game is no longer widely played in the Czech Republic.*" It was no mystery as to why the game is no longer played in the Czech Lands: The community that played it was decimated in the Second World War.

Later that day, December 30, 2015, I received "great news," from Gary. The collector he'd mentioned came by with a copy of a brand-new deck of the original *Franzefuss* cards. I put my order through—$4.50 plus $11.65 USD for shipping—and received confirmation, on January 6, 2016, that my deck had arrived by UPS at my mom's place in the States.

On January 6, Gary forwarded more information from John McLeod: PDF files of the *Franzefuss* rules in Czech and an illustrated Gothic-font German version, published by A. Hartsleben Verlag in Vienna and Leipzig in the mid-nineteenth century. "As for those rules in English," Gary said, "I can't decipher them. Very strange. Hopefully these (the Czech and German versions) will help." Well, actually, no. Though interesting to behold, both versions were unreadable to me. And I knew my mom and I would not be playing *Franzefuss* during my visit the following week.

Maybe when I got back, I mused, I'd have luck with the Czech instructions. M. has a Czech business partner, Miroslav, a native of Brno. But Miroslav, it so happens, is not a card player either. He offered to consult with some of the "old-guard" back home, as he put it, to see if they had heard of the game and might be able to help out. He got back to us with a report similar to Tomás Svoboda's: "*Franzefuss* is very old-fashioned and no one plays it anymore ..."

Good sport that he is, though, Miroslav agreed to step up, join us on a Sunday afternoon at our kitchen table, and give the game a go. At the end of March, he came over for coffee and snacks. I brought out the 32-card deck—which looks little like the decks of hearts, diamonds, clubs, and spades we're familiar with—and the instructions in English, German, and Czech. We drank coffee, snacked on wraps, and didn't get much further than learning the names of the cards and a few of the rules: *Jass* = Queen, *Spodek* = Jack; *Figura*, four of a kind,

Darda, a sequence of three, *Quarta*, a sequence of four. *Fuss*—the eponymous *Fuss*, a sequence of five cards, scores 100 points. All tens score highest—200 points, and the lowest cards—seven to nine—score nothing … baffling. After two hours we decided we'd have to meet again if we wanted to get beyond the scoring system and actually play a game.

I'd already concluded that I myself would not be playing. If anything, I'd take Franz's tack and keep score on the side while Miroslav and M. played. But none of us is drawn to cards. Miroslav and M. were really only going along to humour me. And I was humoured. We all were—by the element of fun that characterizes play, not the elements of contest and competition. Just sitting together over coffee, wraps and conversation, laughing over our ineptitude at getting past even the first steps of resurrecting *Franzefuss* on the kitchen table. Laughing most of all at M.'s jokes and his flair for telling them. Levity and feeling fine on a Sunday afternoon. That was as far as we got with the game, even though we paid a little lip-service to getting together again to resume the pursuit.

I'm about as interested in cards as Kafka was. I can relate to his take on *Kartenspiel* as a waste of time. I'd rather read, write, or paint. But cards are not bound up for me, as they were for Franz, with a profound relational struggle. The rivalry that bound him so intractably to his father, at least from his own perspective, has no personal charge in my life. Yet in a small way I feel that I can access, empathically, something of the impact that that rivalry had on Kafka's life and writing.

And I have this facsimile pack of cards—a deck that was once upon a time used by central-European Jewish communities for playing a game that happens to contain Franz's name. These cards, with their odd, old-world images, represent a kind of skewed connectivity for me; I keep them on the shelf above my workplace.

***

Coda: About a year after this piece was written and then published in the *Humber Literary Review*, I discovered that Franz did in fact name the hated card game—in a letter to Felice on May 8, 1913. "Now look, Felice," he wrote, "you've got our families mixed up! It's yours that plays 66, here they play a different game: Franzefuss." The name was there all along. How I could have missed it escapes me; I thought my search of the *Letters* had been so thorough. Evidently, I didn't see it for reading, which, I suppose, is just as well. If I'd found it, my pursuit of it, which was a big part of the ferment, would have been much diminished.

Two Short Talks

In 2010 I purchased a copy of Anne Carson's first poetry collection, *Short Talks* (first published in 1992), at Toronto's Word on the Street. I opened the tall, slim book as soon as I stepped away from the Brick Books kiosk and stood reading under an oak. I was rapt from the first page of the Intro:

"In a good story, Aristotle tells us, everything that happens is pushed by something else ... the plant called audacity that poets mistake for violets ... I will do anything to avoid boredom ... You can never know enough, work enough, use infinitives and participles oddly enough ..." I felt pushed, prodded, pressed. Oddly undressed.

Carson's short talks have been called essays, narrative verses, riddle-poems. To me they read as micro truths, sometimes tiny splices of auto/biography. Of the 45 pieces in the volume, none is longer than one page and several no longer than a few lines. The shortest, "Short Talk on Gertrude Stein at 9:30 p.m.," is nine words. They look like prose—set in narrow, justified columns—and speak mostly in a plain, laconic voice, yet wax lyrical too, and command the galvanic authority of a prophet on a mountaintop. The topics are as unstrung and quirkily diverse as "Homo Sapiens," "Hopes," "Housing," "Hölderlin," and "Hedonism." In other words, as broad as history and evolution, philosophy, travel, art, illness, and Who You Are.

The whole small volume is an astonishment. But two talks in particular drew me in: "Short Talk on Rectification" and "Short Talk on Waterproofing."

Short Talk on Rectification

Kafka liked to have his watch an hour
and a half fast. Felice kept setting it
right. Nonetheless for five years they
almost married. He made a list of
arguments for and against marriage,
including inability to bear the assault of

his own life (for) and the sight of the
nightshirts laid out on his parents' beds
at 10:30 (against). Hemorrhage saved
him. When advised not to speak by
doctors in the sanatorium, he left glass
sentences all over the floor. Felice,
says one of them, had too much nakedness left in her.

Short Talk on Waterproofing

Franz Kafka was Jewish. He had a sister, Ottla, Jewish. Ottla married a
jurist, Josef David, not Jewish. When
the Nuremburg laws were introduced
to Bohemia-Moravia in 1942, quiet
Ottla suggested to Josef David that
they divorce. He at first refused. She
spoke about sleep shapes and property
and their two daughters and a rational
approach. She did not mention,
because she did not yet know the
word, Auschwitz, where she would die
in October 1943. After putting the
apartment in order she packed a ruck-
sack and was given a good shoeshine
by Josef David. He applied a coat of
grease. Now they are waterproof, he
said.

Both talks are about Kafka—the first about Franz and his fiancée
Felice Bauer (1887-1960); the second about his youngest sister Ottla
(1892-1943). When I first read *Short Talks*, I was actively researching
Kafka for a biography-as-art course, so the content of the talks was
familiar, and resonant. Struggling as I was to distill Kafka's life for an

assigned one-hour presentation, I was amazed anew by what could be contained and conveyed about a subject (and its presenter) through spare foregrounding of information, and ellipsis. Carson's choice omission of detail exerts a potent force—the unsaid looming through the said. A large part of my experience of these pieces has been to "live into," so to speak, the unsaid, the alluded to. To reconstruct the bigger picture.

The "Short Talk on Rectification" is a sonnet-length piece of fourteen lines comprising five sentences. The first two sentences address a Kafka idiosyncrasy and Felice's way of dealing with it: "Kafka liked to have his watch an hour / and a half fast. Felice kept setting it / right." These lines are a rephrasing of Kafka's own words from his diary entry of January 24, 1915. He and Felice had reunited in the bordertown of Bodenbach (Děčín) at the time referred to in this snippet and Kafka wrote openly about it in his "private" writing, which he frequently did of such things—in contrast to his more restrained meant-to-be-published fiction. A translation of the actual entry reads: "I think it impossible for us ever to unite … I yield not a particle of my demand for a fantastic life arranged in the interest of my work, she, indifferent to every mute request, wants the average: a comfortable home … good food, bed at eleven, central heating; sets my watch—which for the past three months has been an hour and a half fast—right to the minute."

"Nonetheless," Carson writes in her next sentence, "for five years / they almost married." The adverb "nonetheless" sums it up. Despite significant differences in personality, values, and goals, Franz and Felice were twice engaged to be married. They carried on a tortuous, mostly epistolary five-year relationship—meeting only briefly for a few days here and there. Felice saved more than 500 of Kafka's letters (Kafka did not save hers), which she sold to Schocken Books of New York in 1955, after ill-health left her financially strapped. They were published in English translation in 1973. At nearly 600 small-print pages, they exceed the length of Kafka's novels combined and provide a wealth of biographical insight.

At the beginning of the relationship, Franz was the active pursuer, Felice the somewhat reluctant target. He admired her business acumen, strength and self-sufficiency—qualities he felt lacking in himself. Felice bolstered his confidence as a writer. She became his Muse. Days after his first letter to her, he penned his "breakthrough" story "The Judgement" ("Das Urteil") which he dedicated to Miss F.B. This gave way to an intensely productive writing period that included the completion of "The Stoker" ("Der Heizer") "The Metamorphosis," and "In the Penal Colony"—all works he was satisfied enough with to have published.

Yet even as he wooed Felice, Franz waffled. She was a straightforward young bourgeois woman who wanted to marry, have children, and enjoy a comfortable home life. In this she embodied the conflict he carried—between himself, his family, his social class, and society at large. As soon as she drew near, she pressed on the tensions, and he backed off. Carson addresses this indecision in her fourth sentence: "He made a list of / arguments for and against marriage, / including inability to bear the assault of / his own life (for) and the sight of the / nightshirts laid out on his parents' beds / at 10:30 (against)." The arguments are listed in Kafka's diary entry of July 21, 1913. Seven in all. And even the argument "for" comes with a hedge. In Kafka's own words: "I am incapable, alone, of bearing the assaults of my own life, the demands of my own person, the attacks of time and old age ... sleeplessness, the nearness of insanity—I cannot bear all this alone. I naturally add a perhaps to this ...": "perhaps" being the operative word. Kafka was aware of his block-and-tackle manoeuvres. He may have admired Felice's strength, and in argument six allows that "through the intermediation of [his] wife," he [too] could be "fearless, powerful, surprising, moved as [he] otherwise [is] only when [he] writes ... But then would it not be at the expense of [his] writing? Not that, not that!" Kafka is exclamatory.

Carson is terse. She cuts to the nub of his argument against marriage in the second clause of sentence four; namely, "the sight of the / nightshirts laid out on his parents' beds ..." The nightshirts signal Kafka's deeper reason for holding onto aloneness: "the fear," as he puts it more explicitly in argument 5, "of passing into the other." Kafka's fear of intimacy, sexual intimacy, dogged him his whole life and the nightshirts on the bed are a shorthand for it. Felice was fine as an ideal figure, kept at a distance. When she was in sight of arriving in the flesh, Franz's angst was activated.

Carson distills Kafka's torment to nine lines, and in her fifth sentence, names the "grace": "Hemorrhage saved him." The longer version of this is that during the night of August 13, 1917, Kafka suffered a pulmonary hemorrhage that led to a diagnosis of tuberculosis. He did not view the disease so much as a disease of the lungs as an indictment of his life: part punishment, part penance. Also, more immediately, as sweet deliverance from Felice. On September 4, 1917, he wrote to Ottla: "There is no doubt justice in this illness; it is a just blow, which, incidentally, I do not at all feel as a blow but as something altogether sweet in comparison with the average course of these last years." On September 15, he wrote in his diary rare words of self-encouragement: "You have a chance, as far as is possible, to make a new beginning. Don't throw it away … If the infection in your lungs is only a symbol, as you say, a symbol of infection whose inflammation is called Felice and whose depth is its deep justification; if this is so then the medical advice (light, air, sun, rest) is also a symbol. Lay hold of it." Kafka was granted medical leave from the Workers' Accident Insurance Institute and went to convalesce under his sister Ottla's care in the village of Zürau, northwest of Prague. He broke the news of his illness to Felice, only when the Zürau plans were set; he meant to orchestrate his escape, and discourage her from coming to visit. She made the journey to Zürau anyway, hoping to console, or help out. In his diary entry of September 21, he wrote: "Felice was here, travelled thirty hours to see me; I should have prevented her. As I see it, she is suffering the utmost misery and the guilt is essentially mine … she is an innocent person condemned to extreme torture." In his last letter to her, dated October 16, 1917, he gave her the self-abnegating version of his ailment: "I don't believe this disease to be tuberculosis, at least not primarily tuberculosis, but rather a sign of my general bankruptcy." Three months after their second engagement had been solemnized, the relationship was over.

Kafka lived seven years with TB and continued to have troubled relations with women—including another broken engagement, before meeting Dora Diamant in 1923. But by this time his health was in rapid decline and he had little strength left, either for writing or for physical intimacy. He and Dora were together for the last months of his life and she was at his side when he died at Hoffmann Sanatorium in Kierling. Carson goes straight to the end-of-days in the final lines of her poem—referencing the "conversation slips" that Kafka wrote in lieu of speaking at the late stage of tuberculosis, when the disease had advanced to his larynx and the pain of speaking so great that silence was prescribed. (The slips are the last record of his observations and feelings as he lay dying. His friend and attending physician, Dr. Robert Klopstock, preserved the slips and later gave them to Max Brod. Some are included in the collection *Letters to Friends, Family and Editors*, published in English in 1958.)

In the declamatory deadpan of the last two lines of her talk, Carson writes: "When advised not to speak by / doctors in the sanatorium, he left glass / sentences all over the floor. Felice, / says one of them, had too much naked - / ness left in her." This is fictional. What Kafka actually wrote on a slip in speaking of Felice, was: "She was not beautiful, but slender, fine body, which she has kept according to reports."

The most fictionalized part of Anne Carson's short talk is "glass sentences." It is also the most revealing and poetically true.

What is glass? A hard yet brittle substance with an irregular atomic structure. Transparent, translucent, shiny and ice-like. Like Kafka. Like Carson, too, who put glass in the title of her long poem, "The Glass Essay," published in the collection *Glass, Irony and God* by New Directions in 1992, the same year that *Short Talks* came out with Brick Books. "The Glass Essay"—a rich and searing piece about the narrator's loneliness in wake of rejection by a lover called Law—bears traces and shades of Kafka. But that's another topic and I won't digress, other than to say that glass in "The Glass Essay" is a substance of transparent entrapment where soul is exposed and has no shield. In the short talk, the "glass sentences" that Carson imputes to Kafka are more like shards. Sharp, hard verdicts—one of which signals the final rejection of Felice by Franz, because of her "naked - / ness." The "nakedness" attributed by Carson to Felice also has a parallel in "The Glass Essay," in the synonym "Nudes." Carson writes: "I find no shelter. / I am my own Nude. And Nudes / have a sexual destiny." Nudes and nakedness are about sexuality in both poems. In "The Glass Essay" the narrator is rejected, sexually humiliated. In real life, Felice was also humiliated—

though this is part of the unsaid in the "Short Talk on Rectification." Felice's sexual destiny, her womanhood, could not be rectified.

As it happened, while reading Carson alongside Kafka, I also read *Kafka's Other Trial: The Letters to Felice* (Schocken Books, 1974), Nobel laureate Elias Canetti's fascinating volume on Franz and Felice's correspondence. I could not help but notice that three of the key words in Carson's talk also appear in Canetti's work—two of them in italics. The first is "rectification," on page 79, where Canetti uses the term to refer to the period of Franz and Felice's relationship after the so-called "tribunal" at Hotel Askanischer Hof in Berlin in July 1914, at which Kafka was confronted by Felice and her friend Grete Bloch. Grete had been recruited by Felice in the fall of 2013 to mediate between herself and Franz in the uneasy period leading up to their first engagement (in June 1914), and ended up becoming a parallel love interest, as it were, to Franz. Kafka was accused by Felice and exposed by the two women at the Askanischer Hof. He had no defense: He'd been maintaining something of a two-track relationship. His engagement to Felice was dissolved on the spot.

But they didn't break off contact altogether, and in August Kafka began writing his novel *The Trial.* Canetti argues, on page 63, that the emotional substance of Kafka's engagement and the "tribunal" at the Askanischer Hof both entered directly into the novel: the engagement became the arrest of Josef K. in the first chapter and the "tribunal" the execution in the last. The rectification period, according to Canetti, was characterized by Franz's attempts to "rectify" Felice; that is, to improve her, to make of her a different, less bourgeois woman: to purge her of the heavy furniture. But, as Carson pinpoints in her short talk, the bourgeois in Felice was secondary to the more basic problem of her female sexuality, and she could not be purged of that. As for Kafka himself, rectification would only come through illness, and ultimately, death.

The word "naked" is also italicized in Canetti, on page 83, though here naked is used in the sense of bare, clear, exposed and exposing— more like "glass." "Glass" appears in Canetti too, on page 117, where he writes of Kafka's last letter to Felice: "his glassy statements" (close to Carson's "glass sentences") do not include Felice and are addressed as to a third person. On page 118, Canetti calls Kafka's description of his and Felice's last visit (at Zürau) "cold as ice" and on pages 115-16 deems the final letter to Felice, as a whole, the "most disagreeable he ·(Kafka) ever wrote."

The concurrence of these key terms—rectification, naked/ness, and glass sentences / glassy statements—in Canetti and Carson is unmistakable, and indicates how keen and common interest in a life can bring authors to coinciding perceptions; how the plane of reading and writing, like skin, can be continuous.

In her "Short Talk on Waterproofing," Carson continues—shifting from Kafka's (troubled) love life to his (troublesome) background. "Franz Kafka was Jewish," she writes in the first sentence of the 18-line piece. It's ironic, as an aside, that 18 is the numerical value of the Hebrew word "chai" which means "life"—as in the toast "L'Chaim" / "To Life"—whereas the poem addresses the relationship of Jewishness to death. Carson surely could not have intended any Hebrew number symbolism for her poem, but, coincidentally, there it is.

The first three sentences are the set-up: "Kafka was Jewish. He had a sis- / ter, Ottla, Jewish. Ottla married a jurist, Josef David, not Jewish." Josef David, despite his Hebrew-sounding name, was Czech (and a Catholic nationalist). Whereas Kafka, partly due to his non-Hebrew-sounding name, was not readily identifiable as a Jew. Neither did his published fiction mark him out as Jewish: Nowhere does he mention Jews or Jewishness. In fact, references to religion in Kafka's fiction are distinctly Christian—reflecting the society he lived and wrote in. But in his diaries and letters—not intended for publication— he bared his soul as a Jew in search of an authentic Jewish experience. Kafka was deeply interested in Yiddish theatre, Jewish mysticism, folklore, Hebrew language, scripture and history, and late in his life, also Zionism. Had he not succumbed to tuberculosis, he and Dora might well have immigrated together to Palestine / Eretz Israel. This was their plan. Ottla might have been persuaded to go that route too. She had a similar interest and would have thrived on a pioneering agricultural collective. Ottla was fiercely independent. She flouted her parents' designs for her, studied at an agricultural college in Germany and tended her brother-in-law's farm in Zürau, where she also cared for her ailing brother in 1917-18. She took the even more radical step of marrying out of the faith in July 1920, in opposition to everyone in her family—apart from Franz who supported her like an ally.

Kafka and his parents did not live to see the rise of Nazism. His three sisters were deported and murdered. But Carson comes in, in sentence four, "When the Nuremberg laws were introduced to Bohemia and Moravia in 1942." At this time Ottla had been married to Josef David for twenty-two years and they had two grown daughters, Vera—twenty-one, and Helena, nineteen. Most of what is available on Ottla in English comes from a few sources. The main source is Franz's *Letters to Ottla & Family*, published in English translation in 1977 by Schocken Books with an introduction by editor Nachum Glatzer. This is where Anne Carson draws details for her short talk. Glatzer describes Franz's youngest sister as "reticent, shy, kind, obliging, friendly, gracious ... living in quiet opposition to the bourgeois society and the petit bourgeois regimen of her family." From this list Carson chooses the word "quiet" to describe Ottla, and completes the fourth sentence: "quiet / Ottla suggested to Josef that / they divorce." And this, says Glatzer, is where Ottla's "real story begins"—which he only knows through an old friend of Ottla's, one Anna Maria Jokl, who published what she knew about Ottla in the *Frankfurter Allgemeine Zeitung* in 1969. And so it goes: Ottla to Jokl to Glatzer to Carson: "Ottla suggested to Josef that / they divorce. He at first refused." But brave, self-sacrificing Ottla, who put the protection of her daughters and their father before herself, "advanced the argument," relates Glatzer, so "that after the divorce, their daughters would retain rights to the elder Kafkas' property. This the lawyer David recognized as a "rational approach" and the divorce was effected. Carson renders it thus: "She / [Ottla] spoke about sleep shapes and property / and their two daughters and a rational / approach." The "property" and the "daughters" and the "'rational approach'" from the Jokl / Glatzer account, Carson retains. But she inserts the enigmatic "sleep shapes," giving the passage a liminal quality, and augmenting its strangeness.

In sentence seven Carson steps out of Ottla's purview and tells readers what they already know: that Jews were murdered at Auschwitz. But "she," [Ottla], "did not mention, / because she did not know the

/ word, Auschwitz where she would die / in October 1943." Carson is very good at pathos in plain-face. The back story, she does not impart, because the talk is short, and adding would dampen the impact. But in real life, Ottla, the ever-good-hearted Ottla, interned at the Nazi show-camp Theresienstadt (north of Prague), was one of fifty-three guardians who volunteered to accompany a transport of 1,260 Jewish children to what she and they believed would be safe haven abroad. They were all gassed the day they arrived at Auschwitz.

The final three sentences of the short talk return to the days before Ottla was transported to Theresienstadt, after she divorced Josef David in August 1942, went to the police and registered as a Jewess. Vera and Helena begged to stay with their mother, but they were turned away since the law did not apply to them as daughters of a Czech Catholic father. And Ottla went to Theresienstadt alone. In what must be the most grimly ironic passage in her book, Carson draws from Glatzer's introduction and Anna Maria Jokl's report, barely altering a word: "After putting the / apartment in order she [Ottla] packed a ruck- / sack and was given a good shoeshine / by Josef David. He applied a coat of / grease. Now they are waterproof, he / said."

Rectification and waterproofing. Two longish, positive-sounding words. Rectification, by definition, is about improvement, correcting an error; repair. Waterproofing means making something resistant, impervious, safe against water. But there is no "safe against" at a Theresienstadt or an Auschwitz. And what might have been the tenderest gesture of love and affection on the part of Josef David, one small thing that he was able to do in seeing Ottla off, reads almost as a nod to savagery. Carson brings the record to its barest, glassiest, brittlest pith in these two talks. There is brokenness. And rectification, or repair, seems a long, long way off. The Hebrew term for repair is *tikkūn*, which, by way of Jewish mysticism, has come to possess connotations of healing work and transformation. It also implies shared responsibility. There's a line in Anne Carson's poem "God's Work" from *Glass, Irony and God* that reads: "From these diverse signs you can see / how much work remains to do." This echoes the close of her Introduction to *Short Talks*, where she writes: "Well you can never work enough."

Weisser Hirsch

IN THE SUMMER of 1903, after writing his final exam in historical law at Prague's Charles University, twenty-year-old Franz travelled to Weisser Hirsch (White Hart) near Dresden to recuperate—at Lahmann Sanatorium—a health and treatment spa founded by celebrated naturopath physician Heinrich Lahmann. Franz was an early natural-health enthusiast and at twenty already a seasoned swimmer, rower, hiker and rider. He was also familiar with the spa culture of the time. One didn't have to be sick to stay at a treatment resort. Anyone who could afford to escape the travails of everyday life could relax, unwind, and undergo "cures" at one of the fashionable spas of Central Europe. Kafka's parents were regular guests at Franzensbad; they also sojourned at Karlsbad and Marienbad—the triangle of popular west Bohemian luxury treatment resorts.

Lahmann Sanatorium was farther afield—in Germany—but Franz, motivated to escape Prague and its clutches, convinced his parents that after working hard and successfully completing his rigorous exam, he was entitled to rest and recuperate at the renowned Weisser Hirsch clinic. Dr. Lahmann's naturopathy was state-of-the-art. He offered a regimen called "Physiatrics" that included hydrotherapy, "air baths" in specially designed "air huts," mud pack purges, inhalations, UV light and electrotherapeutic treatments. There was a social aspect to the Lahmann regimen too. Patients were encouraged to meet mornings for light gymnastic exercise, team sports were advocated, and nutritional meals taken together. The sanatorium was expensive, more than a civil-servant lawyer would have been able to afford, and Franz was still only a law student. His parents agreed to foot the bill for their son's pricey, two-week stay.

***

In July 2016 M. and I took the twenty-minute drive from our hotel on Neumarkt Square in central Dresden to Weisser Hirsch—now a suburb of the city. I, especially, was interested to see what remained of the sanatorium that had had its heyday before World War One and made such an impression on young Franz that he brought home with him a set of newfangled, family-distressing practices. He began sleeping on hard surfaces and performing calisthenics with the windows open, no matter the weather. He consolidated unconventional eating habits, including Fletcherizing (named for American health faddist Horace Fletcher)—a practice of chewing each bite of food, thirty-two times, until it became a liquefied mass. The latter practice particularly irritated his father, to no end. Kafka retained a lifelong holistic approach to health, including a preference for vegetarianism, though later in life he disavowed what he came to regard as the oppressive rigidity of health-spa and sanatorium practices.

M. and I were both astonished by what we found of the former sanatorium. The site, renamed Dr. Lahmann Park, is huge: 36,000 square meters, and since 2011, under renovation by the developer Baywobau—designated to become a compound of luxury condominiums. We arrived at a deserted lot of partially renovated buildings and quantities of neatly stacked building materials, but no machinery or sign of recent activity. We entered the silent site from an opening on a side street, Stechgrundstrasse, and surreptitiously explored—photographing the ruins and the restoration-in-progress. It wouldn't remain this way for long, we surmised, and our photographs would hold the moment: the partly restored "Docktorhaus," Hirschhaus," and "Natura Sanat," and the many ravaged rooms, halls, walls, windows, doors and corridors, staircases, nooks, panels, frames and grilles—still standing derelict. The walk-through felt like a strange trespass into a fractured past: eerie, doleful, remotely composed.

We sat for drinks at a restaurant on Stechgrundstrasse after we left the lot. I asked the waiter if there was much work going on at Dr. Lahmann Park. "It looks like the development is on hold," I said. "Dr. Lahmann Park?" he questioned, looking puzzled. "Yes, the site of the former Lahmann Sanatorium. Over there," I said, pointing out the window across the street. "Oh that," he replied flatly. "Who knows." M. and I were astonished by the find: that it was there at all, that it had withstood two World Wars, that a good portion of it was being preserved, renovated and repurposed. And that it was open for us to explore, unimpeded, upon our arrival. The waiter, for his part, couldn't have cared less.

***

After our visit, I read that the Lahmann site had housed a hospital administered by the Soviet Army, from 1946-1992, which explained why we found Russian books in a few of the ruined rooms. That the books had lain there for almost twenty-five years after the Russians withdrew seemed implausible. Yet there they were. Mouldy but intact. I'd considered taking something from our exploration home as a keepsake: one of the books, or an old metal electrical box I'd photographed hanging askew in a brick niche. In the end I decided that the photos would be keepsake enough. It seemed almost indecent to think of removing any of those artefacts, even if they'd probably be cleared and disposed of anyway. As for Franz, not a trace. Except, perhaps, the fact of what was standing.

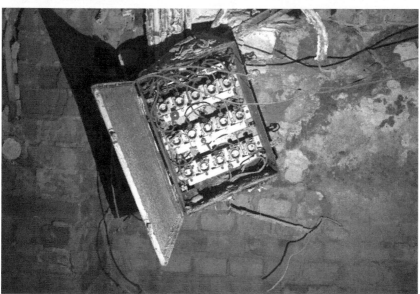

What More Is There to Say of Hearts

I saw the man in the dream—that Franz—
on a bench in the park
consuming fruit: Fletcherizing it—
masticating it
slowly—for his health.

He rose from the bench;
this act in the past
converted the dream-scene
to red—probably through the homophone "rose,"

though maybe through the fruit
he liked to eat.
That colour
in Chotkovny Park, in
a garden of sculpted hearts—

What more is there to say of hearts
that hasn't been said already
by the Romantics
and more baroquely—

Maybe that these hearts in the park
were captured in paint by an artist I like,
that she and Franz and I have strolled
that park in Prague,
though he the most,
and none of us together.
Of dreams: that they conflate and animate.
Of red: that it's the colour across from green.

Back at the Office

IN NOVEMBER 2015, M. and I were in Prague on an indoor leg of my quest. I'd booked a room at 7 Na Poříčí Street in the neo-Baroque building that had once housed the Workers' Accident Insurance Institute—the semi-governmental company where Kafka worked as an insurance lawyer. The building is now Hotel Century Old Town and Room 214, Kafka's former office, a guest suite.

I was thrilled to be staying in the room where Kafka had worked as a respected civil servant for fourteen years—longer than he lived and wrote in any of his many dwelling places around town. By the time he was pensioned off at thirty-nine in 1922, he'd been promoted to the eminent rank of senior secretary. He was a much-admired, highly valued asset to the firm. Yet in his correspondence, he referred to the office as a dreadful impediment to his real life's work—his writing—and complained that "writing and the office cannot be reconciled."

In fact, the office and Kafka's writing could not be *un*reconciled. He lived and breathed the Institute so deeply that his writing became suffused with its stamp and language. The office provided a trove of images, associations, and scenarios that made their way into his fiction. *The Trial* and *The Castle*, in particular, present refractions of the senseless, pedantic, often cruel and absurdly bureaucratic work-world that Kafka knew well, and that has come to be characterized by his name 'adjectivized': Kafkaesque. His restrained, precise, elliptical yet crystalline language can also be traced to the legalistic style required for the office.

Taking a cue from French philosopher Gaston Bachelard's lyrical work, *The Poetics of Space*, my aim during our 2015 stay was to check out the physical features of Kafka's workplace for what they might reveal. Bachelard held that there is active interplay between the mind and its surroundings, that the spaces we live and work in have great power for the integration of our thoughts, and that the rooms a person spends time in can be put to what he termed topoanalysis. Topoanalysis asks: Is the room large? Is it cluttered? How is it appointed, and lit? Does it afford reverie? Reverie was important to Bachelard—as the state for seeding creativity. Kafka would have concurred. For Franz, the boundary between dream, reverie and reality was constantly eroded.

Bachelard's *Poetics* became the hook for "Faithfully Seeking Franz: The Office Stop," a piece I wrote in wake of the 2015 trip that was published in the 2017 Summer Issue of New *Madrid – journal of contemporary literature*. The piece comprised a blend of observations, evaluations and imaginations. In the absence of photographic evidence, I imagined, for example, what Kafka might have had on his office walls. Diplomas maybe, a painting or two … I was reminded of Chapter 7 of *The Trial*, the comedic scene featuring the wily court painter Titorelli. Kafka's stand-in, Josef K., purchases one, then two identical "Sunset over the Heath" landscapes that Titorelli pulls out from the dust under the bed in his studio, sensing a buyer in the chief financial bank officer. "They're beautiful landscapes," the bewildered Josef K. says of the gloomy paintings. "I'll buy them both and hang them in my office." Titorelli, eager to unload his surplus, then extracts all the identical heath paintings he has under his bed and Josef K., nonplussed, agrees to take every one! Ha!

Making sure that I would not be without photographic evidence this time round, I photographed the room—the layout, appointments and furnishings—from all angles. Then, standing before the high open windows, imagining myself like Kafka—fresh-air zealot that he was— inhaling the cool autumn breeze, I was struck by what faced me on the neo-Baroque building across the street: a stone relief sculpture of a beautifully hewn sheep, sitting naturalistically on an altar-like mound. Noble profile, solemn body: grey stone on a golden background.

Relief sculptures are common in Prague and many of the neo-Baroque buildings feature animals on their façades. The buildings are even named for these decorative emblems—as in House at the Unicorn,

House at the Golden Pike, House at the Blue Goose, House at the White Swan. Creatures are pervasive features in Kafka's work as well: dogs, horses, apes, jackals, mice, goats, moles … Creatures that speak, whistle, sing, investigate, and burrow into the issues important to the author: the nature of power and authority, alienation, the strangeness of modern life, the inescapability of cruelty, guilt and shame.

I couldn't, I wrote in my 2015 piece, recall any sheep in Kafka's fiction. In a 1913 diary entry, however, Kafka wrote obliquely: "I am really like a lost sheep … or like a sheep running after this sheep." *This* sheep. I stared at the sheep on the building before me—a building that looked to be of the same vintage as the former Workers' Accident Insurance Institute, that Kafka would have viewed from his office window whenever he looked out onto Na Poříčí Street. I wondered if I was apprehending some thread of connection between the world of the office and Kafka's private diary-writing. (He couldn't have imagined that the body of his meant-to-be private writings would be published after his death and scrutinized by generations of readers.)

"Imagination augments the value of reality," Bachelard writes in The *Poetics of Space*. A part of me wanted to believe that this particular sheep-in-relief spoke to Kafka personally, and that I, all these years removed, was tapping that connection. This part of me wanted to interject insight, to augment the literary value of the sheep for the sake of my search. I wanted to be addressed. I wanted there to be message 'out there' and here for me—one that others may have missed. But plainer thoughts and questions prevailed: What can really be culled from a mutual view? And what can we truly know of the links between the seen, the perceived, the dreamed, and the written-down? These are mostly covert connections and processes, obscured and unknown—even to writers themselves.

I looked long and hard at the sitting figure—the solemn, regal sheep. I took several photos. The stone did not disclose a thing; it remained as enigmatic as Franz. I started to feel warm, thirsty, slightly addled. Then another shadow of doubt descended: that this room was ever Kafka's actual office. Wouldn't a senior civil servant have earned a room on a higher floor ... I wrote in closing my previous piece.

The editor who selected the essay for publication in *New Madrid* liked that open-ended ending, which he saw as my invoking a Kafka-like ambivalence. Thing is: I ended on that note because I really did doubt that Suite 214 had ever been Kafka's office. I wasn't aiming to invoke a Kafka-like device.

***

In 2018, M. and I were back in Prague—on this trip our base for a trek to Kafka-destinations east of the capital. I again booked at the Hotel Century Old Town, though this time I requested a room on the top floor: I wanted to see what view Kafka likely actually had.

The hotel had undergone renovations—the foyer now modernized and shiny, with ambient lighting, chrome-back chairs upholstered in green chenille, matching green carpets and low-standing, circular mirror-top tables. The bronze bust of Kafka, mounted on a stand in an enclave near the ornate railing of the original staircase, appeared to be the only appointment in the foyer that remained from our previous stay. "It was decided," the receptionist, a tall friendly young man named Jan, said, "to give the hotel a more contemporary look." M. mentioned my Kafka-quest and I told Jan that I was not convinced that Suite 214—still being advertised as the Kafka Suite—was ever actually Kafka's former office. "Wouldn't a senior employee at the Insurance Institute have commanded an office on the top floor?" I asked. "You're right," Jan said. "Kafka did have an office on the top floor. But he also had an office on the lower floor. Both locations are actual. You might be interested to know that the Kafka Suite 214 is currently being upgraded. It's not yet open to guests, but perhaps you'd like to see it as it is in progress." Well, of course, I would!

To our surprise, Jan emerged from behind the reception desk, deposited our bags in a storage room adjacent the desk, led us to the elevator, and escorted us up to Suite 214 on the spot, to give us a tour of the renovation-in-progress. It was as if Kafka himself had instantly intervened and directed the motions on our behalf!

Suite 214 looked nothing like it did in 2015. It was enlarged—two or three suites combined—with a sitting room, dining area, entrance nook, separate bedroom, spacious bathroom, and a built-in bookcase containing, disappointingly, only one Kafka title. The décor—black, white and putty-grey—imparted a cool, minimalist look. The renovation was close-to-complete. A painter was standing on a ladder by the window, looking like an actor in an art installation, applying finishing touches. A large black and white portrait of Franz stood propped against the wall of the sitting room, behind it a framed facsimile of a page from his story "The Judgement." And on the wall: a thick black decorative daub of paint.

"How much would it cost to stay here for a night?" M. asked. "About 16,500 Czech crowns," Jan said. I didn't do the math, but it sounded way beyond our budget. It was all fine and large to be having a surprise glimpse into a renovation-in-progress, and to be documenting it in photographs, but I was feeling suddenly fortunate to have had the opportunity, in 2015, to stay in the more economical model of 214. Kafka himself would not have been able to afford a night in his eponymous suite, and most probably wouldn't have wanted to!

All the rooms at Hotel Century Old Town had been renovated to showcase the Kafka connection.

A swishy K logo had been applied to the walls; some also featured a framed fragment of an enlarged Kafka text. The management, clearly banking on international Kafka cachet, had converted the whole hotel into a kind of Kafka central—with a Kafka lounge, accessible from Na Poříčí Street, and conference rooms named for women in Kafka's life: Felice, Milena, and Dora. The restaurant was no longer called The Felice Patisserie, but Kafka's so-called "favourite cake"—Bábovka—was still being served. During our 2015 stay, we were amused to see that Kafka's "favourite" changed daily.

Upstairs, in our small cramped room with its swishy black K above the bed, I had to lean way out the window to get a photograph of the regal sheep relief on the building across the street that I'd readily captured face-to-face on our previous stay down at Suite 214 ... And now a new doubt started to well up in me. I wondered if the building across the street had actually been standing when Kafka worked in this one. Maybe when he stood in his top-floor office, inhaling the fresh air at his high window, he saw an open city vista, no building with a sheep relief at all.

In Berlin

APART FROM VACATIONS, business trips, and his final years of convalescing, Franz Kafka's life centered on Old Town Prague. Escape plans were mustered early and updated regularly, yet one wonders whether Kafka ever really wanted to leave his hometown, even as he protested its grip. In a letter to classmate Oskar Pollak, written in 1902 when he was nineteen, he rails that "Prague doesn't let go ... This old crone has claws ... We would have to set fire to it on two sides ... then it would be possible to get away." Pollak, for his part, did get away. After attaining a doctorate in art history at Prague's Charles University, he lectured at the University of Vienna, then worked as art historian at the Austrian Institute for Historical Research in Rome. When the First World War broke out, he volunteered and died on the Austro-Italian front.

Franz escaped that fate. After attaining his law degree from Charles University in 1906, he took a position at the Prague branch of the Italian-owned Assicurazioni Generali insurance firm with "hopes of sitting in chairs in faraway countries"—as he wrote to Hedwig Weiler, a girl he met over the summer while visiting his Uncle Siegfried in Triesch, Moravia. To Max Brod, he wrote of securing a position through his Madrid uncle, director of the Spanish railway, and of going to "South America, or the Azores, or Madeira." Daydreaming was natural for Franz. And both he and Max had a taste for travel. From 1910 to 1912, they vacationed together in Paris, Switzerland, Italy, and Germany. Kafka's destinations all hold appeal for me and I'm slowly making my way along his routes, staying, where possible, in places he stayed—in pursuit and sympathy. As Franz himself stayed at Hotel Matschakerhof while in Vienna in 1913—in sympathy with one of his own dead literary mentors, Franz Grillparzer, who routinely took lunch at the hotel.

But he "hated Vienna," that "decaying mammoth village"—as he put it in a letter of April 8, 1914. He felt that his best prospects for getting away—from parents, the office, and the old crone claws of Prague—would be in Berlin, where he could make best use of his writing ability. "I choose Berlin" because "I love it," he proclaimed. Berlin was the city-screen onto which he projected his early escape dreams. It's not surprising then that an "empty face" young woman from Berlin became his first, and probably most significant, muse.

On August 13, 1912, the day Kafka met Fräulein Felice Leonie Bauer, a relative by marriage of the Brods, he wrote in his diary: "When I arrived at Brod's, she was sitting at the table. I was not at all curious about who she was, but rather took her for granted. Bony, empty face that wore its emptiness openly. Bare throat. A blouse thrown on. Looked very domestic in her dress although, as it later turned out, she by no means was." Felice may not have had physical beauty to recommend her. But she had the right résumé for Franz. She was a successful professional woman living in Berlin; a shorthand typist and executive secretary at Carl Lindström Inc.—a firm that made gramophone and dictation machines. She travelled frequently and represented her company. She enjoyed transcribing manuscripts and had invited Max to send his manuscripts to her in Berlin. She attended the theatre, read books, was interested in Zionism and learning Hebrew. Kafka had a subscription to the Zionist monthly, *Palästina*, but when they met had not yet taken up Hebrew study. He was astonished by the confluence of qualities. Normally reserved, he suddenly asserted that he was willing to devote his entire vacation the following year to travelling to Palestine and he invited Fräulein Felice to join him. She declared her willingness and they shook hands on it.

By the time Franz was walking Felice back to her hotel, he'd reached an "unshakeable opinion," he wrote in his diary. A week later, on September 20, he penned his first letter to her. And during the night of September 22-23, in an eight-hour marathon, he composed what he regarded as his breakthrough story, "The Judgement," a possible suicide, or dying-into-life tale, which he dedicated to Miss F.B. Felice wrote back to her suitor on September 28 and their five-year, upwards of 500-letter correspondence—punctuated by two broken engagements and fewer than twenty live encounters—tumbled into motion. Felice secretly kept most of the letters Franz wrote to her and only late in life, under financial pressure, sold them to Schocken Books of New York, along with the rights to publish them, for the modest sum of $5,000. *Letters to Felice* was first published in 1967, forty-three years after Kafka's death. Felice's letters to Franz were not preserved.

I'm hardly alone in feeling degrees of uneasiness in reading Kafka's letters—rich as they are in drama, melodrama, and quotidian detail—for he surely intended them for Felice's eyes only. He famously willed the incineration of all his unpublished manuscripts—letters and diaries included. And Max Brod, as executor, famously defied that will and devoted much of his own life to publishing all of Kafka's retrievable writings and promoting the literary legacy of his friend. The letters and diaries—a lion's share of all that Kafka wrote—provide a wealth of insight into how he constructed his daily life: what he did and felt and dreamt, what he thought and saw and read, what he ate and how he ate it, what he wore and what he weighed, how he slept or didn't sleep, where he stayed, for how long, and with whom.

For the duration of his relationship with Felice, Kafka regularly stayed at the Askanischer Hof Hotel, when in Berlin. The *Baedeker* travel guide recommended the Askanischer Hof as one of the more expensive smaller places to stay: 50 rooms with 70 beds, baths, a restaurant, and a garden terrace. Kafka liked it well enough to become a return customer. "My joys and miseries are so entwined with the place," he wrote to Felice on May 25, 1915, "it is almost as though I had left behind some roots into which I could graft myself on my return. Besides, they like me there. On the other hand, it is rather uncomfortable, also fairly expensive; but—I stick to it—I still like it best." With Franz there was always an "other hand."

In my early phase of tracking Kafka, the Askanischer Hof Hotel was at the top of my to-visit-list—the Berlin location most saturated, as it were, with Franz. The site of the most dramatic scene in his relationship with Felice, perhaps in his entire life: the "tribunal," as he referred to it in his diary entry of July 23, 1914, that spurred the writing of *The Trial*.

There's an eerie foreshadowing of the novel in Franz's very first letter to Felice. The last words read: "… you might well give me a trial." He cannot have meant to be predictive. He likely meant nothing more than give this man a chance, but since a trial of sorts did ensue, in which Franz was in the metaphorical dock, these early words to Felice seem oddly ominous. Even though Felice was the one under examination at the start of the relationship, not Franz. Already in his second, long letter of September 28, he was demanding details about her life in Berlin—as if collecting data for a life insurance package, travel prospectus, storyline, or all three: "You must record at what time you get to the office, what you had for breakfast, what you see from your office window, what kind of work you do there, the names of your male and female friends, why you get presents, who tries to undermine your health by giving you sweets, and the thousand things of whose existence and possibilities I know nothing." In the same letter, strange for an opener, he also admitted to mood swings and indecisiveness: "Oh, the moods I get into, Fräulein Bauer! A hail of nervousness pours down upon me continuously. What I want one minute I don't want the next."

In the letters to Felice, Kafka's tone is frequently effusive, his manner extravagant—so unlike the cool, removed style of his fiction. Yet no less deliberate. By November 1912 Franz and Felice were writing to each other almost daily, sometimes more than once a day. Franz is candid about his sleeplessness, his restlessness, especially at the office, "which bears no relation to my real needs." He deems himself "sincere … perhaps also insincere"; says that his "life consists, and basically always has consisted, of attempts at writing, mostly unsuccessful"; that when he isn't writing, he is "flat on the floor, fit for the dustbin." He is abjectly honest. He tells Felice that there's hardly a quarter of an hour of his waking time in which he does not think of her, yet even this, he admits, is related to his writing: "My life is determined by nothing but the ups and downs of writing." Writing, he makes clear from the start of their correspondence, is his life. And Felice—as subject of his romanticized fixation—is subjected to his writing.

On November 9 he drafted a letter he didn't send: "Dear Fräulein Felice, You are not to write to me again, nor will I write to you. I would be bound to make you unhappy, and as for me I am beyond all help." On November 11 he wrote: "My health is only just good enough for myself alone, not good enough for marriage, let alone fatherhood." The story of Franz and Felice might have ended here. But the following week he made an impassioned about-face. "Dearest, dearest!" he exclaimed, switching from the formal German form of you—"Sie"— to the familiar "Du": "The Du stands firm, like your letter when I kiss it."

He was gushing. With Felice in the picture, his writing was suddenly going well. He'd decided not to give up on his novel, *Der Verschollene* (*Amerika*), at least for the time being, and in October completed the first chapter, "The Stoker," to his rare satisfaction.

In mid-December 1912 his first book, *Meditation* (*Betrachtung*), was released with Rowohlt—the collection of short prose pieces he'd been shaping for publication the evening he and Felice met at the Brods'. He was working on his story "The Metamorphosis" and waved off, with sugary pledges of love, an opportunity to reunite with Felice at holiday time: "Where are your lips?" (December 27-28) and "goodnight, dearest, and a long, calm, confident kiss" (December 28-29), countered with rebuff: "You have proved your love with long letters, now prove it with short ones" (December 30-31). He wanted the connection with Felice, as long as it served and didn't detract from his writing. But the connection inevitably came with anxiety over physical intimacy, an issue he broached with Felice, but not to the depths.

Seven months of letter writing passed before the two met again. And in March 1913, leading up to reunion, Kafka went through a ritual round of indecision, writing on March 20 of "newly emerging further threats of possible obstacles to [his] short journey," and the next day: "Still undecided." The equivocating had to have been unnerving for Felice. Yet on March 23 he did arrive in Berlin and then it was his turn to feel unnerved: "What has happened Felice?" he wrote on Askanischer Hof stationery. "You must surely have received my express letter on Friday in which I announced my arrival on Saturday night ... now I am in Berlin, and will have to leave again this afternoon ... and still no word from you ... I am sitting at the Askanischer Hof waiting."

In August 2011, I set my sights on booking a room for M. and me at the Askanischer Hof Hotel. M. was still aloof to my 'Kafka project' as he termed it at the time, though keen on visiting Berlin. I was thrilled to find the hotel listed online, at 53 Kurfürstendamm— the leafy, fashionable street that runs through the centre of the city and leads southward to Grunewald, where Franz and Felice went for a walk on their second meeting and first date.

That first date must have been awkward. Franz cut it short in order to meet up with literary friends at Café Josty on Potsdamer Platz. Yet he arranged with Felice to meet again—at Whitsun in May. Back in Prague on March 26, he wrote to her: "I gazed at you too long in real life ... for your photographs to be of any use to me now ... In the photographs you are smooth ... whereas I have beheld the true, human, inevitably imperfect face, and lost myself in it." They'd sat near enough to each other for Franz to take in Felice's fragrance and get a good look at her imperfect teeth. (She complained of toothaches and had a tooth extracted soon after.) On March 30 he proclaimed: "I love you too much," "I am obsessed by the need for news of you" ... "I press your letter to my cheek and inhale its fragrance ... it is then that you are more firmly in my heart than ever." In typical Franz fashion—of giving with one hand and taking with the other, he continued: "On the telephone from the Askanischer Hof I was closer to you, felt the happiness of our bond with greater intensity than earlier on, when sitting on the tree trunk in Grunewald." In other words, the bond is stronger at a distance—where physical contact can't intervene.

M. and I stayed at the Askanischer Hof Hotel for three nights in August 2011.

During that phase of venturing into the field, I was more wishful and enthusiastic than informed: I thought I'd booked us a room at the hotel where Kafka had stayed. When we checked in, I asked the concierge if she knew whether Franz Kafka had regularly stayed in the same room at the hotel. She smiled politely and told me that this was not the hotel where Kafka stayed. I blushed, suddenly deeply embarrassed; M. suppressed a chuckle. "But this is the Askanischer Hof," I said, suppressing my embarrassment. "Yes, of course, but this is a different branch," she said. "The other building was destroyed in the War." "And there's nothing at all left of it?" I asked. "No," she said. "There's a new building at that location." M. took the key from the reception desk. Impatient from the day in transit, he was ready to go to the room. "I'd like to see where the other hotel was located," I said. "Can you tell us how to get there?" "Take a taxi to the Askanischer Platz," she said.

On April 18, 1913 Kafka wrote to Felice: "I don't think you have properly taken in that writing is the only thing that makes my inner existence possible ... I am awake only among my imaginary characters." And two days later: "Haven't you noticed, Felice, that in my letters I don't in fact love you; if I did, I would have to think only about you, write only about you; but what I do is worship you, and in some way expect your help and blessing." "Worship" is the operative word. Franz did not love Felice for herself; he was not attracted to her physically; he couldn't be. He needed to elevate her to lofty heights, where she would be unreachable, except as a fount for attention and blessing. He expected to be accepted for how he was and for what he required for his writing. From his response of April 28, it's clear that Felice had been offended by his frankness: "So I wanted to hurt you, Felice? Hurt? You? When my one desire is to lessen as best I can all the unhappiness, which through no fault of mine, passes from me to you." Kafka must have realized just how self-righteous he sounded; must have half-expected to be dismissed, and yet he insisted: "All the same you should allow me to come and see you in Berlin at Whitsun, for this journey was far too definite a plan, the changing of which would turn my whole life upside down." His tone of entitlement is unabashed. On May 4, he announced that he would again be staying at the Askanischer Hof.

After exploring our hotel room—furnished genteelly in the manner of La Belle Époque, M. and I went down to hail a cab. Dinner would wait. I was eager to see something of what I'd come for, even if it was only a trace. We climbed into the back of the cab, told the cabby where we wanted to go. I noted the route: Kurfürstenstrasse, Budapeststrasse, Tiergartenstrasse … and asked the cabby if he knew of Hotel Askanischer Hof—that had once stood at the Askanischer Platz. "Yes," he said matter-of-factly. "My mother lived in the building beside the hotel." "Really," I said, surprised. "Yes," he said. "Those buildings were destroyed in the War." "How weird is this?" I whispered to M. "We happen to get a cabby whose mother lived beside the hotel that Kafka stayed at." "It's called a coincidence," M. whispered back. "It means nothing." Maybe not, I thought, but still … "Here we are," the cabby said, pulling up beside a subway station on Stresemannstrasse. "This is Askanischer Platz. The hotel was there." He pointed to a block of buildings. We thanked him, paid, and got out at the subway entrance—marked with a green S: Anhalter Bahnhof.

I took out the camera, photographed the street, the signs, the Askanischer Platz—a parkette of dry grass, shrubs and tall leafy trees. The building where the hotel once stood is now DKV: Deutsche Krankenversicherung—an insurance company, of all things.

During his second stay at the Askanischer Hof—on Whitsun—May 11-12, 1913, Franz met Felice's family at their home on Wilmersdorfer Strasse. They were celebrating the engagement of their son, Felice's brother, Ferri. Franz was anxious about being cast into a family festivity of this sort on a first meeting and cognizant of being on-course for an engagement of his own. Fortunately, the subject of marriage to Felice was not raised. But back in Prague, he wrote a series of self-recriminatory letters—building a case against why Felice would want him as a spouse, then grieving her silence as rejection. On June 16 he penned a singularly strange, long letter in which he asked Felice for her hand in marriage: "Will you consider whether you wish to be my wife? … Fundamentally this is a criminal question … but in the conflict of forces, those that have to pose this question are victorious."

Felice said yes to the proposal without delay, yet Franz continued, throughout July and August, to badger her with letters of dread: "Felice, you have to believe what I say about myself; which is the self-knowledge of a man of thirty who for deep-seated reasons (he cannot specify what they are) has several times been close to madness … To be frank ... it is my *dread of the union* (his emphasis) ... I have a definite feeling that through marriage, through the union ... I shall perish, and not alone but with my wife." And at the end of August he wrote to Carl Bauer, Felice's father, a letter that reads more like a red-alert than an introduction to a future son-in-law: "My whole being is directed toward literature ... I am taciturn, unsociable, morose, selfish, a hypochondriac, and actually in poor health ... I lack all sense of family life ... Is your daughter destined to live with this kind of man? Is she to tolerate a monastic existence ... and in a foreign town, in a marriage that may turn out to be a relationship of love and friendship rather than a real marriage?" Felice intercepted the unhappy missive. But Franz's unhappiness and misgivings did not abate.

On September 6 he travelled to Vienna with colleagues as an official delegate of the Workers' Accident Insurance Institute at the Second International Congress for Rescue Service and Accident Prevention. He was miserable. On September 9 he wrote to Felice that he sits "at meals like a ghost." From Vienna he travelled on alone to vacation in Trieste, Venice, Verona, and Riva on Lake Garda in northern Italy. On September 16 he wrote Felice a letter "overflowing with unhappiness" from Hotel Sandwirth in Venice. He closed by saying: "We shall have to part." The two remained incommunicado for over a month.

When M. and I arrived back at the Askanischer Hof on Kurfürstendamm, the concierge asked us if we'd visited the Askanischer Platz. "We did," I said. "There wasn't much to see. It's a parkette of overgrown grass. But where the hotel once stood there's an insurance company, which is curious, seeing that Kafka was a lawyer for an insurance firm." I felt silly saying that, like I was stretching for connections. "Well," she said, lowering her voice to a confidential pitch, "we do have the desk and chair from the room that Kafka stayed in. Some of the furnishings were saved and brought here." "Really?" I said, sounding incredulous. "Yes, really," she said. "We keep them in our private area at the back. Would you like to see them?" Well, of course, I would. M. was silent. The concierge emerged from behind the reception desk, and, leaving it unattended, led us down a long hallway toward the back of the building. In a room with a window overlooking an inner courtyard stood a large dark wood desk with a carved floral motif around the edges and thick twist legs. The chair was of the same dark wood, with the same floral motif on the arms, upholstered with a heavy red fabric. "Have a seat," she said. I did, and in the moment, I believed that that desk and chair could very well have been the same desk and chair that Kafka had sat at. It seemed entirely plausible.

The period from September 20 to October 29, 1913 marked a turning point in Franz and Felice's relationship. Felice recruited a friend—a young professional woman named Grete Bloch whom Felice had met at a trade fair in Frankfurt—to mediate between herself and Kafka. The assignment was to induce Franz to make the trip to Berlin to discuss the impasse that had arisen between them. Grete contacted Franz by letter, he agreed to meet her, and they met up in Prague at the Schwarzes Ross Hotel (no longer standing). Grete succeeded in convincing Franz to make the trip to Berlin. She also succeeded in drawing him into a lengthy conversation that covered matters far beyond the designated purpose of the meeting.

On November 8, 1913, Kafka took the eight-hour train ride to Berlin, arrived at the Anhalter Station at 8:30 in the morning and again checked in to the Askanischer Hof. He and Felice arranged by telephone to meet at noon for a walk at the Tiergarten. The walk lasted ninety minutes, after which Franz met with his writer-friend, Ernst Weiss. The meeting at the Tiergarten was tense and unpleasant. Felice and Franz could agree on nothing. Kafka put the details into a long letter to Grete Bloch, dated November 10. He also expressed his dismay in retrospect that Grete, who had introduced herself at the Schwarzes Ross as Felice's "close friend," could have spoken about such personal things as Felice's "tooth trouble" and the "breaking-off of her brother's engagement." What truly close friend would be so insensitive as to bring up such private matters at all, let alone at a first meeting with a stranger. He felt "rage and despair" at himself for having "said too much during their conversation"; that "in addition to having wronged Felice so deeply already, [he] had betrayed her as well." He realized from the start of his correspondence with Grete—which lasted from October 1913 to October 1914 and is preserved in *Letters to Felice*—that the exchange with Fräulein Bloch as intermediary for Felice was dubious. Nonetheless, he took it up. And in many of the letters it's difficult to discern, from tone and content, the prospective fiancée from the girlfriend of the prospective fiancée.

On January 2, 1914 Franz renewed his request of marriage by letter—with pledges of love, along with a plea to Felice to let him be: "Let's do it. Marriage is the only means whereby the relationship between us—so very necessary to me—can be maintained ... You are not satisfied with me ... want me to be other than I am ... Why try to change people, Felice?" Kafka wanted to be accepted for who he was: a writer who desired a supportive but sexless marriage. He idealized the benediction of marriage, valued the stability and appearance of normalcy and respectability that marriage could afford him, but was repelled by inadmissible "deep-seated reasons" by the idea of marital sex.

The two met during Kafka's fourth visit to Berlin—February 28 - March 1, 1914. Felice voiced her "fears about a joint future": She might not be able to put up with Franz's idiosyncrasies and fluctuations, forego Berlin—marriage would entail a move to Prague—and the lifestyle she was used to. Franz promised, against his will, to change his ways, but was conflicted. He spent a sleepless night at the Askanischer Hof. He would rather live in Berlin as a writer than in Prague as a civil servant, writing on the side, but he could not (for the time being) expect Felice to marry him, give up her well-paid position and have her face the prospect of a diminished lifestyle in a foreign city.

Meanwhile the correspondence with Grete Bloch continued. The letters to Grete are warm and playful, also eerily similar in pattern to the early letters to Felice. Kafka requested details of Grete's work, health, friendships, travels and reading habits. He recommended books, places to eat, performances to take in, and suggested vacationing together: Grete, Franz and Felice. It was a triangle that was bound to collapse. Yet the marriage plans stood. On April 7, Franz announced to Felice: "I am coming at Easter ... I shall be staying at the Askanischer Hof." On April 9, he added: "It would be better if you came to the Askanischer at about 7:30, but punctually, I beg you." (Franz couldn't bear to be made to wait.) And "No, Fräulein Bloch is not coming. I like her very much." Felice must have been feeling uneasy about the intermediary arrangement she herself had trustingly arranged.

The unofficial engagement took place on Easter, during Kafka's fifth visit to Berlin—April 12-13, 1914. The next day, Kafka wrote to Grete: "Dear Fräulein Grete, it would be nicer if instead of the telegram I were holding your hand." And the day after: "Dear Fräulein Grete, I feel an unmistakable and true longing for you." On April 17 he added: "I do want to go to Berlin. Berlin does me good in every way. But it would surely be taking a great risk if I were to give up my safe job now. On my own I could have done it, or rather, I should have done it. But now, with Felice? Am I entitled to persuade her to give up her good job to which she is so attached, in order perhaps to suffer hardship with me in that same Berlin?" Marriage and Prague were presented by Franz as a package deal. On May 1, Felice arrived in Prague. She and Franz rented a three-room apartment at Langegasse 923/5. Franz suggested to Grete that she come live with them, make it a threesome. On May 8 he wrote: "... once [Felice and I] are married you are to come live with us ... (and from the beginning) ... We shall lead a pleasant life, and in order to test me you shall hold my hand, and I, in order to thank you, must be allowed to hold yours." Another fantasy.

The official engagement was held on Sunday June 1 at the Bauer apartment. On June 6 Franz confided to his diary: "Was tied hand and foot like a criminal. Had they sat me down in a corner bound in real chains, placed policemen in front of me ... it could not have been worse. And that was my engagement ..." During the following month, he wrote twelve letters to Grete; none to Felice.

The indelicate balance collapsed on July 12 at the Askanischer Hof—in a back room with a window overlooking a courtyard: Felice, her sister Erna and Grete Bloch in attendance. In his diary entry of July 23 Franz called the ordeal the "tribunal in the hotel"; Felice "said very studied, hostile things she had long been saving up," he wrote. And added: "devilish in my innocence"; "Fräulein Bloch's apparent guilt." "Devilish" because he knew he'd been operating deviously on two tracks, though Felice did not—not until the beginning of July, when Grete shared with her friend what Franz had written to her. "Innocent" because he maintained his love for Felice—however skewed and fettered to his head. There must have been tension between Felice and Grete as well, but Grete managed to save the friendship at the eleventh hour by handing over to Felice most (not all) of her correspondence with Franz. The passages implicating herself for having led Franz on were excised, while Kafka's indiscretions were underlined in red. These Felice read aloud at the tribunal. Franz had nothing to say in his defense. The engagement was broken off and the parents informed. Felice's mother, distraught, put the blame squarely on Grete.

On the last day of our stay in Berlin, I came across a small red volume on the bookshelf of the hotel breakfast room: *Kafka in Berlin* in German by Hans-Gerd Koch. I brought it to our room to examine the old photographs, most of which were new to me. I was intrigued by two in particular: one of the foyer of the original Askanischer Hof—a cramped, dim, cave-like room with curved-arch wall-recesses, a few round tables and light armchairs (of the plain Deutsche Werkstätten style that Franz favoured), and a staircase descending directly into the sitting area. I imagined Franz hunched glumly in one of the wall-recesses, waiting impatiently for Felice. The other photograph—captioned "a letter sheet of the hotel used by Kafka"—shows the hotel's façade, with the byline *Quiet family house. Comfortable Living.* The date, "13 VII, 1914," is written in Kafka's hand. July 13 was the day after the "tribunal." This is the letterhead of the letter Kafka wrote to Felice's parents in wake of the breakup: "Now I no longer know how I shall address you. I shall not come to see you. I know what you would say to me. You know I would take it. So I am not coming. I shall probably go to Lübeck this afternoon … Farewell, you have won my unconditional admiration … don't think badly of me."

With the marriage off—for the time being: the two would meet up in January 1915—the prospect of quitting his job and relocating to Berlin acquired renewed appeal for Franz. In this he was encouraged by Ernst Weiss, who disliked Felice and did not approve of the match. In a letter to his parents, following the dissolution of the engagement, Franz asserted that his life in Prague could lead to "nothing good" and that he wasn't "finished with Berlin." He declared his plan to resign his position at the Institute, leave Prague and live on his savings while pursuing his literary work in Berlin. But then War broke out and the plan was not put to the test.

After the fateful day at the Askanischer Hof Hotel, Kafka did not see Berlin again until 1923. In August he began writing *The Trial*, which Klaus Wagenbach has called: "a punishment fantasy" and Elias Canetti: *Kafka's Other Trial*. Canetti, in his book-length study, draws a direct connection between the engagement and arrest of Kafka's cipher, Joseph K., in chapter one of the novel, and the tribunal and dissolution of the engagement with the guilty verdict in the final chapter.

I ended up taking the small red volume, *Kafka in Berlin*, home with me. I'd intended to put it back on the breakfast room bookshelf; it found its way into my suitcase instead. I felt mildly guilty for having removed it from the hotel but gave it a place on my Kafka shelf at home where it sat, unopened, until 2016, when M. and I again visited Berlin. We were with a tour group this time, staying at the Crown Plaza City Center on Nürnberger Strasse. I suggested to M. that we take our free afternoon to walk over to the Askanischer Platz; my fascination with the location had not abated.

***

We walk along Kurfürstenstrasse, cross An der Urania and Potsdamer Strasse, pass through the sprawling sports park—Park am Gleisdreieck, cross Schönberger Bridge over the Landwehr Canal, continue along Schönberger Strasse, and cut across a field in the direction of the Askanischer Platz. We stop in our tracks as a massive brick ruin comes into view.

Approaching it from the field, we pass through the rectangular gateway and come to a memorial column in front of the broken façade:

It is the surviving central portion of the Anhalter Bahnhof, where, on arriving from Prague, Kafka repeatedly disembarked and walked across to the Askanischer Platz on what was then Königstrasse and is now Stresemannstrasse. Anhalter Bahnhof, we read on the plaque, was one of three stations from where over 50,000 Berlin Jews were deported to extermination camps in Nazi-occupied territories of Eastern Europe. Today the S-Bahn subway station is the only remainder. It is still called Anhalter Bahnhof, though the aboveground terminus was closed over a half-century ago.

We're puzzled. How could we not have seen this huge ruin on our previous visit? We'd stood at the S-Bahn subway station at Askanischer Platz, I'd photographed the parkette, the street and the signs. We walk from the ruin across to the Platz—still a dry-grass parkette. I sit on one of the park benches and M. photographs the setting. The Anhalter Bahnhof terminus ruin isn't visible through the tall leafy trees. That's why we hadn't seen it. And we'd approached Askanischer Platz from the northeast on our previous visit, and walked back to our hotel in the same direction—by way of Potsdamer Platz. Askanischer Platz itself yields nothing new; I didn't really expect it to. But now I want to retrace our steps—to revisit the Askanischer Hof Hotel at Kurfürstendamm 53. We take the hour-long walk only to find that the hotel is closed.

I learn that the original Askanischer Hof ceased operating as a hotel in 1923, and the building was rented out to commercial enterprises. By 1924 it no longer appeared on the hotel list of the Berlin Address Book, and in World War Two the building was destroyed by allied bombing. According to Hans Gerd-Koch, author of *Kafka in Berlin*, a former staff member of the original Askanischer Hof operated the hotel at Kurfürstendamm 53 under the same name. It was a family-run hotel, a bel étage representative of typical old Berlin. "Of the original furniture nothing remains today," Gerd-Koch writes: "You can't sleep in Kafka's bed, but you can perhaps read or write in the light of a lamp which served him during one of his visits." The Kurfürstendamm hotel closed permanently in June 2015. It strikes me as fortuitous that M. and I got to stay there in 2011; that I'd sat in the light of a room at a desk that Kafka never sat at. The concierge—she must have been a member of the family that ran the hotel—made up that story to please me, and it did. And I took the little red book from the breakfast-room shelf.

K.

You sang the ancient wail of the sad animal,
made it always modern.
Like infinite wind, the dark at dusk—

elegant as number.
Gaunt blossom, hungry son:
got none of the food you liked and slowly starved.

Your gaze, the weight of slate and mail,
still vaster than The Castle—
Why did you arrive if not to remain …

Never were you photographed in profile,
or behind—the back of your head,
bat thin-tip ears, thick horsehide hair,

I imagine. Absolute hands,
the vaporous
shade of your nails.

I sat at the hotel chair you sat at,
set my arms upon the desk;
could not procure a word.

But the wood that beat in the heart
of the wood is the same brown
grain that might have touched your paper.

Isn't it felicitous—this furniture, this silent set—
was spared when fire rained the sky,
flattening more than half the city to ash.

At Marienbad

Up before dawn, I'm standing at the French windows of our Nové Lázně Hotel room. The view is a flat gravel roof, a row of opaque windows—blank rectangular eyes staring back at me from the opposite wing of the building. Small commotions of dry leaves circle the roof in the fall breeze, the desiccated eddying is almost ghostly. A fuggy smell of onion hovers in the mist—the kitchen must be beneath us. And on the road to the right, a passing car swooshes like water.

This is Mariánské Lázně, formerly Marienbad. The waters are everywhere: sixty or so cold-water springs, each with its own properties. The Cross and Ferdinand are rich in purgative salts. The Rudolf is alkaline. The Karolina and Ambrosius Springs have high iron content. (I will sip Ambrosius water from a tap in the hotel garden and spit it out; the taste is heavily metal.) These waters were once touted as treatment for any array of illness: liver, kidney and lung diseases, gynecological disorders, urinary tract infections, intestinal catarrh, boils, abrasions, obesity. Whatever the ailment, the waters could heal it.

Among the world's grand health spas that have slipped from general memory, Marienbad, nestled in west Bohemia, was once the grandest of all. In its golden era—from the late nineteenth century to the outset of the First World War—Europe's royalty, intelligentsia and celebrities came to take the curative waters, enjoy the natural beauty and the architectural splendours of the town. Among those who came and came again: King Edward VII, Emperor Franz Joseph I, Tsar Nicholas II, Prince Friedrich, Friedrich Nietzsche, Goethe, Chopin, Wagner, Mahler, Sigmund Freud, and Franz Kafka—

Marienbad was a neutral destination for Jews—assimilated western Jews as well as rabbis and their entourages from Eastern Europe. Many of the spa doctors were Jewish too. Maybe it was the beneficent effect of the waters that fostered inclusion, at least for a time. The town remained a popular destination during World War One and into the interwar period. After 1945, the ethnic Germans of west Bohemia—the heart of German-speaking Sudetenland—were expelled, and the area emptied of the majority of its population.

Today the area is Czech, but German can be heard in the streets and spas of the former Marienbad.

When M. and I arrive at the Nové Lázně Hotel, on November 18, 2015, the receptionist greets us in Czech-inflected German, assuming we are German guests; we don't hear any native English during our two-day stay. When I order tuna salad without onion at the hotel's Wiener Café, the waitress blanks at my English and I have to resort to my stilted German: "Ohne Zwiebeln, bitte." She gives me a look as if to question why anyone would want their tuna salad without onion. The Apfelstrudel we order for dessert is nothing like the strudel we've had in Vienna either. But that's another story.

We haven't come to Marienbad for the strudel, or for the cures. We've come to see the place where Kafka came, for business in May 1916, then, delighted by the spa-town's peace and quiet, returned to two months later—to reunite with Felice Bauer. The two were between engagements at the time and kept separate but adjoining rooms—at the Schloss Balmoral Hotel, from July 3 to 13. After Felice departed, Franz stayed on for ten more days. It was during his extended stay that he met up with Georg Mordechai Langer—his Hasidic friend from Prague, with whom he shared an interest in Jewish mysticism, folklore, Hebrew language and literature, and who just happened to be at Marienbad at the same time.

Langer was with the entourage of the ailing Rabbi of Belz and the two friends met for evening walks. In letters to Max Brod, Kafka writes at length and in detail of his time with Langer. Felice is mentioned in letters from Marienbad too. After an uneasy passage, this was one of their more agreeable meetings, and at Marienbad they apparently worked out a formula for re-engagement. Yet in one of his letters to Brod, Kafka recalls how he had been "hampered by the reality of this girl … When she came toward me in the big room to receive the [first] engagement kiss, a shudder ran through me. The engagement trip … was sheer agony for me, every step of the way." Kafka embraced contradiction in both life and writing. Did he love Felice, as he sometimes claimed in his letters? Did he honestly want and intend to marry her? Or was their five-year, chiefly epistolary relationship mostly an agonized mystification? This will probably never be known for sure.

What is known is that Kafka was generally conflicted where women and physicality were concerned. In *Franz Kafka: The Poet of Shame and Guilt*, Saul Friedländer assesses Kafka's letters and diaries, attending to lines that were excised by Brod in his capacity as literary executor. Friedländer emphasizes the personal anguish that informed Kafka's oeuvre, and maintains that the issues torturing him for most of his life were of a sexual nature. This may well have been so.

Although he declares his love for Felice in a number of his letters, he also refutes this love, and refers to himself as "monkish," "by no means extremely sensual," and stresses his *"dread of the union,* even with the most beloved woman, above all with her." In a 1918 letter to Brod, he writes, "You are right in saying that the deeper realm of sexual life is closed to me; I too think so." Kafka idealized marriage and parenthood as the highest moral attainments, yet was terrified by the idea of marital sex. He sabotaged every relationship he had with a potential mate. His two engagements to Felice, in 1914 and 1917, ended badly, as did his third engagement to Julie Wohryzek in 1919.

The one relationship with a woman that Kafka did not actively sabotage was the last one—with Dora Diamant, the young free-thinking woman he met in July 1923 while vacationing on the Baltic. Dora was his companion during his last months. She considered herself Kafka's wife, yet loving and dedicated caregiver would be a more fitting descriptor. They didn't marry, and Kafka was too enfeebled in his final months for any test of deep physical intimacy.

The train ride from Prague to Marienbad is a slow three hours. The weather is cool on the day of our trip, the countryside grey, the Mariánské Lázně Station quiet on our arrival. There are no taxis at the station stand, so we opt to walk to the hotel. I need the air anyway; I've been nauseous since Prague.

The first views of the town are cheerless—bars and diners, a funeral parlour, store fronts displaying kitsch. Ten minutes into the walk, I cross the street—to bend and retch behind a clump of shrubs. We plod on and the structures become more decorous. Parkland opens before us; ornate buildings to our right and left. The Nové Lázně Hotel, where we're booked for the night, glints with a renovated splendour. We check in and are welcomed in the room with sparkling water and a plate of fresh fruit. I'm still feeling wonky and need to get horizontal. M. wants to sample the free Roman bath waters advertised in the spa area. But he hasn't brought a bathing suit. He goes back out to purchase one and returns with shiny blue Speedo trunks—1970s vintage. "Don't laugh," he says; I can't help myself.

The hotel provides a map of Mariánské Lázně: The Schloss Balmoral Hotel—our destination—is nowhere on it. According to the tourist office in Prague, the Schloss is scheduled for restoration under the name Lázeňský Dům Balmoral. This, we thought, would be enough to guide us. We inquire at the front desk. No one at the Nové Lázně has heard of the Schloss Balmoral or the Lázeňský Dům Balmoral. I pull out a copy of a photo I've brought from home: the building, circa 1910. The receptionist examines it and says, "Maybe you want the Osborne." I recall the letterhead on letters from Kafka to Brod, July 1916: *Schloss Balmoral & Osborne, Marienbad.* "Yes, that would be it," I say. She circles the location on the map and we set out.

We take the winding indoor corridor that joins the Nové Lázně to the adjacent hotel, the Centralni Lázně Spa Resort, exit to the spring pavilion and try some curative water. *Feh!* We pass the orthogonal Assumption of the Virgin Mary Church, the grand colonnade, the singing fountain—now silent for fall and winter, the statue of Goethe by local sculptor Vítezslav Eibl. Beyond Goethe, the plaster is crumbling on the hotel where King Edward VII once had a suite. The shattered windows stand out like black teeth in a pale face. We peer in; the interior is sacked.

Marienbad is a faded lady, a time tunnel. I'm reminded of the Alain Resnais film, *Last Year at Marienbad*: the connecting passages, halls, high windows, doors, partitions, thresholds and steps. We pass through a peopleless street of shops and restaurants, come to a narrow lane at the edge of town, woodland beyond. "We have to be close to it now," M. says, studying the map. We approach a shabby peach-tinted building with a red roof and spired cupolas; a two-wing edifice. On the façade of the wing to our left, high up, we see the inscription *Osborne* in thin, pale lettering. And to the right of the entrance to the building before us, a small bronze sculpted head—mounted too high to touch. The plaque beneath it reads, *Franz Kafka*. So, this is it: the once Schloss Balmoral Hotel.

We enter the narrow front door and come to a dark foyer. The woman at the desk doesn't speak English, or German, and we have no Czech. I call on a young man sitting on the far side of the room. "Do you speak English?" I ask. "Of course," he says. "We're looking for the Schloss Balmoral Hotel," I say, "where Franz Kafka stayed." "This is a student residence and there's no Franz Kaka here," he says, mispronouncing the name. "Franz Kafka," I reiterate, "the author. He stayed here with his soon-to-be fiancée in 1916" … my voice trails off. "Please translate for the receptionist," I say. "Maybe she knows which rooms they stayed in." "Ja, Ja, Franz Kafka," the woman chimes in, nodding enthusiastically from her place behind her desk as she hears me repeat the name. The young man translates something, but it amounts to nothing.

Yes, this is where Kafka stayed, for a few pleasurable weeks in 1916, when the building was a spa-hotel. Now it's a residence for foreign students taking Czech language courses to qualify for university admission. "Where are you from?" I ask the young man. "Dubai," he says. "What are you studying?" I ask. "I'm preparing for entrance to medicine at Charles University," he says, looking somewhat doubtful. I don't bother telling him that Charles University is where Franz Kafka obtained his doctor of laws degree in 1906. "I wish you well," I say. "Thank you," he replies, pressing his palms together at chest level in a gesture of prayer. "Let me take your photograph," he offers, as if by way of consolation. I hand him our camera and M. and I pose by an arch in the lightest spot in the dim room. The image is too dark to show our faces. "You can get a good picture of the buildings from down the hill," the young man says, pointing to the Osborne side. "They look really nice from down there." We thank him, smile at the woman behind the desk, and exit.

I want to climb the hill on the side of the former Schloss Balmoral. We've come this far, located the place, I need to see the view from above.

M. remains below. He's not interested in negotiating the climb. I try to envision, on making my way up the steep and slippery incline, in which of the rooms Franz and Felice may have slept ... The idea becomes intrusive. I reach the top of the hill on which the Schloss amongst the spruces is set, short of breath and muddied from slipping and sliding. Near the rear of the building, at the top of a rounded façade, the year of hotel's construction is etched in white: 1905. Seeing this date somehow vindicates the climb, the trek across town, the trip to Marienbad as a whole. The view from the hilltop is tangled and brambly, the plaster on the building distressed. Nonetheless, it's a beautiful view, one that transcends any relevancy.

We board the train at 4:55 p.m.; it promptly departs. It's dark on the way back to Prague, but the city is teeming with life upon our return.

So Good at This

I've wished to step into the black atoms of midair,
be ambient
and present to a figure.

My shoulders twitch like lift-off
at Benétská and Na Slupi Streets—
a crow alights, indicative,
and drops
beyond a wall.

This way lies a hospital, a pharmacy,
remembrance.
That way to the room where clerks
were stripped and whipped,
and whimpered.

Pieces filter through the trees
like feathers to a well.

Can you tell by the pen
I seek a yard and garden in Nusle ...

A tall man shed his hat and jacket,
got down
dirty in the earth, darker here than he was
in the sun:
déclassé
for a friable while,
the soil beneath his nails.

Dark man to a bird on a roof.
Draw him as he's gone—
    so good at this

he doesn't die
but consecrates in creatures.
Through storyline and dream—
the flatlands of confabulation:
literature, and illness.

Mary Lou Paints the Little House on Her iPad

1. Hypersensitive to noise, Franz seeks a quiet place to write—
after his hectic workday at the office.

2. November 1916, he and his sister Ottla rent a tiny cottage
on Alchemisten Lane, the Castle Quarter of Prague.

3. They use the cottage frequently through spring of the following
year. Ottla secretly meets here with her lover.

4. Almost all the stories in the volume, *A Country Doctor*,
are written in the little medieval house.

5. 1917, from March till August, Franz also rents a room
at Schönborn Palace, near the Moldau. He sleeps by the river
and writes by night on the hill.

6. Writing by night is key to fighting fears that interfere
with sleep. All the meddling spectres.

7. He awakes in the Schönborn bedroom on the night of August 13.
Coughing up blood. A date with an eerie echo: August 13, 1912,
exactly five years prior, he meets Felice—with whom he carries
out his anguished fantasies of marriage. In over 500 letters, for five
tormenting years. Twice engaged, they never wed. At last
it is the hemorrhage that frees him. Diagnosis—tuberculosis—
blend of penance and grace.

8. Mary Lou paints the little house on her iPad. She gives it
a greyish roof, no windows. Bright leek-green front door. The house
is set between two bigger, rose-red-roofed abodes. Mary Lou is intuitive.
Her palette matches a screened-motif in the story "A Country Doctor":
the doctor modelled on Kafka's uncle—country doctor at Triesch.

9. The doctor in the story lies in bed beside the patient—his treatment for the wound: a wormy rose-red opening in the hip. A naked man pressed up against the bloody groin of a boy. What is Kafka getting at? Perhaps.

10. The tale does not end well for either hero. The patient dies, the doctor flees. Yet Rose, the girl in the story, is called the victim.

Franz Among the Animals

THE TINY VILLAGE of Siřem is located 78 km northwest of Prague. By Route 6 on a clear day, driving time from the capital is under two hours. When Franz made the trip in 1917, the village was known as Zürau, and travel time by train to the nearest station, Michelob (Měcholupy), was almost four hours. Zürau, six and half km from Michelob Station, could only be reached by horse and cart.

Kafka spent almost eight months in Zürau during the War—from September 12, 1917 till April 30, 1918. The village then had a population of 350; a church, a pond, a smattering of country buildings on rolling hills, farmland, hops gardens, and animals—whose number, including the mice, far exceeded the number of residents. There was no electricity, no running water, no restaurant or inn. No paved streets and no post office. The postal address for Zürau was Flöhau, Bohemia—six km away. Letters and packages from Prague took three to four days to arrive. Tiny, rural Zürau was a complete contrast to Prague. Exactly what was wanted.

Following a pulmonary hemorrhage during the night of August 13, Kafka was diagnosed with tuberculosis and approved, on September 7, for a three-month medical leave from the Workers' Accident Insurance Institute where he then held the position of vice secretary. He'd felt the illness lurking in him for years. Finally, fatefully, it broke out and his life took an abrupt turn. With the doctor's consent, he put himself under the care of his sister Ottla, who was tending the Zürau acreage of their brother-in-law, Karl Hermann, while Karl was on duty in Hungary on the eastern front.

In a letter of August 29 to Ottla from Prague, Franz termed his illness a "mental disease." In his diary, he referred to it as "a symbol whose inflammation is called Felice." In his first letter from Zürau, to Max Brod, he wrote: "Things can't go on this way, said the brain, and after five years the lungs said they were ready to help." Franz and Felice were still formally engaged when he left Prague for Zürau, but an end would soon be put to the tortuous relationship. The TB diagnosis provided the reprieve. Felice had played the role of felicitous muse for his creative breakthrough in 1912; also discordantly, for the writing of *The Trial*. But those roles had played out.

In August of 2017, deep into my quest, I'm eager to visit the setting of one of Kafka's happiest periods—the place where he connected with the land, lived side by side with his favourite sister in peace, and produced a body of short, introspective writing that has come to be known as *The Zürau Aphorisms*. Kafka kept his Zürau writings secret, even from his closest friends, though the manner in which he transcribed and ordered the pieces indicated that he might have been considering publication. In his study, *Kafka's Castle and the Critical Imagination*, Stephen D. Dowden holds that the Zürau literary miniatures should be regarded as finger exercises for *The Castle*, which Kafka started writing in January 1922. Kafka himself suggested no such connection and the short texts, first published in 1931, stand alone as distinctive in the oeuvre.

I'd perused old photos of the village and knew what I was looking for: first and foremost, the house where Franz and Ottla had dwelled. There's a photo of brother and sister standing at what could be the entrance to the dwelling, Franz wearing a fedora, overcoat, white shirt and tie—looking like he's ready for his workday at the office; Ottla dressed plainly in a long dark skirt, her hair pinned-up and out of the way. The photo shows only a portico with a small transom and passage to an inner courtyard. The plaster on the steps and doorway appears eroded, even in 1917, so I can't be sure the building is still standing. The *Ringplatz* (village square) and the goose pond that Franz refers to in letters is near the house, adjacent the onion-domed church. The church appears in a number of old photos, also on Google maps; I'm hoping to be able to enter it.

The morning is warm and sunny when M. and I depart Prague in our rented Škoda. Within the hour we pass through the brew-town of Krušovice, population 615, turn north onto Route 221 and pass through the hamlet of Krupá on the two-lane road that leads to Siřem. The land is flat and stark, dotted with clumps of wild grass, the occasional tree. Hardly another car.

Two men in bright yellow vests come into view as we approach a level crossing. They're standing at the roadside—one in front of the other, one close, the other farther away. It's an odd scene: empty fields, no traffic, only these two yellow-vested men, facing each other at a distance. They're holding instruments and I realize in the moment that they're surveyors. "Land surveyors!" I announce, and quickly grab the camera.

"So what? What's so special about land surveyors?" M. says, not slowing to look. "You know," I say, snapping quickly as M. drives past them. "K., the stand-in for Kafka in *The Castle*, identifies himself as a land surveyor. And he has two look-a-like assistants, Artur and Jeremias," I add, as if to invoke some kind of transposition from the novel to the road.

Seeing these two look-a-like surveyors on the way to Siřem feels significant to me and I say so. M. is unresponsive. "How many times in your life have you seen land surveyors on a country road?" I ask as he drives on, eyes on the road. "I don't know," he says, "maybe never." I ignore the deadpan. "Exactly," I say. "You don't see land surveyors every day, but today, on the road to Siřem—where Kafka lived happily for eight months and later wrote *The Castle*, in which K. is a land surveyor, with two assistants"—I stress the latter point—"we see land surveyors." "Right," M. says. "Maybe it's a sign … I don't know what it signifies, but maybe it's a sign." "It's an affirmation," I say, "a nod from literature." "Right," he says again, laconically.

I disengage and turn to view the shots I managed to snap in passing: two shots of two surveyors in bright yellow vests. In one of the shots, one of the men is obstructed by a road sign. In the same photo, the other is holding his instruments in front and I got the shot when we'd already passed him, so the instruments are obstructed. The second photo shows only one of the men—facing us with his instruments slung over his back. Both views are partial and I'm feeling a little denied. My photographic 'proof', despite the 'live-sighting', is less than compelling.

We pass through the village of Svojetín, slowing for a lone dachshund. The road wends through the village of Velká Černoc, where we pass a country church, a small roadside chapel (kaplička), then another: each with a cross on top, Madonna, Son, and flowers in the niches. We come to Soběchleby, population 129, the hamlet Kafka would sometimes walk to—2.6 km from Zürau. We're close; I've got the camera in hand.

Trees border the winding road, fields of hops extend beyond. We pass a new-looking cemetery, several red-roofed buildings on the hillside, then the road sign: Siřem. The onion-domed church comes into view at the bend, blue sky showing through the slats of the broken cupola, tufts of wild grass rising from the tower stone. I zoom in, capture the dilapidation.

Ottla attended to her brother here, while shouldering responsibility for cultivating fifty acres of farmland. She'd broken away from the family shop in Prague to pursue her dream of living a simple agricultural life in the country. It was an arrangement that for a time served both her and the family well, especially Franz. Ottla bore her brother up "on her wings," as he put it in a letter to Max: "I live with Ottla in a good little marriage." It was the solicitous, unsexed kind of marriage that best met Franz's requirements for happiness.

Some of the buildings on the road into Siřem—ramshackle and abandoned—look to be of Kafka's vintage. Others are more recent, giving the place a patchwork appearance. There's a bus stop at the *Ringplatz*, a taxi. Not a person in sight. M. parks the Škoda near the church and we step out to gauge the lay of the land. The "goose pond outside the window" that once claimed Franz's hat in its ice is now a rectangular concrete pool surrounded by a tattered chain-link fence. The water is stagnant, a bright lurid green, thick with scum. There are no geese, nor do we hear the sounds of any of the many other animals that Franz names in his letters from Zürau. There's a phlegmatic stillness to the village.

"I am thriving among the animals," Franz wrote to Max in a buoyant tone three weeks after his arrival. "This afternoon I fed the goats." Franz was in retreat among a veritable Noah's Ark of farm animals: geese, pigs, cows, goats, dogs, horses, cats, rats, mice. There was a din in the village, largely due to the animals, and Franz was hypersensitive to noise. But he wasn't complaining. In Zürau, a pro offset every con: His room faced northeast and was "not sunny and not quiet," but it was "well-furnished." The mice in the house "carried on outrageously," but the weather was mild and there was this "marvelous spot" where he would lie "like a king," "sunbathing in semi-nudity" in his "reclining chair." As for his illness, he reported "no fever" and "no pain." He was "short of breath, but didn't feel it when lying or sitting." And though he had "no appetite," "all the things he was supposed to be eating were in good abundance." By the end of September, he'd "already put on a little weight."

The disease, in its initial stages, was "more like a guardian angel than a devil," Franz wrote to Felix Weltsch on September 22. Especially with regard to Felice. Before coming to Zürau, he hadn't been able to muster the resolve to tell her that he was breaking off their engagement. On September 20, she made the gruelling thirty-hour trip from Berlin to Zürau to see how her fiancé was doing, likely expecting to find him wanting consolation. Instead, he was more at ease than ever, and from the evidence of his letters, distinctly disinterested in her. She must have left feeling dejected and humiliated. The day after her departure, his mention of her in a letter to Felix has the tone of a brisk aside: "... my room is not as good as my sunbathing spot ... but I can perfectly well go somewhere else ... as I did yesterday when Felice was here."

Their second engagement—only five estranged-months old—was formally terminated in Prague, at the end of December 1917. After that they never saw each other again. Franz used the disease to cut the ties that bound him to Felice. Max was aware of it, so was Ottla. TB was the official explanation for the breakup given to Felice and the parents as well: A healthy woman cannot be expected to marry an unwell man. Franz was all too well-aware that he had wronged Felice, and he did cede her the high ground, though not without a serving of self-righteous histrionics. In his last letter to her, dated from

Zürau, October 16, 1917, he wrote: "You were unhappy about the pointlessness of your journey, about my incomprehensible behaviour, about everything. I was not unhappy … a bit of an act is something for which I can readily forgive myself, because the spectacle before me … was so hellish that one was bound to try to help the audience by introducing some diverting music." A straightforward apology would probably not have blunted the blow very much, but it would have been far less distasteful than a theatre piece.

I'm thinking of Felice, the long trip she took to Zürau, only to find, definitively, she'd been dumped. Where is the dark northeast room she slept in, while Franz was dreaming in another room? Where is the dwelling that he idealized as part of his peaceful life here? I open the copy of *Letters to Ottla & Family* I've brought along. It includes a photo of the *Ringplatz*: the church, the pond and a few houses. The caption indicates that "Kafka and Ottla lived in the house to the right of church." I'm standing in front of the church. Stone angels on the gate columns gaze out over my head, into the beyond. The church windows are shattered, the plaster exterior cracked, the churchyard overgrown with weeds. The house to the right of the church can't be where Franz and Ottla lived, and Felice stayed—for one very unhappy night in 1917. It's a newer building and doesn't match the placement of the house in the photo.

I pass through the rusty church gates. M. is off on an exploration of his own. The churchyard is a gravesite of crumbling monuments—gravestones that were no doubt once quite grand, engraved in

German, Gothic lettering: Josef Steidl, born 15 February, 1834, died 12 December, 1909; Paulina Wallenta, died 15 November, 1910; Anna Quoika, died at 82 on November 14, 1908 … Franz would have viewed these monuments when he entered the yard, which he did on at least one occasion during his time here. At the beginning of February 1918, he wrote to Felix that he'd recently attended a sermon at the church: "It had a business-like simplicity. The text was Luke 2:41-52, and three lessons were drawn. 1. Parents should not permit their children to play outside in the snow but should bring them into the church (see all the empty seats!) 2. Parents should be as tenderly concerned for their children as the Holy Family was for their son (and this even though he was the Child Jesus, about whom they did not need worry). 3. Children should speak piously to their parents as Jesus did to his. That was all, for it was very cold, but there was a kind of ultimate power in the whole thing." The tone is jocular—it often is in Kafka's letters, but one takes from it a certain acknowledgement of the place of the church in the village society, though attendance may have been spotty, even in those days.

The church is locked, so I won't be entering. But the keyhole in the wooden door is huge. I peer in. There are a few chairs in the left transept, no pews; an altar draped with a red-edged cloth, topped with pots of artificial flowers; a thin, wooden cross rises fraily from the floor. The wooden sanctuary—ark of the Host—must be empty: There's no chancel lamp. A rustic rendering of a half-armless, bleeding-heart Jesus swathed in yellow, is tacked to the wall. The church is decommissioned.

A Czech-language leaflet posted to the door reads: "Help us save the Church of the Immaculate Conception of the Virgin Mary in Siřem. We will be happy upon request to send tax receipts. Roman Catholic Parish, www.Liběšice.com. Restoration is supported by the Ministry of Culture for the Czech Republic with the assistance of the Ministry of Culture for Archeological Heritage." Perhaps a resurrection is in the offing …

M. has spotted something of interest—a small brick building with a clipped-gable roof and slatted-wooden doors, located outside the churchyard. The plaque above the door reads *Spritzenhaus, erbaut 1927*. We figure the little building could be connected to the church, but it too is locked, and windowless. A Spritzenhaus, I find out, from the word spritzen—to sprinkle or squirt—is an old German word for fire station. This station doesn't look big enough to hold anything more than buckets and hoses, maybe a small cart. I'm reminded of Kafka's couched humour in the "fire-brigade festival" passage in *The Castle*, in which the all-male fire department volunteers greet the castle's donation of a new "Feuerspritze"—fire-engine—with great glee. The segment turns farcical through repetition of the word "Spritze," and castle official, Sortini's, persistent handling of the "Spritze" and "Spritzenhebel," translated as "shaft" in the Oxford edition.

A small square building set into the slope behind the church draws our attention next. This building is identifiable in the old photos. Once upon a time it had windows. Now they're bricked-in, and there's no door. Chairs like the ones in the church are visible in the semi-dark of the opening, sitting in litter. The words *Unauthorized Entry Forbidden* in Czech are etched above the lintel—giving the place the appearance of a kids' rundown clubhouse. Who knows what purpose it served originally, and there's no one to ask.

Beyond the little square building, there's a sports court—the newest-looking addition to the village. We check the photos. Evidently, the court is located where the house that Ottla and Franz lived in once stood, where Franz began his "new life with a measure of confidence," as he put it in the early days of his stay here. He'd stocked up on blue octavo notebooks in preparation, and announced to Max: "What I have to do here I can only do alone. Become clear about ultimate things." He intended to write in Zürau, and did: over fifty letters in the house-no-longer-standing, and over one hundred short texts that Brod arranged for publication in 1931 under the rather grand-sounding title of *Reflections on Sin, Hope, Suffering, and the True Way* (retitled *The Zürau Aphorisms*). Yet during his stay in Zürau, Kafka kept his writings about "ultimate things" undercover, even claiming mendaciously to Max that "his will is not directed to writing," and "since I am not writing at all I don't have to strive for quiet."

The quiet in Zürau was violated most often and insidiously by mice, of which Franz expressed terror: "Certainly this fear, like an insect phobia, is connected with the unexpected, uninvited, inescapable, persistent secret aim of these creatures," he wrote to Max at the beginning of December. "The night is theirs and because of this nocturnal existence and tininess they are so remote from us and thus outside our power." The mice—and the cat that was brought to Franz's room to control them—became a running theme in his letters from September through December. To Felix, he wrote that he "controls the mice with a cat, but how shall I control the cat?" The cat, a necessity, was less vexing. "Overnight I leave the cat in the empty room next to mine, thereby preventing her from dirtying my room," he wrote to Max; yet despite her "excretions … strewed over rug and sofa," he admitted to growing fond of her, to holding her "warmly in [his] arms." He even came round to calling her "a very good little creature," though he was uncomfortable if she jumped into his lap, and he "didn't like being alone with her … it's considerable nuisance to undress in front of her, do one's exercises, go to bed …" That was Franz: uneasy with the opposite sex, even in the body of a cat.

By January 1918, the cat was no longer being brought to Franz's room. Traps had been acquired and mice ceased to be a theme in his letters. He emphasized to friends that he was doing well in Zürau—health- and other-wise. The packages of reading material that he regularly received kept him up on current issues, and he had as much freedom to read as daylight permitted. He read extensively and eclectically: biographies, correspondence, the Hebrew Bible, a theatre journal, a pacifist journal, Tolstoy's diaries, works by Dickens, Mann, Buber, Hans Blüher, Schopenhauer, and Kierkegaard. By spring of 1918, he was steeped in Kierkegaard: *Either/Or, Fear and Trembling, Repetition*, and *Stages* are named in letters to Max in March and April.

It's not hard to imagine that Kafka would have found space for reflection in Zürau. There's little in the village to distract one from a task at hand. Even today: one main road, a few dirt footpaths. No inn, no coffeehouse. We return to the pool in front of the churchyard. M. goes to check out the buildings across the way. I take a seat on the bench inside the pool area and gaze out over the green water. Still not a villager in sight, not a goose. Quiet like a counterpane.

I take out the book of Kafka's 109 aphorisms that I've brought along. The short texts have been described as contemplative, conceptual, metaphysical, philosophical, Kabbalistic. Several are poetic, and cryptic: "A cage went in search of a bird"; "A faith like a guillotine, so heavy, so light"; "A. is a virtuoso and Heaven is his witness." "A." is mentioned in three of the aphorisms; who "A." is, is not spelled out. (Perhaps A. stood for Arthur, as in Schopenhauer ...) Lord, God, Heaven and Paradise are thematic; evil and the Evil One appear no fewer than ten times. The Tree of Life also appears, as does the Fall, the Tower of Babel, the Last Judgement, sin, prayer, and the singular, oft-quoted phrase: "the indestructible within." The frequent use of theological terminology in the aphorisms contributed to a presentation of Franz Kafka as a Jewish writer with distinctly religious concerns, though the writings themselves put the divine-sublime quite out of reach. In this sense, a connection can be drawn between the aphorisms and the castle in *The Castle*: Whatever it represents, cannot be reached. But perhaps it was not meant to represent anything, nor to be reached. Perhaps the castle is simply a device for holding the novel together: a kind of through-line. Not a metaphor, nor a symbol. In any case, Kafka abandoned the work mid-sentence, never reaching an ending.

I open the slim volume of aphorisms and read the first one aloud to the air above the stagnant green water: "The true way passes over a rope which is not stretched high up, but just above the ground. It seems to be intended more for stumbling than for crossing." I can't help but chuckle a little, though Kafka surely did not intend his words to be humourous. Sitting before the former goose pond in Siřem, I'm reminded of a neighbour back home who installed a low rope enclosure around his front yard to prevent the Canada geese from coming up from the nearby pond to feast and defecate on his green lawn. The low rope served the purpose of preventing their crossing, and the grass was kept pristine. The geese could not step over the rope, and they didn't have the wherewithal to fly over it.

M. beckons me to the other side of the pool—over to a low-standing house with a large bay window. Taped inside the windowpanes are the Zürau photos of Franz and Ottla. There's the one of them standing in a field near the village. Kafka's secretary, Julie Kaiser, from the Worker's Accident Insurance Institute appears in this one, so it can be dated to early November 1917: Franz mentioned in a letter to Max that the girl from the office came for a visit—at Ottla's invitation. There's the one of Franz and Ottla standing side by side at the entrance to what might have been the house they lived in; also a panoramic postcard view of the village. A bulletin in Czech taped to the inside of the window announces "the opening of a permanent exhibition about Kafka in the countryside in the New Galleria in Siřem." The opening date is cited as August 19, 2017—two days from the day of our visit: We were in Siřem on August 17. I peer into the room. It's empty and decrepit. There's no sign of an imminent exhibition.

We walk around to the other side of the building—to see if there's a better view. A wooden fence, stone parapet, high grasses and shrubbery obstruct passage. We could try negotiating the brambles and climb over the parapet, but that would be trespassing—even if there's no one living here anymore, and no one watching us … But there is: an orange tabby cat, peering at me through the grass. We lock gazes and stare each other down. It occurs to me that this is the only animal we've seen in Siřem, and that s/he is quite possibly a descendant of the cat that sat on Kafka's lap. I want to believe that.

Ottla

Zürau, Bohemia, 1917

The world at war,
    the village where you till

the land is still. Sister with your practical granting

hands and understanding,
      you are just this close to having wings.

I envision you over pots and in the fields

with your primitive implements; what would the simple tools

do without your movement …

All around you animal chatter—this the natural

clamour. I want to have a glimpse into the quiet

of your mind, plain pacific face,

beneath the pictured thick and pinned-up hair.

Earringless and ringless in this *good little marriage*

to Franz. You knew what he needed and bore him up—

Ottla, most beloved.

It is fall,
    it is not fall in the ranges of your heart—

large enough to hold a failing farm, a lover,

a brother. His eyes the trouble-colour;

yours opaque as the pool in the *Ring*, and shrine-like.

Surfacing Behaviour

Váňovský Pond, Třešť, Czech Republic

The pond alive with them—leaping, thwacking like paddles
upon re-entry. The sound of it loud and out of the blue: You don't

expect these fish—they look like carp—to breach like humpbacks.
You don't expect this tranquil water to clap. I like the way

you call from the car, roused as much as I am by the action.
I am at the pond-side with the camera, poised to shoot the proof.

Swans are on the water also—whites and pale grey juveniles—
approaching. It's possible I've never had an accurate sense

of distance, which is to say I fear their teeth on my toes. I snap
the jumpers—fish at once so fully of-the-water / oddly not; I

capture golden bodies aloft—mid-wriggle. Gleeful in the leaping,
or at least it seems to me. Maybe it's display, a sign ...

Perhaps they're on their way to whale—with imminent lungs
and blowholes. It's possible I've never had an accurate sense

of mystery, which is to say their realness is their glee. The swans,
emerging at the grass, back me to the Škoda (you haven't left).

Anyhow, we're good to go. We've seen the small Czech town
where young Franz Kafka came in summer, to visit Uncle

Siegfried—country doctor of Třešť (at that time, Triesch). *Lay
naked by the pond,* he wrote, *rode his uncle's motorcycle,*

*herded cows and goats, played quoits; fell for a shortsighted
girl by way of her fat foreshortened legs, and went to temple.*

The Mammoth Village & Gmünd

THE RELATIVELY STRAIGHT line a seeker hopes a search will take veers sometimes—suddenly and unexpectedly—to yield thrill and delight. Or disappointment. Stephen Collis brings this observation to *Almost Islands*, his sage and spacious memoir of literary friendship with late legendary Canadian poet and broadcaster, Phyllis Webb, whose search included abandonment of a long-pursued poetry project on Russian anarchist prince, Pyotr Kropotkin, and Collis's shimmery idea of picking up where Webb left off—to write his own Kropotkin poems "as a gift to the unwritten." I've had the picking-up idea in my search as well, which has yielded its share of thrill and surprise, and has also veered to disappointment.

Perhaps it's the disappointments that have prodded me on. I can say this now, years after first venturing into the field, faithfully seeking Franz. Seeking when I'm not in the field as well—in the way that reading, sleeping and dreaming are part of writing, and writing part of thinking: of figuring out what it is that one thinks. There's a continuum, and the field feeds the yield, with hope against disappointment, for thrill, surprise and delight.

***

In March 2019, M. and I are again in Vienna—the city Franz called "that decaying mammoth village"—to visit and revisit K. locations. This time we drive northwest from the capital to Gmünd—a railway-crossing town on the Austrian-Czech border. The hub of the former Austro-Hungarian Empire and the border town both became bound up with Kafka's complicated un/happiness picture. I'm interested in what, if anything of that picture, will be mirrored to me.

Kafka hated Vienna, so he claimed. His hometown was just "barely bearable." Vienna is "desolate," he wrote to Felice in April of 1913, six months into their courtship. Berlin was the place to be, especially for a writer; Vienna was steeped in the past—a flatter, bleaker, bloated version of Prague. Kafka's longest intersection with the city came in

1913, from September 7-14. He was on official business with colleagues from the office: a delegate of the Workers' Accident Insurance Institute attending the Second International Congress for First Aid and Accident Prevention at the hall of the Viennese Parliament. It was a difficult time in his generally fraught relationship with Felice. On-course for marriage and dreading it, his stay—recorded in cards and notes—was overshadowed by his moodiness, which he attributed to the city. He found fault with almost everything: the weather ("heavy rain"); colleagues he met up with over dinner and coffee ("inane gossip"); meetings of the Eleventh Zionist Congress he attended ("fruitless German speeches"); a day at the Prater amusement park ("incessant headaches"); and sitting through hours and hours over five days of insurance-conference proceedings with two of his superiors from the Institute. On the last day he wrote to Felice: "It would be best if the days I have spent in Vienna could be obliterated—one and all. I am leaving for Trieste tomorrow." He'd be taking his annual vacation in Italy, solo.

The one bright Vienna-spot might have been Hotel Matschakerhof. In sympathy with author Franz Grillparzer, who'd routinely dined at the hotel, Kafka booked a two-room suite with his travel companion from Prague—poet and translator, Otto Pick. Hotels usually gave Kafka a feeling of ease and freedom, but due to Pick's noisy comings and goings, even Franz's off-hours at the Matschakerhof were disrupted and marred by insomnia and headaches.

The September trip is remembered in February 1914 in a letter to Grete Bloch—the young woman Felice recruited in autumn of 1913 to mediate between herself and Franz, who fast became an exciting new pen-pal. "For my part I wouldn't want to be in Vienna even in May," he wrote to Grete, then residing in the city. "It was far too unpleasant for me, nothing on earth would induce me to set out again for the House of Parliament … sit at the Cafés Beethoven or Museum, and never again would I feel like wandering around the gardens of Schönbrunn … The Grillparzer Room in City Hall is the one thing I should like to see, I missed it, not having heard of it until too late. Do you know *The Poor Musician* by Grillparzer? That one can well and truly suffer in Vienna was truly proved by Grillparzer."

Franz Grillparzer was one of four authors Kafka named as his "true blood-relations." (The others were Dostoevsky, Kleist and Flaubert.) Grillparzer's 1848 novella, *The Poor Fiddler* (*Der arme Spielmann*, a.k.a. *The Poor Musician*), was dear to him. He'd read it aloud to his sisters and knew it almost by heart. He recommended it to Felice, to Grete and to Milena Jesenská, his Czech translator, and gifted copies of the book to the latter two.

The Poor Fiddler apparently held messages from Franz for women. I ordered the book from AbeBooks, planning to read it ahead of our trip, by way of preparation. It arrived the day before our departure—a slim, discharged library copy from St. Mary College of Leavenworth Kansas. The old-style Date Due card glued inside the back cover showed that only one person had ever borrowed the book: a woman with neat cursive writing named Mary Kenan Wolff. That Mary Kenan and I share a surname—with the same uncommon spelling—felt like a little convergence that can't mean much, yet seems to signal something. I packed *The Poor Fiddler*, now planning to read it aloud to M., as Franz had read to his sisters, but on location—where the story was written and set.

The Grillparzer sites—Hotel Matschakerhof at 5 Spiegelgasse and the Grillparzer Room at the Vienna City Museum—are at the top of my visit-list, along with places connected to Kafka's second longest stay in the city—from June 29 till July 4, 1920—when he came to meet up with Milena Jesenská, who, like Felice, fast became an epistolary love interest.

The relationship between Franz and Milena began as a business correspondence in April 1920. Franz was convalescing in the northern Italian spa-town of Merano. Milena was living unhappily in Vienna with her husband, Ernst Pollak, with whom Kafka was acquainted through the Prague Jewish literary circle. Franz and Milena were introduced in the fall of 1919, at Prague's Café Arco, probably by Pollak. It was Pollak who encouraged his wife to translate Kafka's stories into Czech and she became the first person to introduce Kafka to non-German readers. She initially translated "The Stoker"—the opening chapter of *Amerika*.

When the translation appeared in the small leftist weekly *Kmen* on April 22, 1920, Franz wrote to tell Milena that he was "moved by [her] faithfulness toward every little sentence." In the same letter he was already providing details—at her request—about his romantic status. He was still officially engaged to Julie Wohryzhek—the young Prague woman he'd met early in 1919 while the two were convalescing at Pension Stüdl in Schelesen (Želízy) north of Prague. Their marriage, planned for November 1919, was strictly opposed by his father (on grounds that Julie, daughter of a synagogue beadle, was not of the Kafkas' social standing). Franz told Milena the engagement was "still alive although without any prospect of marriage." In July 1920, urged on by Milena, he formally broke (messily) with Julie.

By the end of May, Franz and Milena were corresponding daily. She invited him to Vienna. "I don't want to come," he wrote on May 31—in a manner reminiscent of his teetering with Felice: "I couldn't stand the mental stress." But he was building up to the trip. On June 11, he asked her to address him by the familiar German form of "you": "Du"—also reminiscent of his patterning with Felice. Despite their age and ethnic differences—he was thirty-seven, she twenty-four; he, Jewish, she, Christian, and married to a man Kafka claimed he admired—the attraction was real. They were both writers, both tubercular, both engaged in lifelong conflict with their fathers, and both averse to Vienna. Milena wrote of her struggles of living in the city, with the pain of a philandering husband. They became entangled in each other's grievances.

Kafka arrived in Vienna from Merano on Tuesday June 29, 1920. At 10 a.m. he sent Milena a letter poste restante—as per arrangement—to the Bennogasse Post Office near the Pollaks' apartment. He was sitting at a café near the Südbahnhof, he wrote, and would be waiting for her at 10 a.m. the next morning in front of Hotel Riva, next to the train station. In the meantime, he would check out the sites: "Lerchenfelderstrasse (the apartment where the Pollaks lived) and the post office, while trying to remain as invisible as possible."

Lerchenfelder Strasse and the Bennogasse Post Office are on my itinerary too, along with the Volksgarten (where Franz and Milena went for a summer stroll), the train station, and two cafés—The Herrenhof and Café Central—both frequented by Ernst and Milena. Milena resented the café culture that held her husband in thrall, and

Franz was not at all interested in café culture by 1920, especially not in Vienna. But The Herrenhof is adjacent the breakfast room at the renovated Hotel Steigenberger, Herrengasse 10, where M. and I are staying, and Café Central on the next block.

We deposit our bags in our room and head down to The Herrenhof Café—a pale version of the ornate art nouveau original. Large black-and-white photos mounted on the white walls evoke some indefinite time-past—nothing of the café in its heyday, when Ernst (enthralled) and Milena (bored) sat in the company of his circle of friends, keeping abreast of literary and art news. The Herrenhof that M. and I enter is empty. We order lattes and use the tabletop to map our route for the afternoon.

Our first stop is Herrengasse 14—the former bank building housing the café that had already acquired cult status when Ernst and Milena were regulars. Rebuilt to traditional grandeur, Café Central now has cult status of the tourist kind. There's a long lineup outside, so we defer our visit and walk around the corner to the Volksgarten. The historic public park is surrounded by a high spiked-iron fence and a sign on the gate that reads (uninvitingly) *Achtung!*: Opening hours: 7:00 till 17:30. We enter.

Franz and Milena strolled here at the end of June 1920, when the chestnut trees were in bloom. At the end of March, for our visit, the cherry trees are in blossom, the profusion pink. In addition to the many specimen trees, the Volksgarten is home to a small-scale replica of the Athenian Temple of Hephaestus, Triton and Nymph Fountains, elaborate rose gardens, and several august monuments. It's an elegant public park, impeccably maintained, but M. is less-than-interested in imagining Franz and Milena's circuit here, or in sitting on any of the many benches to take in the attractions—including the grand statue of Franz Grillparzer.

We depart the Volksgarten, before I'm done with it, and continue on our route. Within the hour we're standing in front of Lerchenfelder 13, which I've noted as Milena and Ernst's address. It's a handsome neoclassical building—much more upscale than what I've imagined for the couple, who struggled with funds. But perhaps this building, like Hotel Steigenberger and Café Central, has undergone renovation. I photograph it for the record—it yields no secrets—and we continue on to the Bennogasse Post Office: a fifteen-minute walk—not as "near" the Pollaks' apartment as Milena indicates in her letters.

When we arrive, M. is on edge. "It's a post office," he says. "You knew we were going to a post office," I reply: "It's not just any post office. It's historic. This is where Milena came every day in the summer and fall of 1920. It was part of her ritual of sending and retrieving letters from Franz." "Go inside then," M. says, waving me off. "We're here, you may as well check it out, see what it yields." I glance into the fluorescent glare of the crowded hall. It's sterile, ordinary, completely charmless. I don't feel like going in. I cross the street instead, photograph the building in its setting. M. photographs me standing at the entrance, my enthusiasm tamped. I'm feeling like I imagine Milena must have felt on days when she emerged from the building empty-handed, not having received a letter from Franz.

Shadows are lengthening as we head back. M. breaks the silence that's settled between us: "The afternoon would have been better spent at the Kunsthistorisches Museum—with Brueghel, and the Rothko retrospective you've touted as a bonus for this trip," he says. "This trip isn't only about Kafka," I say. (We both know that, largely, it is.) "We'll see Brueghel and Rothko tomorrow." M. is not assuaged. And as we're passing Shakespeare & Company Bookstore on the way to where we're going for dinner, I suggest we step in quickly, since we're here, and buy a Vienna memento. M. gives me the grim look and stands sentry at the door while I step in and make a snap purchase: *Party in the Blitz*, Elias Canetti's memoir of his wartime exile in England. The Nobel author had had no doubt as to the biographical provenance of Kafka's novel of trial, judgement and punishment: In *Kafka's Other Trial*, he draws direct connections between Kafka's life and writing, and his case is persuasive. On our way to the restaurant, I try sparking a conversation about how places, people and their ordeals get written into books. M. is too cranky to engage.

Luckily the restaurant—Alef Alef—is just around the corner, at Seitenstettengasse 2, and dinner, along with the owner's light house wine, brings us both up. On leaving, I notice two plaques mounted high on the side of the building, both commemorating Adalbert Stifter—a poetic realist and another of Kafka's literary mentors. I photograph both plaques—one worn, one shiny—to translate the inscriptions later, and we proceed to Spiegelgasse 5: Hotel Matschakerhof. It's no longer a hotel, but the building is standing, well-preserved, with the name affixed to the façade—along with another commemorative plaque. The inscription, at eye-level, is translatable on the spot: *Franz Grillparzer 1791-1872 was a regular guest at the Matschakerhof tavern.* I feel a clinch of literary sympathy, and a tingle in knowing that in this building, Franz slept.

Back at Hotel Steigenberger I translate the inscriptions on the Stifter plaques. The older one reads: *In this house lived Adalbert Stifter, in the years 1842-1848*; the newer one: *At this location Adalbert Stifter observed, on July 8, 1842, the only total solar eclipse that occurred in modern Vienna.* Stifter—whose oeuvre has largely faded into obscurity—was witness, at Seitenstettengasse 2, to a cosmic wonder. The cosmic connection gets the better billing.

In reviewing my notes from the day, I discover what I'd half-suspected: I had incorrectly copied Milena and Ernst's address. They lived at 113 Lerchenfelder Strasse, not 13. According to Google Maps, walking-time from Lerchenfelder 113 to the Bennogasse Post Office is 5 minutes; the distance from Lerchenfelder 13 to the post office is 1.1 km—not exactly "near." That's why Milena's reference to the post office being "near" their apartment seemed off. I don't bother telling M. that I'd mixed up. I know we won't be going back to view Lerchenfelder 113. (What would it yield?) He's relaxed now. We're in bed, weary from the day's trek, and he's ready to hear me read from *The Poor Fiddler*. I open the book and start reading aloud:

In Vienna the Sunday after the July full moon is a genuine people's holiday ... On this day the people of Brigittenau celebrate the dedication of their own saint's church, and with them those of Augarten, Leopoldstadt and the Prater, all linked together in one unbroken chain of jollification ... There was a woman harpist with repulsive, glassy eyes ... a cripple with a wooden leg who labored away at a frightful, obviously homemade instrument ... a lame, misshapen boy, hunched inextricably over his fiddle ... and finally an old man in a threadbare but decent overcoat of Molton cloth and a smiling, self-congratulatory expression ... He sawed away at an old, much cracked violin ... What he played seemed nothing but a disjointed sequence of sounds, keeping to no time or tune ... For all that he was utterly absorbed in his task.

I'm soon reading to myself; M. is fast asleep.

I can see from the opening pages how this tale would have appealed to Franz. The narrator and the fiddler are both bachelors, one the observer, one the performer, outsiders heartened by art. Kafka would have identified with both—with the narrator and his curiosity, and with the poor fiddler's ardent absorption in his art. But unlike the fiddler, who was oblivious to the discordant sounds he produced on his cracked violin, Franz suffered recurring doubt about the merit of much of his art, and considered himself especially lacking in musical talent. "Unmusicality ... I inherited from my paternal grandfather," he wrote to Milena from Merano. He repeatedly professed his unmusicality, his "inability to enjoy music connectedly," he confided to his diary. Yet music is emblematic of humanity in his most iconic story, *The Metamorphosis*, and thematic in his last, "Josephine the Singer, or the Mouse Folk," which, like *The Poor Fiddler*, addresses the themes of what constitutes art, the relationship of artist to audience, and artist to legacy. On these thoughts, I notice that M. and I are breathing in-sync; we've become synchronized, and I too drift off.

***

Next morning there's no lineup outside Café Central. We're quickly ushered in and begin our day under the vaulted ceiling of the elegant coffeehouse with smoked salmon plates and pots of strong coffee, served efficiently by a young waiter from Israel with a Barack Obama smile. We hear little German and most of the breakfast guests are tuned to their devices, not engaged in coffeehouse conversation or reading a newspaper. On our way out, M. photographs me standing beside a large brass newspaper stand—a nod to yesteryear set at the far side of the room, by a serving station. The newspapers, undisturbed, are hung like neatly folded coats.

Around the corner, we join the long lineup outside the Kunsthistorisches Museum. It's worth the wait. The Rothko retrospective is comprehensive, beautifully curated. I'm moved by the huge, prayerful colour field paintings, the way the canvases resist my attempts to capture them, the camera lens zooming in and out, unclear on what to focus. It's as if the spirit of the work will not be contained, that to be in the presence of a Rothko colour field demands one's undivided attention. M. is far more impressed by works of Pieter Brueghel the Elder in the Museum's permanent collection: *The Tower of Babel*, *The Return of the Herd*, *Children's Games*, *The Peasant Dance*, *The Peasant Wedding*. The two exhibitions—mounted in adjacent halls—could hardly be more divergent: Brueghel, Renaissance master of exquisitely detailed, realistic depictions of biblical themes and peasant scenes; and Rothko, the abstract expressionist who eschewed the term, and in painting floating zones of colour was most interested in expressing basic human emotion.

From the Kunsthistorisches Museum we make our way to the City Museum, Karlsplatz—the one site in Vienna that Franz was sorry to have missed. On April 7, 1914 he sent Grete Bloch a copy of *The Poor Musician*. The following month he instructed her not to leave Vienna until she'd been "to see the Room at the City Museum and written to tell him about it." On April 26, 1914, as she was relocating to Berlin for work, he was still insistent: "You are about to leave ... Don't forget the Grillparzer Room."

We reach the City Museum only to find it *geschlossen*—closed—for renovations. A notice indicates that some of the exhibitions from the Wien Museum, Karlsplatz, have been transferred to the MUSA Museum on Felderstrasse for the remodelling period. I dash off an email to the City Museum asking if the Grillparzer Room is one of the exhibitions temporarily at the MUSA. M. is certain I won't be getting a response any time soon, if at all. And now he wants to pass on walking to the Südbahnhof, since I'd found out at the hotel that the south station, once Vienna's largest railway terminus, was demolished in 2010 and replaced with a new station—the Hauptbahnhof. He sees no point in walking to a place that's no longer there, and after the Lerchenfelderstrasse miss of the previous day I can almost agree.

But we aren't so very far from the station and I want to see where Franz sat at a café and wrote to Milena about the poor pastry and disappointing cocoa—even if the station and the café are no longer standing. Even if the fleabag Hotel Riva "next to the garage at the Südbahnhof"—where he and Milena met up on the morning of June 30, 1920—isn't there either. Would I feel greater sympathy for a presence than for an absence? Absences can impart messages as well. And maybe something synchronous will happen—that can't be ruled out. But I don't share these thoughts with M. I point out that we're seeing the city, enjoying the day, and will be stopping in at the Belvedere Palace Gallery to view the visiting Klimt exhibition on the way to the station. M. begrudgingly concedes and we proceed—first to the gallery, where we crowd in with the other visitors to view pieces by Munch, Gerstl, Schiele, and Klimt, including his famous Kiss—larger and shinier in life—and afterwards sip lukewarm, overpriced lattes at the Gallery Café.

The Hauptbahnhof is glassy, ultramodern. We walk through the station—from Canettistrasse at the north entrance to the Südtiroler Platz on Laxenburger Strasse. There's a bus terminal on the south side, a sausage stand, and a stretch of drab apartment buildings along Laxenburger Strasse. No hotel—Riva or other. Not a trace of Kafka— except perhaps in the sign, Canettistrasse—the street named for Elias Canetti on the north side of the station. "Now you're really reaching," M. says when I pull up the camera to photograph the sign. "So what if Canetti wrote a book about Kafka, then had a street named for himself next to where Kafka once in his life got off a train. Even if Canetti

Street were Kafka Street, what would the connection to Kafka be?" "Maybe your mood," I say. "You're sounding as cranky as Franz." "Can you blame me?" M. says. "We've walked for over an hour to see a street sign and a sausage stand." He's not exaggerating by much and we both fall silent. Truth is, I'm feeling moody too, and not much sympathy for an absence.

We hail a cab back to the hotel. I suggest stopping in at the MUSA Museum on the way—to see if the Grillparzer exhibition is set up there. "The Grillparzer Room is, after all, what Franz most wanted to see in Vienna," I say. "It's the main K. attraction here." M. again begrudgingly concedes. But, of course, there is no Grillparzer exhibition at the MUSA, and, as if to rub it in, one of the staffers informs us that the City Museum renovation is scheduled to take five years. I have to laugh. In April 1914, Kafka wrote to Grete Bloch: "Even if I were Viennese it would probably be impossible for me ever to get to the Grillparzer Room."

On the walk from the MUSA back to the hotel, an email from the City Museum pings into my cellphone Inbox: *Dear Ms Wolff—I am sorry—the Grillparzer apartment is currently not on display as the Wien Museum is closed. At the MUSA we are only showing temporary exhibitions. The exhibition rooms are too small, it is not possible to show also our permanent exhibition. Best regards, Andrea Glatz.* "At least I got a reply. You didn't think I would." I cast a sidelong glance at M. "And how synchronous with Franz is that! He didn't get to see the Grillparzer apartment either!"

Of his days with Milena in Vienna, Franz wrote to her that "the first was unsure, the second was oversure, the third remorseful, the fourth was the good one." They visited the Volksgarten, went to a stationer's shop, spent hours walking in the Vienna Woods on the outskirts of the city, and lay side by side on the "wretched bed" at the "vermin"-ridden Hotel Riva. This can be pieced together from their correspondence. Franz wrote repeatedly of his "fear" (angst). The word "fear" trolls through his letters to Milena; through his letters to others as well. Milena wrote that she tried to help him overcome his fear of the physical. But she was respectful. Their affection did not extend to sex. A month after their togetherness in Vienna Franz came as close as he would to speaking to her of his "fastidiousness: … between this day-world and 'that half-hour in bed' of which you spoke contemptuously as 'men's business', there is for me an abyss which I can't bridge, probably because I don't want to." On July 5, the day after his return to Prague, he sent her a copy of *The Poor Musician*: "not because it means so much to me," he wrote, "although it did once years ago. Rather I'm sending it because it is so Viennese, so unmusical, so sad, because he was looking down on us in the Volksgarten." Kafka had respect for that which touched him from the beyond.

Dusk is falling by the time we reach the Volksgarten. I want to walk through the park again—to view the Grillparzer Monument up-close this time—to sense impressions, as I put it to M. He wants to go straight to the hotel room, rest, then go for dinner. I tell him I'll meet him back at the room. After I've explored the park. We part abruptly and I'm on my own.

Being in a fenced public park five minutes from the hotel isn't really being on my own, but I'm the only one here, and it's quiet. I walk to the far end of the park and stand before the imposing Grillparzer Monument, the author sitting silently, book in hand. I'm waiting for I-don't-know-what when the quiet is broken by a loud caw. A crow lands on a bench to my left, cocks its dark head and caws again, emphatically. I've seen crows at other Kafka locations and as 'kavka' is the Czech word for jackdaw—the smallest member of the crow family—a coincidental appearance of a 'kavka' inevitably suggests to me a feathered manifestation of the author himself. This time I ignore him—at least I try to; I'm focused on Grillparzer. The crow flutters up to the tree next to me, releases another loud, unmusical sound. He can't be ignored. I look up; he stares me down. I'm tempted to ask him what he wants. I snap his picture instead, turn and head briskly for the exit. The sun is setting, I'm feeling uneasy. Surely the gate won't be closed as long as there's someone still in the park. I pick up my pace, break into a jog, hear fluttering close above. It's the crow, as if to usher me out. I reach the gate, depart the Volksgarten. The crow remains inside. I'm ruffled. I don't slow to a walk until I've turned the corner toward the hotel.

"It's getting dark," M. says as I enter the room. I know from his tone that he's glad I'm back. I'm glad too. The abruptness between us has passed. "Did you get to see what you wanted to see?" he asks. "Yes," I say, but I don't mention the encounter, and he doesn't press me.

When we turn in, I take out *The Poor Fiddler*. "You'll have to start again, I don't remember a thing," he says. So I start at the beginning and again, before long, he's asleep. I continue reading aloud to myself—to where the fiddler reveals to the narrator that he calls his playing "improvising," then "falls silent for shame at having given away his inmost secret"; namely, that improvising is like prayer, and "prayer is private." The narrator—beguiled by this odd old man, asks if he can join him at his home—to listen in on his "solitary exercises." The fiddler reluctantly agrees to receive the narrator at his lodgings—where he shares a divided room with two journeymen. I pause to underline "prayer is private." In autumn of 1920, soon after Franz refreshed his connection to Grillparzer's novella after giving it to Milena, he wrote in his diary: "writing is a form of prayer"—a line that's been cited as characteristic of Kafka's thought in general.

***

Early next morning we set out for Gmünd. We drive past the district where *The Poor Fiddler* is set—Leopoldstadt, which together with Brigittenau, forms a large island in the Danube Canal, the Danube River to the north. We haven't planned to stop at places mentioned in the novella: neither the Augarten nor the Prater amusement park, which Kafka recalled unfavourably from his 1913 visit. We have to be back from Gmünd by evening and given the time constraint, I'd rather stop in at the former Hoffmann Sanatorium in Kierling, north of the city, where Kafka spent his last days.

M. and I had weathered the trek to Kierling in January 2014—by train, bus and foot—and managed by serendipity to arrange, on the spur of the moment, a visit to the Kafka *Gedenkraum*—Memorial Room—on the threshold of its closing for renovations. Our guide, Herr Norbert Winkler, former secretary of the Kafka Society of Austria, met up with us in the Hofer supermarket parking lot next to the sanatorium—now a residential building—to give us a tour. He unlocked the front door, led us upstairs and showed us the sad, stark Memorial Room (not the room Kafka actually stayed in), and the antique elevator (no longer in operation) that Kafka used on arrival and departure. "Do you want to see the bathroom in the hallway?" Herr Winkler asked. M. has got a lot of poke-mileage from the fact that I said yes, then sat on the toilet that Kafka himself may well have sat on. It still worked—at least it did in 2014.

The staid three-storey building at 187 Hauptstrasse, with the strangely placed front door—at the far right of the building—is as I remember it. M. parks the car in the Hofer parking lot. We get out, like déja vu. I photograph the back of the building first—the balcony on the top floor that Kafka used when weather permitted—to rest, chest bared to the sun, and view the Vienna Woods beyond. The Woods, green and serious, are as I remember them as well—trees have a kind of constancy. But on this visit, I notice just how narrow the building looks from the side—almost like a façade only. We walk around to the front; the door of course is locked and we haven't arranged a tour so we won't be entering this time round.

Visits to the *Gedenkraum* are now limited to certain hours of the month—listed in a glass box next to the entrance. The Memorial Room has a Facebook site now too, where Kafka events are posted, and one can watch a short video—filmed in the renovated room. We watch the video clip on M.'s phone. Medical records and antique instruments are still on display, as are books by and about the author. The room looks brighter in the video, the wall texts and photos more attractively mounted. A metal bed has been added, which one can't believe was ever seen by Franz.

The two-hour drive from Kierling to Gmünd is leisurely. We pass through slumberous towns with unfamiliar names—Tulln, Krems, Limbach, Kirchberg, Ullrichs, Nondorf—places with pastel-coloured churches, tiny roadside chapels, cramped and patched plaster houses, crumbling buildings whose use or former use is undiscernible. I divide the drive between window-gazing, snapping pass-by shots, and reading aloud from *The Poor Fiddler*—this time continuing from where I left off.

The narrator visits the fiddler at his residence—to observe his "solitary exercises," "the old man scraping away" on his cracked violin. His section of the room at Gärtnergasse 34 is modest, yet neat. There's a bed and table for music and writing materials, the "equator of his miniature world" marked in chalk to separate it from the shambles on the side of his roommates. Fascinated though he is by the fiddler's "sensuous enjoyment in playing," the narrator can bear the dissonance for only so long. He "spares the reader a description of the infernal concert" and the plotline is redirected. "I'm curious to know your story," he says, "how it is that you became a street musician."

"You see," M. says, "I'm listening, and I'm following. This is how you should read to me—when I'm awake! But for now, take a break. We're nearly there. I have to watch the road."

The WAZE App is programmed for the Gmünd train station. Kafka wrote at length to Milena of "the amazing story" of his layover at the station on his way back to Prague, after their four days together. He was detained at passport control for not having his papers in order. He might have been required to spend the night at a hotel near the station and return to Vienna the next day to obtain the necessary visa—if not for the "angelic intervention" of Milena: is how he put it. "It's as if you had run up and down knocking on all the gates of heaven to plead for me," he wrote to her. For suddenly, inexplicably, and miraculously one of the inspectors let him through to Prague without a valid visa. "Moments like that make one choke with emotion," he told her. I can relate.

Franz and Milena met for the second time in Gmünd, for several hours on Saturday, August 14, 1920. The four days in Vienna brought mostly happiness; the afternoon in Gmünd brought only pain. They met at the railway station, went for a walk—probably on Bahnhofstrasse— the main street that leads to the Stadtplatz—Old Town Square. They lay in a meadow—probably at Schlosspark—a two-minute walk from the Square, and talked. All the anticipation of the previous weeks collapsed into an afternoon of agitation and misunderstandings. Franz was nervous and arrived even less able to express affection than he'd been on their first day in Vienna. But in Vienna he'd had three days to come round. In Gmünd they talked in circles. Milena still believed in the "indissolubility of her marriage" and was both concerned about "infidelity to Ernst" and uncertain about Franz's feelings for her. "What does this 'infidelity' matter compared to my eternal bond," he asked her, by which one has to understand (and Milena surely did) that he meant a bond of souls, not a physical bond between man and woman, not sex.

On August 24, he wrote of the Gmünd meeting: "On that day we spoke and listened to each other often and for a long time, like strangers." He felt abandoned by Milena for "something he did wrong" there. What was it exactly? At the end of August, he reached out to her; he wanted to "write or talk about Gmünd." He wanted some kind of closeness, and oddly asked her to "send [him] a view of [her] apartment." Was it love? Maybe some kind of love. But on September 14 he wrote "perhaps it isn't love when I say that you are what I love the most— you are the knife I turn inside myself, this is love." At the end of the month, he conceded that "few things are certain, but one is that we'll never live together, share an apartment, body to body, at a common table, never." The following day the sentiment was reiterated. Then the letters dropped off—to two at the end of October; on November 20 he asked that they stop writing to one another altogether: "These letters do nothing but cause anguish ... They can only evoke a day in Gmünd, produce misunderstandings and shame ... I am powerless toward you as well as toward myself ... and all the causes lie buried in darkness." (Again, the deep-seatedness, the dark and buried causes.)

After Gmünd they didn't see each other for a year. But Milena was not able to hold to Franz's request and in January 1921 she wrote to him in Slovakia, where he was convalescing at Villa Tatra, Matliary. She wrote to him there again in April, despite a renewed promise not to. Then in July she wrote to Max Brod asking him to retrieve all her letters from Franz; they were never recovered and their fate is unknown. She visited him in autumn of 1921 at his parents' home in Prague where he handed her his diaries to that date. She already had in her possession the manuscript of his first book, *Amerika*, and the "Letter to His Father"— the long and scathing letter (never delivered) that he wrote in fall of 1919 at Schelesen (Želízy) in the wake of his father's opposition to his engagement to Julie Wohryzek. Even after the breakdown in their relationship, he still had full trust in Milena as a writer.

In August 1920—just before the Gmünd rendezvous, Milena wrote to Max: "Frank (she called him Frank) is unable to live. Frank will never recover ... Frank will soon die ... He lacks even the smallest refuge: he has no shelter … He is like a naked man among the dressed … His asceticism is completely unheroic … here is a man who is forced to be ascetic because of his purity and inability to compromise … His books are amazing. He himself is far more amazing." I type these words, Milena's words, as snow falls on the windows of my study. Clear, pure, honest words. They make me tear.

M. and I approach Gmünd from the southeast. We come to a green inn with a red tile roof: Zum Schachner. "The train track runs next to the hotel," Franz wrote to Milena of his Vienna-to-Prague escapade. Zum Schachner is next to the tracks but it's too new to be a hotel that Kafka could have referred to. "Let's go in and ask," M. says. "Maybe the operator knows of an older hotel." As it happens, he does, and we're directed to Pension Botzi, "the oldest hotel in Gmünd," located near the tracks on the other side of the station.

Pension Botzi—a corner-building that looks like it was designed by committee—is clearly not an original structure. It's hardly older than the Zum Schachner. We enter and are greeted in a small foyer by an elderly lady in a bright red sweater. I tell her we're visiting Gmünd for the day and are particularly interested in Pension Botzi as the oldest hotel in town. Her face lights up and in halting English she escorts us in to the adjacent room—a private living space cramped with furniture, household items, knickknacks, art, and *alte sachen*. She introduces herself, Helga, and then her husband, Albert Botzi, a frail old man, hunched over his meal at a table in the corner. He looks up at us, nods, and returns to his food. Helga invites us to have a seat, steps behind a high counter and quickly returns with several old photos that she spreads out in front of us, as if they'd been awaiting our arrival.

"Pension Botzi has a long history," she tells us. "My husband's grandparents opened the hotel in 1913. It was then called Losert." She points to a creased sepia photo. "This building, where we are sitting now, was not the first one. The first one was wood." She points to an antique postcard—Gruss aus Gmünd—featuring thumbnail images of the old train station, a tobacco stand, and the original hotel, captioned *Leopold Losert's Gasthaus*.

I wonder aloud if Kafka ever stayed at Losert's Gasthaus. "Franz Kafka the writer?" Albert Botzi says from his spot at the corner of the room. Till now he hasn't uttered a sound. My mention of Kafka piques his attention. "Yes, Franz Kafka stayed here," Botzi says in English more fluent than his wife's. "But the hotel has been renovated more than once since then." I don't know whether to take the man at his word or not. But the unexpected, compressed turn of the conversation—as in a Kafka story, where things often happen suddenly, oddly, and by seemingly accidental, leaping advancement—makes me think it's quite likely that Kafka did indeed stay at Losert's, which would make Albert Botzi a living link, if not a direct one, to Franz. Botzi, this frail old man, carries a trace.

"Can I take photos of these photos?" I ask Helga. She readily says yes and I photograph the photographs. She then turns to M. and asks him to take a picture of us—meaning her and me. She wants to be documented. We thank the Botzis and say our good-byes. Both M. and I are quite astonished by what we've been brought. I have the sense we've been helped—in the way that Franz felt he'd been helped on his stopover in Gmünd between Vienna and Prague.

After departing the Botzis, we walk along Bahnhofstrasse toward the town centre—past a billboard announcing Tom Jones LIVE in concert in Gmünd: 18.07.19; past a large red tile-roofed high school, a turreted church and several well-maintained homes of early twentieth-century vintage. We turn on to Schremerstrasse, pass the Town Hall, and then on to Muhlgasse. I photograph some very rustic-looking dwellings covered in moss.

We follow the street northward and emerge at the Stadtplatz—a quaint cobblestoned Town Square of shops, restaurants, tables and chairs; no one in sight. The town in March is virtually empty. We rejoin Bahnhofstrasse, which becomes Schlossgasse, pass through an arched opening in a brick wall and we're in Schlosspark—a long stretch of grass bordered by a river, the Lainsitz. The name of the river in Czech is Lužnice—derived from an old Czech word for water flowing through meadows. "Perhaps this is the meadow that Franz and Milena came to," I say, "where they rested and talked and felt in the end like strangers." "This has to be the place," M. says; he's persuaded, and I believe him. One can almost feel their sadness ensouled in the air.

***

We take an alternate route from Gmünd back to Vienna—through Böhmhöf, Frankenreith, Grafenschlag, Elsenreith, Ötzbach, Ötz, Muhldorf—Austrian wine country, places with castles in the hills, the Melk Abbey perched on a rocky outcrop above the medieval town. I recall Melk from Umberto Eco's theological murder mystery, *The Name of the Rose*. I'd like to see inside the abbey but by the time we reach the fortress gate, it's closing.

"Read to me from the *Fiddler*," M. says when we get back to the car. I pick up, reading aloud from where the old man tells the story of how he came to be a street musician. His father was the Hofrat (I'm compressing here)—a mean, ambitious, authoritarian man who upbraided his son for his poor academic performance and threatened to apprentice him to some manual trade. The fiddler "would have liked nothing better than to have become a turner or compositor," but that would have "hurt his father's pride," so he was made a "copy clerk in the court of public records" and virtually banished from the family. "The fiddler had serious father issues," M. interjects. "Yes, just like Kafka," I say. "Kafka's father was also domineering, and his stature as a paterfamilias and successful businessman produced in Franz a sense of inferiority and guilt."

"Go on," M. says. Well, one day while sitting in the dark (I'm continuing to compress)—the fiddler heard singing in the neighbour's yard and "it was as if the finger of God had touched [him]." He "fell upon his knees and prayed aloud." It was the baker's daughter singing. He liked one of the songs so much that he took up the playing violin, with a passion. He fell in love with the girl because of a tune, overcame his timidity and claimed his inheritance in hopes of marrying her. But the plan fell through. He lost his copy job and then had nothing concrete to offer. "You'd have to find a regular occupation," the girl told the fiddler. "You're a child ... you would have to change. I hate effeminate men." "That's harsh," M. says. "Harsh, and also kindred to Kafka," I say. "You can see how this story would have affected him, on several levels. He too spoke and wrote of feeling timid, weak and effeminate, also childish. Child is a word he uses repeatedly in his fiction." Dusk is falling as we near Vienna; it becomes too dark to continue reading.

After dinner we pack for departure. Our four days in Austria are coming to a close. Tired, we shower and turn in. M. scans the news on his phone; I flip through Franz's letters to Milena. On July 13, 1920 he wrote: "What you say about *The Poor Fiddler* is entirely correct. If I said it didn't mean anything to me I was only being cautious, since I didn't know how you would like it, also because I'm ashamed of the story, as though I had written it myself ... and it does have a number of defects, ridiculous moments, dilettantish features, and deadly affectations (which are especially noticeable when read aloud), and this way of practising music is a lamentably ridiculous invention; it is enough to make the girl (myself included) so extremely angry that she hurls everything in her shop at the story." Clearly the tale struck in Franz a deep, lasting, ultimately discordant, chord. Like the relationship with Milena.

In October 1922, Milena sent Franz a letter via a friend. He replied briefly with news of his summer at Planá in south Bohemia, where he'd been staying with his sister and working on his castle story. In May 1923 she again sent greetings, to which he replied with a postcard from a pension in Dobřichovice, southwest of Prague. She'd been working on a translation of his story "The Judgement," which appeared in the periodical *Cesta* in mid-1923. This was the last of Milena's Kafka translations to be published. On December 25, 1923 Franz sent his final letter to her—from Berlin-Steglitz. He was living at Grunewaldstrasse 13, Dora Diamant by his side.

He didn't mention Dora by name but did write that he was "being cared for gently and well to the limit of earthly possibility." He lamented that his "only source of news about the world—but it's a very vivid source—is the rising cost of living." He was receiving no newspapers from Prague, couldn't afford the ones in Berlin, and asked Milena to send him "an occasional clipping from *Národní listy*—the kind that once gave [him] so much pleasure"; namely her own lively articles on sundry subjects.

Max brought his very ailing friend back to Prague from Berlin on March 14, 1924. Three weeks later, Dora accompanied him to the Wienerwald Sanatorium outside Vienna where he was diagnosed with laryngeal complications to his pre-existing tuberculosis. From Wienerwald he was brought to a clinic in Vienna where the diagnosis was confirmed, then to the Hoffmann Sanatorium in Kierling. Milena's extraordinary obituary appeared in *Národní listy* on June 6, three days after his death. Her tribute recognized Franz Kafka the person, his singularity as a writer, and demonstrated that, despite the painful turns in their relationship, she held no antipathy.

"Look at this," I say to M. from my side of the bed; my iPad is open to Google Maps. "There's a Franz-Kafka-Gasse—a Franz Kafka Street in Gmünd. We could have walked there if I'd seen this earlier. It's less than twenty minutes from the meadow at Schlosspark." M. doesn't lean over to look. "What could we have found on Franz Kafka Street that we didn't find in the meadow?" he says. This may be his roundabout way of saying that our trip to Gmünd wasn't fruitless. I don't try to clarify and he segues to the fiddler: "Why don't you read to me from the story." "I'm too tired," I reply. "Another time. Anyway, you can already guess. I've read to the end: The fiddler and the girl don't end up together, but he's memorialized in her heart, by way of his violin. Maybe this is the message Franz meant for the women he recommended the book to—that the artist must remain physically unattached, must be loved for his art alone. His happiness can fundamentally and admissibly only be bound to his art."

Vienna, "the mammoth village," came to represent a four-day idyll for Franz, also for Milena. In other words: an impossibility. Gmünd, the railway-crossing town, confirmed this. A gloomy afternoon soured whatever remained of the idyll, and the fraction of happiness could not be recovered. But this I already knew from letters. So what was added by tracking a path? What was mirrored to me from our own four-day trip? Probably, that we see our own reflections—transposed. The left eye is right, the right eye left, and since none of us is purely symmetrical, we all appear in some way skewed, hardly, if ever, as we'd wish to see ourselves, or be seen.

I think of Stephen Collis, his memoir of friendship with Phyllis Webb. The doubt, as he puts it, that one inescapably finds oneself caught up in, in midst of a search or obsession. (Is this an obsession?) Do I even know what I'm after at this point, or am I just ploughing on because I've been ploughing up till now? Should I stop, let go of the ghost? And if I do, what becomes of what I've gathered? Do I abandon the work, as Franz himself repeatedly did? These thoughts bear down on me, muddle me up.

But there are two of us in this, M. and I together—at least in the field. And we've come to mirror each other en route—each transposed in the other's eyes, not always, or even mostly, as we'd want to see ourselves reflected. This, too, is coming through the search. Little breakdowns and breakthroughs in relationship. Glimmerings and the yields of close encounters. The other in oneself—adumbrated, refracted. Traces uncovered and brought along. Pieces in a long concatenation. The not yet sought, not yet written. The beckoning within and call beyond. The complicated un/happiness picture we carry and don't discard.

Snapshots from Pension Stüdl

Schelesen / Želízy, Central Bohemia

Here you are at table slowly masticating your meal, little Minze
at your left—a fellowship of lungs.

That's you in contradiction wrapped in blankets on the balcony—
your chest exposed to cold December sun.

Here: six postcard drawings for your sister:
scenes from a country life, or inner country life with dog—

the yappy Pomeranian to blame.
Hard to say what this one is—some indistinct excitement:

gnats around the oil lamp in your room?
Here: a list of Hebrew grammar-points penned in Hebrew script,

preserved—like everything else you wrote—by Max.
Postmarked 1918, *Schelesen bei Liboch.*

Here you are with Julie in the yard, 1919. You hardly left
the pension at new year, due to the cold. You and Julie

would look at each other and laugh. At meals, in hallways
while passing each other, you laughed. As if the laughter

could palliate you both. I'm glossing over the hard parts
that go on for another year—after you wrote from here

the scathing letter to your father. After you sent a lawyer's
letter to Julie's sister, Käthe, defending your decision

to disengage. After you gave the letter meant for your father,
to Milena—that she might better understand your angst.

You weren't always clear; you were lucent.

Here I am in front of the house in 2017. A family with children
live here now. If I'd had the gumption, I'd have asked to view

the view you had inside. Behind your Star of David face,
attached to a plaque by the door, like a tourist doodad.

Sanatorium Hartungen

Riva del Garda

WE STOOD AT dusk before the abandoned former sanatorium. All I wanted, again, was a simple answer. Are you here? Not that I expected it in diction. If a building would speak, what could it utter?

Wind inhaled and yawned, we heard a bang from the second storey, then another. I looked at you, you looked at me—as if to check the weather. I couldn't say, before I did, we heard a third—whatever it was—bang shut.

This banging feels like comradeship with Kafka / Gracchus / the hunter—who fell to death, but couldn't complete the crossing. According to the story, he's been sailing the in-between, unsettled in his vessel ever since. Maybe he's in Riva now—battling death's rejection, banging his drafty language in a place he once sought healing and was granted some reprieve.

"How he came to bang out loud, without a lung or larynx, must be natural magic." I'm humouring you with lines like these when nature calls and urgently I dip into a bush behind the building. From in-between the leaves, I glimpse a boat in misty cloud-roll over the lake. You call—as loud as you dare from your watch: "A man with a dog is crossing! Keep your cover!" What kind of crouching creature am I?—flank and ankles nearly touching soil—

Down by the moat we watch two swans embracing, neck to neck. Sudden undulations: moon-white ripples over the hazy harbour, up to the hydroelectric plant. The monumental structure looks fascistic in the distance. Even more imposing from up close. We meet a youthful couple there, strolling in the night, like us, and enter into friendly conversation. We tell them we're from Canada. They tell us they're from Poprad, by the Tatras.

"Gracchus was in the Tatras!" I exclaim. "He went for the mountain air and stayed from winter of 1920 till summer of '21!" I blush at my eruption. How loopy I must sound—alluding to Kafka's Gracchus in his un-dead hunter story.

But then they say: "We know the place, Tatranské Matliare." So they do. Every ounce of oddness makes their answer feel replete: a comradeship of wings, of interlinking time and place. Atemporal in-betweens. What more need even be said.

We part, they stay in the mist by the massive hydroelectric plant. The night is windless, still, Lake Garda dictionless as ink.

Merano, 1920 / 2019

How to explain the shape he takes in penning his many letters, sitting on the *balcony, sunk into the garden, birds and lizards* bidding his gaze: a liquid shade of grey.

The room at Villa Ottoburg is low. Thousands of higher balconies, not a single one to be had. A sparrow on the ledge comes looking for crumbs. Over the threshold, into the room, more in than out he hops. Then frightened by the writer, flies away.

***

All this sun, Tyrolean slopes, the river rocking the riverbed, cars becoming dragonflies with immaterial wings. Some transcendental factor. We turn at Holy Spirit Church, onto Via Maia—toward the villa where Kafka convalesced.

***

He'd rather sit alone and eat his vegetarian meals in peace but can't avoid the invitation to join the communal table: a colonel and a general, two rheumy maiden ladies—all of them German guests. He's German-speaking too—from Prague, not Czech. How to explain what he truly is to these blue-eyed, watch-face men. German-Bohemian, one of the women suggests. The topic is dropped for dinner. But the general—with his critical ear, schooled in the Austrian army—isn't finished. After dinner he questions the writer's foreign German again—bothered, perhaps, by what he sees more than by what he hears. The other 'admits' his 'difference' and the bantering comes to an end.

The ethnic thing will take its mortal course.

***

Villa Ottoburg isn't Villa Ottoburg anymore. An upscale condominium now, and gated. The evergreens conceal their rings in their trunks.

***

The grey-eyed writer comes at night and leads me to the river. I rest my aching ankles on a rock. I'm tired, so is he. He climbed to Principesco Castle—"Yesterday," he tells me, to view the alpine vista from the loggia: He says this in my morning dream, by way of his liquid eyes.

***

You and I beyond the fence can see the room; he dreamt there. And slept (and didn't) and dithered. In letters from Merano to Milena in Vienna: *I'm coming / I'm not / I probably won't / I cannot come / don't want to … Coming would tax my mental strength. But if at the end of 14 days you want me to come as you do today, I will.*

The horrid inner voices and the trusting her like no one else in the world. Her *faithful* first translations. His being led in Czech along the sentences: his long and limpid subterranean passages.

***

I'm sliding here, I'm coming to at Via Maia 12 beyond the gate. Something small and greyish falls and settles on my coat. You see it first and point: "A sparrow feather." Flitting like a flag attached to my chest. You reach to lift if off, before you do, it flies away.

Concatenations: Hotel Gabrielli-Sandwirth, 1913 / 2019

IN THE NEAR-INVISIBLE city, under a super-sensible realm, a steamer docks, a man steps off. He's brought to a top-floor suite with a rain-lit view of the blue lagoon, the archipelago shifting in the mist. He scripts a farewell letter to his unsuspecting girlfriend. The rain does not abate, sadness floats like shadow listing slowly over the boats: Riva degli Schiavoni is sheathed.

M. and I arrive by vaporetto: sounds of minstrels singing, motors, smartphones, churning turquoise waters. We wheel our luggage across the promenade and enter the old hotel. Clerks—like two supporting actors—face us from behind the desk, nod in unison, smile, and take our papers. "The short one looks like Louis de Funès," M. says under his breath. "Get ready for a comedy."

Eleonora enters: She's summoned from an inner room by 'Louis' to settle our reservations glitch. "The online firm you booked with— failed," Eleonora says. We paid in advance, we're here, but have no room. Nonetheless, we mean to stay ... we end up staying twice:

I lie supine, sleeping, palms on my chest; M. is turned away from me, deep in sleep. A breath and shiver jolt me awake. I feel the breath again, and unmistakably, in my face. The shadow at the ceiling, listing, doesn't call for fiction. Only sympathy with ...

M. enjoys the minibar, the double bathrooms / two bidets, the king-size bed and sateen cotton sheets. I, as through a mist, inhabit absences and fragments—another time revived. But why should you believe: that breath is like a host.

Eleonora sailed in like a sloop, or biblical angel—bearing information and the keys to open suites. People can surprise you—how they shimmer in, and give.

M. and I—we sneak up on ourselves between our luggage, cramped inside the tiny hotel lift; then again in the courtyard under hanging

Murano lamps; and in the hidden garden that we only see on leaving, my ankles—after days of walking the old, uneven streets—heavy as that melancholy letter from Franz to Felice.

***

Kafka documented his September 1913 stay in Venice: his arrival from Trieste by steamer, four days at Hotel Sandwirth—now Gabrielli-Sandwirth, his gloomy mood, the parting letter he wrote to Felice, his departure from Santa Lucia Station, heading for Verona. Venice impressed him as "beautiful," but he wrote very little of how he passed his days in the watery city, and he didn't record the number of his room. I was happy to stay at any room in the old hotel, tour Venice, and see what would be shown to me—if anything—of Franz. I was holding openness … together with desire to be surprised.

M. and I did not expect—why would we?—that the firm we'd booked with for Venice and Brescia would go bankrupt on the eve of our trip, that we'd lose our reservations and have to appeal to Visa for refunds. But this in itself was Kafkaesque, and might have been a harbinger of Franz. So when we arrived at Hotel Gabrielli-Sandwirth on September 20, 2019 and it was confirmed at the front desk that we had no booking, Eleonora Giacomazzo, Reservations Manager, had to be called on to sort things out. Gracious and conciliatory, Eleonora reviewed our pre-trip emails, apologized for the unfortunate turn, and offered to show us two available "economical" rooms.

In the elevator, M. urged me (under his breath) to tell Eleonora why we'd come to the Gabrielli. He'd taken to calling me a groupie (if only between us) and I'd become self-conscious about mentioning anything of 'the quest'. But I did. "We're here," I said, "because Franz Kafka stayed here and I … actually we … are following in his steps." Eleonora's eyes lit up. She said she too was a Kafka enthusiast, had studied German literature at university, including Kafka, and that yes, she knew he'd stayed at the hotel—when it was the Sandwirth—in Suite 518 in fact: a large suite with a terrace and full view of the lagoon, one of the best in the hotel. All this before we'd reached the top floor. Of course, as Reservations Manager, she *would* be privy to such information. But what a conjunction. I was surprised, *and* delighted. Suddenly budget was no object: I wanted Suite 518.

Unfortunately, 518 was not available that night. We chose a small, angled attic-room for its partial view of the lagoon, the inner courtyard, a strip of Riva degli Schiavoni, and the hotel's rooftop lounge. I had to take care getting in and out of bed, lest I bash my head on the downslope of the ceiling, but other than that, the room was charming.

Suite 518 was available for only one night during our time in Italy: Monday, September 23—the night we'd planned to stay in Brescia. Kafka visited Brescia in 1909, with Max and Otto Brod. The three attended an air show and both Franz and Max wrote articles on the event. Kafka's piece, "The Aeroplanes at Brescia," published in the newspaper *Bohemia*, in September, 1909, is considered the first description of 'aeroplanes' in German literature. I wanted to visit Brescia, perhaps even see the field where Franz, Max and Otto had witnessed the making of air history—who knows what can be found in a field?—but we no longer had the Brescia reservation, so we'd be returning to Venice instead, after spending one night—Sunday the 22nd—in Merano, northern Italy, where Kafka convalesced in spring of 1920. And we'd be sleeping in the same hotel room as Franz had. The whole zany zigzag was ironed out so seamlessly, it felt like a comedy preternaturally scripted.

Eleonora played the angel-part—in the sense of biblical messenger. I told her so, and she didn't seem to think it sounded ridiculous. We met up with her once more—on the afternoon of our first stay, unexpectedly, in the dimness of a back staircase. Apparently, both she and we were avoiding the slow-moving elevator. She led us into a long narrow room—no longer in use for its original designation as dining hall. M. took our photo. Eleonora and I, sitting side by side, smiling. For the record.

On the way out, M. and I spotted memorials to Kafka's stay at the hotel: a book in a vitrine by the elevator, opened to a page showing a facsimile of the letter he wrote to Felice under Hotel Sandwirth letterhead. And outside, by the door to the patio-restaurant, a plaque inscribed (translated from Italian): *Franz Kafka stayed at this hotel in September 1913 and wrote here a love letter to his girlfriend Felice Bauer.*

The plaque was probably mounted on the occasion of the hundredth anniversary of Kafka's stay, which the hotel celebrated with a special event on September 15, 2013. The stilted English version of the online press release (here excerpted) reads:

> *Hotel Gabrielli Sandwirth celebrates the 100th Anniversary of the visit of Franz Kafka, who wrote on 15 September 1913 on the letterhead of the hotel one of the famous love letters to his mistress, Felice Bauer ... On this occasion the Perkhofer family who runs the hotel since 1856 invites to a matinee, Klaus Wagenbach, Kafka expert from Berlin and often referred to as "living widow" of the writer, reports on the trip of Kafka to Italy, his extensive correspondence with Felice Bauer and their significance for Kafka's oeuvre ...*

The choice of the terms "love letters," "mistress," and "living widow"—the latter in reference to Kafka scholar, Klaus Wagenbach—is amusing. Franz's letter to Felice can hardly be called a "love letter": He wrote that he was "overflowing with unhappiness," "unable to go forward," "ensnared"; and closed with the declaration, "We shall have to part." The two were incommunicado for two months and, when Kafka wrote again, on December 29, 1913, he confessed to "falling in love" with a Swiss girl he'd met at Hartungen Sanatorium at Riva del Garda in the wake of his stay in Venice. Felice could never properly be called Franz's "mistress" either. Their relationship, by all personal accounts, was fraught *and* chaste. He might have aimed to marry her, but he wasn't able to muster the will—for what he called "deep-seated reasons"—despite two engagements and a correspondence-courtship of over five hundred letters.

The marketing department at Hotel Gabrielli no doubt prevailed in dubbing Kafka's September missive a "love letter," and "mistress" added a spicy touch. Spicier still, or else scrambled in translation, is the blooper "living widow"—a woman who has lost her spouse by death and not remarried—in reference to Klaus Wagenbach.

***

From Italy, M. and I flew to Tel Aviv to visit family. When I could cocoon a bit, I reviewed the Italy trip, the photos and my notes—especially the ones on the mysterious 'night visitation' during our second stay at Hotel Gabrielli. It might have been a dream, if I hadn't been jolted awake by breath in my face—then to feel the breath again and that hanging, listing shadow. My first thought, there in the dark hotel room—with M. fast asleep beside me—was, *Franz is here, hovering …* Once I'd registered that, I was all right, and could slip back into sleep.

On one of our walks, M. and I browsed the third-floor bookstore at the labyrinthine Dizengoff Center mall. There's a good selection there of books in Hebrew and in translation, and always some kind of buy-two-get-one-free type of deal. M. chose a scholarly work. I came away with *The Little Prince* in Hebrew, and another small volume: *The Dove on the Roof* (*Ha-Yona sh'al Ha-Gag*)—a Hebrew translation by Ilana Hammerman of selections from Kafka's late *Writings and Fragments* (*Nachgelassene Schriften und Fragmente*)—the authoritative German Critical Edition published by S. Fischer Verlag in 1992. A few of these late pieces have become part of the Kafka canon but most are unknown to non-specialists.

I flipped through the Hammerman translation and my eyes fell on a vowelized name in a piece near the end of the book. Hebrew poetry is vowelized, but not prose, so the name stood out on the page: "Eleonor"—El-eh-on-or (four syllables, stress on the last syllable, unlike the three-syllable pronunciation in English). Kafka rarely gave names to characters in his short pieces. Yet here was "Eleonor"—the same name, apart from an 'a' at the end—as the Reservations Manager at the Gabrielli-Sandwirth. Immediately I felt there had to be a connection between the events at the hotel, only days prior, with Eleonora as intermediary, and my happening upon this Hebrew translation of a previously unseen Kafka text.

M. and I translated Ilana Hammerman's version of Kafka's untitled story together, rendering the short piece—only six sentences—as directly as possible from Hebrew into English. But I had questions about some of Hammerman's choices, especially her translation of Kafka's long and complicated final sentence. So I ordered *Nachgelassene Schriften und Fragmente*, Volume 2 of the Critical Edition late stories, and slowly made my own way through Kafka's piece, written in autumn of 1923 or winter of 1924, in Berlin, only months before his death. Working with Hammerman's Hebrew, Kafka's original, dictionaries, and finally a number of email exchanges with my German-speaking friend, Hanna Grünfeld, I settled on a rendering:

> *I am stating this here clearly: Everything that has been said about me is false, if it comes from the assumption that I am the first person to have been the soulmate of a horse. It is strange that this immense claim is being disseminated and believed, but even stranger that the matter is being taken lightly, disseminated and believed, yet dismissed and with little more than a shake of the head, laid to rest. Here lies a secret, that would actually be more tempting to examine than the minor thing I really did. What I did, was only this: I lived for a year with a horse, as a man with a girl he reveres, yet who rejects him, would live, if he had no external obstacle to arranging everything that could bring him to his goal. So I locked the horse Eleonor and myself in a stable and did not leave this common dwelling place except to give the lessons through which*

*I earned the funds to support us both. Unfortunately, this took
at least five to six hours daily and it's not by any means out of the
question that this loss of time caused the final failure of all my
efforts, and may the gentlemen whom I asked in vain to support
this undertaking of mine, and who could have given only a little
money toward something for which I was so willing to sacrifice
myself, as one sacrifices a bundle of oats that one stuffs between the
molars of a horse: May these gentlemen let this be said.*

In a Kafka story, both protagonist and reader are regularly and
quickly plunged into unexplained, baffling circumstances. For the
reader, the bafflements are further complicated by ambiguous analogies
and complex grammatical structures. Meaning seems to be clear, then
slips away like a dream upon waking, even if the language is vivid.
Kafka stories also seem to stow hidden psychological content, just
beneath or beyond the text, which can bring a reader to thinking the
hidden can be unpacked, if only probed closely enough.

In the above-piece, the narrator seems to inhabit an unnatural
relationship: claiming to be the soulmate of a horse. But does he actually
mean what he says? And if he does, is the claim so very unnatural, in
psychological terms … the psyche, after all, has its own logic. And the
small connective words, modals, and adverbs that Kafka was so fond
of using—"if," "but," "yet," "may," "could" or "should," "except," and
"probably"—colour the text this way, then that, then this way again. In
listing the things that happen, or appear to happen, one soon becomes
entangled in syntactical and interpretive k/nots:

So the narrator is *not* the first person to be the soulmate of a horse,
and to assume so would be false. The inference being that the relationship
itself is not *so* singular, although the claim is *"ungeheuerliche"*—
"immense" or "monstrous." (I settled on the former word, though the
latter harkens back to the description of the bug in *The Metamorphosis*).
And the strangeness lies not in the man / horse soul relationship, as one
would assume, but in the fact that this relationship has been taken so
lightly by others, believed, and then dismissed. What is Kafka getting
at—with this back-and-forth on strangeness, temptation, secret /
soulmate / relationship, and failure?

Although he despaired of metaphor, he was innately strong at it, and could not avoid it. Translator Mark Harman (who newly translated *Amerika: The Missing* Person in 2008) has argued that metaphor in Kafka carries his deepest personal obsessions—in an intricate web of interconnections. The connection, via metaphor, between the story above and others in the Kafka canon can readily be pinpointed. The horse is a recurring emblem. The word horse is embedded in the name Karl Rossmann, the Kafka stand-in in his first novel: "Ross," meaning horse, is thus Karl "Horseman." And horsepower in *Amerika* alludes to desire, travel, and freedom: Karl Rossmann, naïve teen, leaves his homeland under scandalous circumstances, travels across the ocean to seek freedom and fortune in the new world. Horses and horsepower in "A Country Doctor," the title story of the collection, *Der Landarzt*, join riding / travel with erotic drive—suppressed, misplaced, and defeated. In "The New Advocate" ("Der neue Advokat"), the short opening story in the same collection, the character of Dr. Bucephalus—Alexander the Great's valiant war steed, now proud of his human achievements as a lawyer—is a transposition of Kafka's workplace self.

The horse Eleonor could very well be a stand-in for the narrator's / Kafka's deep inner self—the "soulmate" ("Seelenfreund"), or desire, he keeps obliquely locked in the inner stable, while his social self is impelled to engage with the unsympathetic world of "the gentlemen" ("*die Herren*"), who could (or should) have supported him in his "undertaking" ("Unternehmens"). Blame for his "final failure" ("endgiltigen Misserfolg") is externalized to "the gentlemen," to whom the text is periphrastically addressed.

As he lay dying, Kafka may well have been penning a final pronouncement. He always regretted having to spend too much time at his office job, which deprived him, he repeatedly lamented, of enough free time to write. The conflict between allegiance to his inner self and the demands of his social self was thematic in Kafka's life, and is expressed in his fiction. He also lived with fear of sexual failure and / or discordance, which he documented in his letters and diaries. An element of erotic discordance seems to underlie the 'confession' in this piece as well: "Here lies a secret, What I did, was only this: I lived … with a horse, as a man with a girl would live, if …"

***

After months of wrangling with Kafka's eccentric late text—hoping to find some sort of message embedded within it—I again asked M.: "What could be the connection between Eleonora of Hotel Gabrielli-Sandwirth and Eleonor the horse in Kafka's story? And why do you think I happened upon the Hebrew translation precisely when I did? What could this convergence mean?"

"*Klotz kashas*," M. said, using a Yiddish term. "These are stupid questions. Stupid because there is no definitive meaning—beyond the fact that you drew a connection in your head. You saw the name Eleonor in the Hammerman book, you were reminded of Eleonora in Venice, and you were inspired to translate an obscure Kafka text. Isn't that meaning enough? And wasn't it meaningful that we got to see Venice two months before the worst flooding in the city in fifty years? We were fortunate to have stayed at the Gabrielli-Sandwirth when we did—before the floods, before the coronavirus hit. That was pretty convergent, I'd say. And Kafka probably had nothing to do with it."

Tacitly / Translating

It's windy in the walking field, and two or three
coyotes. Did I say the wind had fallen?
                    Seelenfreunde—

fewer birds, no minnesingers—
none. I've tried
to bring them back with nuts & crumbs; instead
                    a squirrel comes—

with half an ear, a tattered coat, his tail
striped lightning-white: *Vermutung*:
                    He was probably actually struck.

The other day he came in stormy weather & sat on the sill;
eyed me *deutlich* through the *Fenster*:
                    I at the kitchen sink with dishes; he
                    completely drenched.

I photographed him—close-up on my cellphone.
—*Geringfügigkeit* is what he didn't say to that. Nonetheless

there's tacit understanding: I slipped him a bowl
                    of *Hafer*,
                    crumbs & nuts.

Franz of the Magic

FRANZ KAFKA AND Thomas Mann never met. But they might have. Their years overlapped, they shared a mother tongue, a literary world, and they knew of each other's work. On October 17, 1917, Kafka wrote to Max Brod that Mann was one of the authors for whom he "hungered." Kafka was thirty-four at the time, ailing, and had published little. Mann's praise of Kafka came decades later—in a long introductory homage to the Knopf 1946 edition of *The Castle* in which he deemed the novel "very remarkable," brilliant," and "among the best worth reading in the world's treasury of literature." It was this edition of Kafka's unfinished work that contributed to the rise of his star in North America.

Mann was the epitome of the successful author. Just twenty-six when his first novel, the august family saga, *Buddenbrooks*, put him at the forefront of German letters and paved the way to the Nobel Prize. Mann's scope is sweeping, his realism grand, his irony parodic and symbolic. Kafka's scope is parabolic, his realism surreal, his irony dry and sly. Kafka eschewed Mann's grandiloquence but both authors gravitated toward some of the same big themes: art, the artist in society, the seductions of illness, eros, and death. Both contended with sexual ambivalence and guilt. Both were bourgeois men critical of bourgeois codes, yet amenable to bourgeois comforts. Both were aficionados of sanatorium culture. Kafka might even have been a cast member in Mann's monumental sanatorium novel, *The Magic Mountain*.

Mann began writing *The Magic Mountain* in 1912, during his wife Katja's six-month stay in the high woodlands of the Wald Sanatorium in Davos, Switzerland, where she was recuperating from catarrh of the apex of the lung—the same diagnosis that Kafka initially received following pulmonary hemorrhages in August 1917. Inspired by his impressions while visiting Katja, upon returning to the "flatlands" Mann started writing a novella in which the hero, Hans Castorp, is quickly initiated into the feverish atmosphere of life at the heights and ends up staying at the International Sanatorium Berghof, ostensibly ill in the lung, for seven symbolic years. When he eventually shakes the disease, and leaves the protective decadence of the sanatorium to serve in the world below, his life is obliquely disrupted by the War. Mann's work on the novella was likewise disrupted, and after a hiatus informed by the weight of that disruption, he returned to complete a much longer, much enriched work that was published to great acclaim in 1924—the year that Kafka died at Hoffmann Sanatorium in the low woodlands of Kierling, north of Vienna.

It's ironic (and has been overlooked) that a certain Kafka plays a small, wholly odious role in *The Magic Mountain*. In the early chapter titled "Satana," the Kafka character is profiled by the voluble Italian humanist character, Settembrini, who scoffs at the business acumen of the owner of another sanatorium in town—a Professor Kafka, who, "every year would suddenly be called away promising to take care of his discharges upon return, but then would stay away for six weeks while the poor things waited and their bills increased." The *"celebrissimo* Kafka … did not keep his syringes sterile," and "infected his patients with other diseases" as well. Mann's Kafka is a minor character— named only on pages 60 and 61 of the translation by John E. Woods. But the name Kafka, distinctive as it is, stares glaringly from the pages (at least at this reader), especially as Mann's Kafka is tardy and greedy, conceited and callous, sneaky and possibly murderous too. Given that Mann knew of Kafka's work and his rising reputation among discerning literati during the protracted period in which *The Magic Mountain* was written, it seems odd that he should have chosen to give an odious minor character the same name as a colleague. One wonders what was behind the choice …

Sojourns at sanatoria and healing retreats were an integral part of Franz Kafka's biographical map—outlined in his diaries and letters to friends and family, though not, as with Mann, taken up as subjects and backdrops in his fiction. In the summer of 1903, at twenty, Kafka spent two weeks at Lahmann Sanatorium in Weisser Hirsch near Dresden, recuperating from a rigorous law exam. The pricey, state-of-the-art establishment, directed by renowned naturopathic doctor, Heinrich Lahmann, left a deep impression on young Franz and he remained a lifelong natural health enthusiast. In 1905 he summered at Sanatorium Schweinburg in Zuckmantel (Zlaté Hory) on the border with Poland,

and liked it so much that he returned the following summer. In 1911 he stayed at Erlenbach Sanatorium at Lake Zürich, and in 1912 he spent three weeks at Sanatorium Jungborn in the Harz Mountains, Germany. In 1913 he stayed at Sanatorium Hartungen in Riva on Lake Garda in northern Italy (Mann also stayed there), and in 1915 he spent ten days at Sanatorium Rumburg (now Rumburk in the northern Czech Republic). He visited Marienbad in west Bohemia twice in 1916 and, after being diagnosed with tuberculosis, was in and out of pensions and sanatoria for the last seven years of his life. The cumulus of sanatorium culture hovered close to Kafka's writing, even if it never entered his fiction.

***

At the end of August 2018, M. and I again fly to Prague, this time to extend my Kafka quest to elevations east of the author's home base: to Špindleruv Mlýn (Spindelmühle) in the Giant Mountains of northeastern Bohemia—the resort town where Kafka stayed for three weeks in January and February of 1922 and began writing *The Castle*; to Zlaté Hory, the location of early sanatorium romance; and to Tatranské Matliary in the High Tatra Mountains of Slovakia, where he received treatment at Villa Tatra for nine months in 1920-21. We log upwards of fourteen hours in driving-time on our circuit to the borderlands and back to the capital—not counting stops and stayovers.

Our first stop is Troja—now a northern suburb of Prague. In the summer of 1918, a year into his illness, Kafka was spending afternoons here—at the training Institute for Pomology, Viniculture, and Horticulture—his hands in soil in pursuit of fresh air reprieve from hours at the office. Gardening was one of the 'health' activities he'd engaged in over the years, not only as a means of offsetting office work, but also—along with the study of Hebrew—part of his interest in the Zionist movement for Jewish renewal in Palestine / Eretz Israel. In 1913, when he first pursued gardening—at the Dvorsky Market Garden in the Prague neighbourhood of Nusle—Zionism was already a force in the lives of many of Prague's young Jews. Kafka was only peripherally interested at the time, but he took up serious study of

Hebrew during the War. By 1919, in the wake of his eight-month convalescence in the west Bohemian farm village of Zürau (Siřem), a simple agricultural life on the land had acquired great appeal, and by November 1920, antisemitic upheaval in Prague had tipped his sympathies toward Zionism. He wrote to Milena Jesenská: "I've been spending every afternoon outside on the streets, wallowing in anti-Semitic hate ... Isn't it natural to leave a place where one is hated?" Despite his illness, or rather in the face of it, he was thinking of putting his horticultural training (and Hebrew) to use, if he could actualize his simmering plan of exchanging Prague for Palestine. (He'd humoured Felice Bauer on their first meeting with the invitation that they vacation together the following year in Palestine, and they shook hands on it.)

Troja, a ten-minute drive from downtown Prague, is home to the seventeenth-century Troja Palace with its orchards and botanical gardens—renovated in the 1970s and '80s and open to the public. In planning our trip, I'd found no information on the Pomological Institute—online or in print, but I'm assuming that someone at the palace will know something about the Institute. As it turns out, none of the palace reception staff has heard of it. But they're helpful, and with online searching of Czech sites, are able to ascertain that Pod Lisem Street—the highway over the Vltava River, joining Troja to Prague-centre—was once named for the Institute. This becomes our tip to locating the place.

We drive along Troja Street, turn onto Pod Lisem—a thoroughfare that permits no stopping—find parking on Povltavská, a narrow street of old country homes nestled against the hillside just north of the Vltava crossing, and get out to explore. A barking dog sends me scooting from the first house I approach. The adjacent homes show no sign of life. At the last house in the row, a young woman is puttering in the long sloping garden. I call out to her; she comes to the gate. I tell her what we're looking for; she invites us up to the high porch of her house. It's a serendipitous meeting—as if Kafka himself had arranged it. She goes inside and brings back a large book filled with glossy photos of old Troja and botanical drawings of fruit and fruit-bearing trees. The Pomological Institute is pictured on several pages—the way it would have looked to Franz: the fields, the buildings, the hills, the river. I photograph the photographs, looking closely at the horticultural students in one of the shots, though it was taken before Kafka's time here.

The young woman, Štěpánka, granddaughter of the owner of the house on whose porch we're standing, tells us that the Institute ceased operation long ago, its lands sold to a private winemaker. She herself is interested in Troja's history; not everyone is. She's not surprised to hear that the staff at Troja Palace knew nothing of the Pomological Institute, let alone Franz Kafka's connection to it. "Kafka is not so important to Czech people," she says. I don't dispute her view. A person's passions are personal, not necessarily national. We find common interest in local architecture, and I'm thankful to Štěpánka for admitting us to her garden and advancing our search. She directs us to what remains of the Pomological Institute: an abandoned building where Troja and Pod Lisem Streets meet.

M. and I walk up the hill to view the building. It looks more like a derelict church hall than a former horticultural school. I'd photographed it on the drive from the palace to Povltavská Street, not knowing what it was; the distinctive lancet windows had intrigued me. I photograph it again—its solemnity and solitude. The door is locked, the windows boarded. There's likely nothing left inside the building. Still, one wants to be able to see inside: the walls, the floors, the doors, the dust. The shadows.

***

Špindleruv Mlýn is two hours northeast of Troja by car. For our drive, the road is clear, the early September weather sunny. When Kafka arrived in what was then Spindelmühle, on January 27, 1922, it was evening and snow was falling. There's a photograph of the arrival— Franz standing by the rear runners of a two-horse-drawn sleigh, leaning on a walking stick; his physician from Prague, Dr. Otto Hermann and the doctor's wife and daughter, bundled up inside the sleigh. Franz is wearing a fedora, his coat open, neck and chest exposed to the snow. Hardly dressed for January in the Riesengebirge (Giant Mountains), he's counting on the high mountain air doing him some good, if he doesn't catch pneumonia first.

Hotel Krone had mistakenly registered him as Josef K.—his stand-in in *The Trial*. He must have viewed the blip as an indication. He wrote in his diary: "Despite my having legibly written down my name, despite their having written to me twice already, they have Joseph K. down in the directory. Shall I enlighten them, or shall I let them enlighten me?" Kafka was open to indications, and this one pointed directly to his eponymous other. In the same entry, he also wrote: "The strange, mysterious, perhaps dangerous, perhaps saving comfort that there is in writing ..." And with the prospect of some "saving comfort," he began writing *The Castle*:

> "It was late evening when K. arrived. The village lay deep in snow. There was nothing to be seen of the Castle Mount, for mist and darkness surrounded it, and not the faintest glimmer of light showed where the great castle lay. K. stood on the wooden bridge leading from the road to the village for a long time, looking at what seemed to be a void. Then he went in search of somewhere to stay the night."

The Castle has been called Kafka's supreme creative effort, his most auto-biographical work—replete with references to people, places, and events in the author's life. The protagonist, K., is most clearly a cipher for Kafka himself and the circumstances of his nighttime arrival in Spindelmühle can be seen to be reprised in the novel's opening lines: the hour, the snow, the village, the bridge. K. brings with him a walking stick, too, just as Kafka is pictured arriving in Spindelmühle, walking stick in hand.

As for the titular *Castle*, biographer Ernst Pawel notes in *The Nightmare of Reason* that it could be modelled after the imposing seventeenth century castle in the north Bohemian town of Friedland— where Kafka spent two weeks in 1911 on company business. Or it could be modelled on the castle in Wossek (Osek) in south Bohemia, where Kafka's father was born. Klaus Wagenbach, in *Kafka: A Life in Prague*, concurs. But there is no castle in the tiny hamlet of Wossek. The closest castle—a Gothic fortress—is 11 km away, in the town of Strakonice. Moreover, the castle in the novel bears no resemblance to anything grand. Thus, biographer Reiner Stach's conjecture that the castle in *The Castle* could be modelled on Prague's great Hradcany Castle—because the latter occupied a prominent place in Kafka's daily landscape—doesn't tally either. In fact, K.'s castle "was neither a knightly castle from the days of chivalry, nor a showy new structure, but an extensive complex of buildings ... crowded close together. If you hadn't known it for a castle you might have taken it for a small town ... a poor collection of cottages."

The castle in *The Castle* is nothing much to behold, yet it's been read, in the vast exegetical literature, as representative of many things: locus of divine grace (Judaic and Christian), higher consciousness, universal cosmic truth, symbol of bureaucracy and secular power, embodiment of an authoritative Law that no level of reason can ever hope to decode. It could be modelled on the locked chambers of the author's own psyche. *Das Schloss*, which means both "The Castle" and "The Lock," is allusive and elusive, not definitive, and elusoriness is part of what has made the work, and its central emblem, so prodigious and inexhaustible.

K. is a man who arrives in a village, seeking access to the castle Count. K. "may be staying for some time" in the unnamed village, with its rigid hierarchical structure—from peasantry to officialdom; Kafka is characteristically noncommittal. Aside from the opening lines, the village does not resemble the busy winter resort town of Spindelmühle. If it's modelled on any actual village, it could be Zürau—where he dwelled happily among German peasants under his sister's care in 1917-1918 and became enamoured of a rural way of life. But Zürau is not a close approximation. There were no inns there, no poor collection of buildings crowded close together on the heights, as in the novel. Zürau was a rustic farming hamlet in the rolling lowlands of west Bohemia. Now known only as Siřem, it still is.

K. is no romantic hero on a noble quest. He extemporaneously presents himself as a land surveyor summoned by the castle Count. (Coincidentally, as later comes to light, a land surveyor had been summoned years earlier, which renders K.'s claim credible, at least to some of the villagers.) Yet he comes unequipped with any instruments, none are ever supplied, and neither he, nor his two so-called assistants, Artur and Jeremias, ever demonstrate any surveying skills. And the closest K. comes to the mysterious castle is near the end of the novel, in chapter 23, the night he enters an unlocked door at the Gentlemen's Inn and gets into bed with a naked castle secretary named Bürgel. Bürgel offers K. assistance in achieving access to the castle, but K. is either too tired or too resistant to accept. Chapter 23 contains a strange dreamy sequence in which K. struggles with the naked Bürgel, "tickling" and "foot holding" under the sheets, and emerges from the bed at daybreak, induced by a "sense of total futility ..." One wonders who Bürgel might have been modelled after ...

K. is unheroic—by turns cantankerous, calculating, quizzical, indecisive, and manipulative. He's a dissembler, or at least someone holding back his truth. Or maybe someone suffering from what, in today's psychiatric terminology, might be diagnosed 'identity disturbance': a person who exhibits incoherence in his / her sense of identity and finds it difficult to commit to a course of action. K. is indeed noncommittal: his brisk engagement to Frieda (who may or may not have been modelled on a composite of Felice Bauer and Milena Jesenská) lasts only days. His sense of identity is sketchy. In chapter 2, in a comical telephone exchange with the speech-impeded castle official, Oswald, K. asks: "Then who am I?" though the answer—"That everlasting land surveyor"—has been provided. The label "surveyor" persists throughout the novel, though K. takes work as a school janitor, never as a surveyor, and at the end is offered room and board as stable groom for the coachman Gerstäcker—possibly in exchange for K.'s influence with the castle. But K. has not been shown to have any influence with the castle, at least none that he's been able or willing to rally on his own behalf. On the penultimate page, just before the story breaks off, mid-sentence, the landlady of the Castle Inn asks K., "What is your profession?" "I'm a land surveyor," he says. "You're not telling the truth," she says. Why don't you tell the truth?" K. says. "You're not telling the truth either … You are not just a landlady as you make out." And with this bit of tit-for-tat, the puzzle of truth and identity is upheld. As for entry to the castle, K. has already been told (in chapter 2), so the reader also already knows: It can't be allowed.

K. may remain in the village, gain some acceptance and become a part of the community—though in chapter 1 he speaks of bringing something worthwhile home to his wife and child. This claim, made only once, was likely a ruse on K.'s part. Or maybe it was an inconsistency on Kafka's part … A reader has only K.'s monopolized perspective to rely on, and Kafka never did prepare his novel for publication. Max Brod did that, and even with Brod's interventions it's hard to accept his portrayal of K., in *Franz Kafka: A Biography*, as "a man of good will through and through." K. is not a saint, not even a particularly good man, but he is a figure whose poses and patterns a reader may relate to. He presents a murky, shadow-side of personhood—hidden impulses, cover-ups, projections and deflections. For who has never dissembled, circled, been muddled or gone astray? Whose pursuits are invariably consistent, clear, straightforward, always admissible and reachable? And the question K. raises: "Who am I?"—as much plea as provocation; both will to know and challenge to answer—is timeless.

In his introductory homage, Thomas Mann writes that *The Castle* "is not quite complete; but probably not more than one chapter is missing." Mann reports that Kafka told Brod that K. dies at the end of the story from sheer exhaustion, before he can get in touch with the castle. But at the last moment, as K. is on his deathbed, an order comes down from the castle to the effect that although K. has no legal claim, he is granted permission to live and work in the village. This is the 'grace bequeathed' version favoured by Brod—one that sees Kafka as the good and lonely wandering Jew, though the word Jew does not appear anywhere in the text (nor in any of Kafka's fiction). Brod accorded Kafka's work a distinctly Jewish quality—of a stranger in a strange land, seeking to settle and be accepted. I recall reading somewhere a quite different claim: that Kafka told Brod *The Castle* was a novel for writing only, for himself, not for finishing …

***

I was hoping to stay at Hotel Krone in Špindleruv Mlýn. Following a photo in Klaus Wagenbach's monograph, *Kafka*, I searched online. I found no Krone. Hotel Savoy—a modern, mock-half-timbered building with a rooftop lookout came closest to looking like Hotel Krone, so I booked us a room at the Savoy for the night of September 2.

When M. and I check in, I ask the receptionist if she knows of Hotel Krone—where author Franz Kafka stayed in 1922 and began writing his novel *The Castle*. I show her the photo in the Wagenbach book I've brought along. She looks at it closely and says she's quite certain that Hotel Savoy is Hotel Krone—not the same building, of course, but built on the same spot, in a lookalike style. She introduces herself as Iveta

Vošahlíková, the hotel manager, takes down my email and says she'll look into it for me. This is the second serendipitous stroke of the day: this time a manager who happens to be at the front desk when we arrive (we don't see her again), who's willing to do some extra-curricular scouting on my behalf. She had no idea that Kafka had stayed at Hotel Krone, but she knew of the author and seemed intrigued.

M. and I deposit our things in the room and go out to explore. I feel a frisson of excitement in crossing the bridge over the Labe (Elbe) River to the other side of town. It's a wooden bridge, old and stolid, and I'm imagining the "wooden bridge leading from the main road to the village"—where "K. stood for a long time gazing" in the first paragraph of *The Castle*. I pause, mid-bridge, and gaze, like K.—at the mountains, the sky, the water, the lay of the land. It's a moment of the aesthetic kind that validates having arrived.

We take the path by the river and make our way up the hillside—past an abandoned hotel, others still in business, tidy private homes, an old church with a gold clock tower, and sit on a bench to rest. There's a conscientious quality to the town: a new adventure park, an environmental forest trail, a state-of-the-art ski lift to the peak of Medvědín, alongside remnants from the past. And the mountain air is fresh—maybe almost as fresh as it was in the snow a hundred years ago.

Our overnight at Hotel Savoy is pleasant, the room comfortable, if generic, the staff solicitous. After breakfast we ask at reception if we can access the cupola lookout—to view the town from the rooftop. The top floor is a spa suite, closed at this hour, but one of the receptionists takes us up, and, surprisingly, leaves us there on our own. We check out the treatment rooms, the health and relaxation products (why not?), then ascend the spiral staircase into the octagonal rooftop lookout. The photos on the cupola wall are a throwback. Captioned in German, they recollect the past—when the town was known as Spindelmühle: the Riesengebirge in snow, the Riesengebirge von der Böhmischen Seite, Hotel Wiesenhaus, Hotel Esplanade, Hotel Erlebach, the guest hall at Peterbaude, and Hotel Krone—all no longer extant, preserved in print in this inner capsule.

His stay in the Giant Mountains had a salutary, almost magical, effect on Franz. He ate well, stopped agonizing over his illness, stopped taking his temperature, went hiking and tobogganing, tried skiing, and socialized. He wrote in his diary of "the happiness of being with people," of "happy little B.": "towards evening he wanted to go home with me." I wonder if Barnabas, the young white-clad messenger whose arm K. holds onto in the snowy night, and for whom in chapter 2 "the only reason for being together was to keep going," might be a nod to "happy little B." of Spindelmühle. All this social activity and still Kafka found time, requisite strength and inspiration to start writing *Das Schloss* in his Hotel Krone room.

He continued working on the novel in Prague, read the first chapters to Max in March (as per Brod's recollection), and brought the manuscript to Planá, south Bohemia, at the end of June when he was pensioned off from the Workers' Accident Insurance Institute. He continued writing at Planá—in the house rented for the summer, with his sister Ottla, her husband and their baby daughter—until the end of August or beginning of September when he wrote to tell Max that he'd suffered a breakdown and would have to stop work on the "castle story" for good.

***

It's worth noting that Max Brod wrote a stage adaptation of *The Castle* in German that was translated into Hebrew and published in 1955 by Schocken Books, Tel Aviv, though not performed at Habimah Theatre—where Brod was artistic director—until 1970, two years after his death. M. happened across a yellowed, stapled copy of the play among his grandfather's books. It was like a missive from beyond— sent to be received precisely at the time I was drafting this piece. For his dramatization, Brod made castle secretary Bürgel into a main player, whereas, as editor of the novel, he'd maintained that the Bürgel chapter was too inconclusive to include. He thus left the Bürgel 'bed episode' out of the manuscript he prepared for publication—the version published by Kurt Wolff in 1926, two years after Kafka's death. The first English edition of *The Castle*—published in 1930; the second edition— published in 1935; and the 1946 edition containing the introduction by Thomas Mann, all following Brod's edited version, conclude before the Bürgel episode. Not until 1982 was a restored, critical edition of the novel completed by an international team of Kafka scholars and published by S. Fischer Verlag. The first English edition of *The Castle*, based on the restored text—the text as Kafka had left it—was not published until 1997 (in Britain by Penguin, translation by J.A. Underwood; introduction by Idris Parry). Mark Harman's translation was published by Schocken Books in New York a year later.

The incorporation of the Bürgel episode into his play might have marked Brod's belated acknowledgement of its importance to the story. The account of K.'s intimate, ultimately futile, nocturnal meeting with Bürgel could not be suppressed, especially under the eye of growing Kafka scholarship. Nonetheless, Brod 'sanitized' the episode in his play—placing a desk in the room that K. enters at night, whereas in the novel there's no desk, only a bed in the room. In Act 2, Scene 14 of the play, Bürgel is sitting at the desk, writing when K. enters, whereas in the novel, Bürgel is lying naked in bed. Brod evidently could not bring himself to put K. on or in the bed of a man from the castle, no matter how dreamy and surreal the sequence. That would have put a spin on K., and on gaining entry to the castle, that would not have tallied with his near hagiographic presentation of his friend. (This is likely actually why he edited out the chapter of the novel in the first place.) In Act 2, Scene 15 of the play, Bürgel appears as the narrator of a scene that Brod imports from *The Trial*—the discussion of the "Before the Law" parable in which a man from the country tries to gain access to the Law, spends his whole life before the keeper of the gate, waiting to be admitted, and dies there, but not before glimpsing in the dark beyond the keeper a glowing light. Brod's play ends at Scene 16, with K.'s death. K. does not gain entry to the Law / the Castle, but in light of his untiring diligence, is granted posthumous permission to stay in the village. Dead and buried, however, permission for K. in the play is sadly moot.

***

M. and I depart Špindleruv Mlýn for Zlaté Hory on the morning of September 3. Before long, traffic grinds to a halt on the two-lane country road. Our WAZE App shows a serious accident ahead and directs us off-road, onto a meandering roundabout—through a farmer's field, then through Czech towns and villages: Mladé Buky, Trutnov Nový Rokytník, Komárov, Proruby, Velký Trebešov; across the border and through Polish towns and villages: Jeleniów, Szczytna, Bardo, Suszka, Kamieniec Ząbkowicki, Złoty Stok; back to Czech lands—through Javorník, Horní Heřmanice, Velká Kraš, Mikulovice, Ondře Jovice, and finally, five hours later, to our destination: Sanatorium Edel—the former Sanatorium Schweinburg, Zuckmantel, located on the edge of town and surrounded by woods and a gurgling brook.

The original complex, still standing and well-kept, is now a hospital for children with respiratory diseases. When Kafka summered here it was a naturopathic establishment under the direction of Dr. Ludwig Schweinburg. Dr. Schweinburg—author of *Handbook of General and Special Hydrotherapy*—was considered a water specialist, though he prescribed for his patients a mixed regime of hydrotherapy, electrotherapy, air-bathing, gymnastics, daily walks, and controlled diet. Franz at twenty-two, and not yet a patient per se, had become a natural health enthusiast during his stay at the Lahmann Sanatorium in Weisser Hirsch near Dresden two years prior. The more economical Sanatorium Schweinburg provided similarly elegant accommodations and treatments, plus—importantly for Franz—the opportunity to socialize freely, far from the eyes of Prague. Near the end of his first stay at Sanatorium Schweinburg—from August 3 to 27, 1905—he wrote to tell Max: "I am frivolous … mingling a great deal with people and womenfolk and have become rather lively." (Here and elsewhere, the word "people," as distinct from "womenfolk," is another word for men.)

Reiner Stach deems Zuckmantel one of the most "significant blanks" in Kafka's biography. Yet significant it was. He returned the following summer and stayed from July 23 to August 29. A picture postcard, addressed to him in Prague, had arrived in a closed envelope.

It read: *That is a forest, and in this forest one can be happy. So come!* The signature is illegible and Franz maintained lifelong silence on the identity of the sender, but he kept the card—unlike most of the many cards and letters he received—and he noted "that time in Zuckmantel" in his diary. Ten years later he also recalled to Milena Jesenská, the intimacy he'd experienced there: "... but she was a woman and I was a boy." Ernst Pawel holds that Kafka's memory of "unambiguous happiness" was probably a "quasi-maternal affection." Reiner Stach writes that "the guest list at the sanatorium seemed to indicate that she was not a patient there." Could that mean that there were no female guests at the sanatorium during Kafka's stay? Or perhaps she was an employee and not a guest, or a local resident ...

The Zuckmantel relationship, cloaked in mystery, is coyly memorialized in "Wedding Preparations in the Country," the fragmentary novella Kafka began writing upon his return to Prague. In the story, Eduard Raban, a city-dweller, sets out on a trip to the country to visit his fiancée, "Betty, an oldish pretty girl." Raban is not looking forward to the demands of the journey nor to spending time with his wife-to-be. On the way to the train station, he meets an acquaintance, Lement, who tries to persuade him to postpone the trip, but Raban, feeling guilty, decides to go through with it. The manuscript breaks off after he arrives at the country train station and no one is there to greet him. The title-word "Preparations" suggests that a wedding in the country will not be taking place, and indeed it did not. Nor did Kafka keep up with the "oldish pretty girl," or whomever he met at Zuckmantel.

The first version of the novella was written in 1906 and 1907, two shorter re-workings in 1909. All three fragments were published in 1953 as part of Max Brod's definitive edition of Kafka's work. In his introduction to the 1995 Schocken edition of *The Complete Stories*, John Updike calls "Wedding Preparations in the Country" an "opaque," even "repellent" work: a far cry from Mann's praise of Kafka's "objective, clear, correct style" in his introductory tribute to *The Castle*. In fairness, "Wedding Preparations ..." has to be viewed as an exploratory work that never came close to being completed. The value of the text, even with pages missing, lies in what it reveals of Kafka's process, and as an early iteration of some of his characteristic motifs: bachelorhood, guilt, 'non-arrival', and doubling—including a signal pre-*Metamorphosis* scene in which Eduard Raban imagines sending the figure of his dapper persona out to meet the challenges of the world, while his more insular self—in the shape of a large beetle—stays at home in bed, dreaming.

M. and I stroll the paths through the manicured gardens surrounding Sanatorium Edel, then cross into the forested area beyond, where according to the message on the postcard, *"one can be happy."* We encounter no one. And the staff at the Edel reception desk speak no English, though we do manage to communicate through broken German and end up getting a pamphlet in Czech that contains the name Franz Kafka. Evidently, Kafka's stay is remembered as part of sanatorium history, if only for advertisement purposes. It's gratifying to see these grounds—where Franz experienced happiness over a century ago—so well-maintained. Yet there's an odd stillness to the place. This is a hospital for children, with no children in sight. No young voices, no play things. No noise. There's a kind of sterile quiet Franz would have found ideal for writing.

M. is eager to get back on the road. It's been a long day already, but we've come this far and I don't want to leave town without seeing the train station: point of dis/embarkation. I'm imagining Franz, like Eduard Raban, coming to the country and making his way from the station by coach. From the Edel, by car, it's a four-minute drive. The station building is locked, boarded, and grafittied. A smaller building adjacent the station houses a set of outhouse-style toilets and a storeroom with an old sofa. I photograph the sober tableau. Clearly people don't arrive and depart Zlaté Hory by train anymore. The station—like so many defunct structures in the Czech lands—has been left to languish. The historic gold mining town is not what it once was. Apart from a few refurbished buildings on the main street— notably the parish church, which bears a restoration plaque inscribed in German and dated 1937—much of the centre is also languishing. On the terrace of a lone open restaurant, men—men only—are sitting, smoking, keeping company. Across the street, Hotel Minerál, is closed. We booked a room for the night at Hotel Monopol in Katowice, Poland—partly because Katowice is on the way to our next stop, but also for lack of options in Zlaté Hory.

***

Kafka never visited Poland, but Felice Bauer was born in former Upper Silesia, in Neustadt: now Prudnik—four miles northeast of Zlaté Hory, in Opole, west Poland. I inform M. of the fact as we pass through

Prudnik, twenty minutes into the drive to Katowice. He asks if I'd like to check out the local cemetery—to see if any Bauers are buried there. He's poking me. But I might have wanted to stop, if the hour weren't late. Cemeteries are some of my favourite places. Yet only so much can be fit into a K. day and the aim is to reach Katowice before nightfall.

We arrive at the Hotel Monopol at dusk, weary and leery of what to expect. It's billed online as a boutique hotel with unique cultural-historical significance: built in 1902, awarded the gold medal at the hotelier's exhibition of 1904, the most expensive hotel in Katowice by the mid-1930s. After that the building fell on hard times (a euphemism) and ceased operating as a hotel—until it was bought up by the Likus group in 2001, restored and reopened in 2003. Hotel Monopol exceeds expectations. It's as comfortable as any hotel we've stayed at in Prague and we welcome the comfort. After a good night's rest in the burled-wood room, we set out early in heavy rain for the High Tatras of Slovakia. We pass four exits to Oświęcim—which appears on the same green highway signs as the city of Kraków. Oświęcim, a town in southern Poland, like any other. But not.

***

Kafka stayed in the High Tatra Mountains from mid-December 1920 till the end of August 1921—his longest stay away from home base. At the end of August 1920, the family doctor recommended treatment at a specialized sanatorium. The last thing Franz wanted was to spend weeks, or months, among sick people. "Those institutions are exclusively for the lung," he wrote to Milena, "houses that cough and shake with fever … where you have to eat meat, where former hangmen dislocate your arm if you resist injections." A specialized sanatorium was something different from the many health resorts he'd stayed at over the years—most recently Villa Ottoburg in Merano, Italy where he'd convalesced from April till June. But the latter stay had not helped, and by fall of 1920 he was short of breath, constantly coughing and running a low-grade fever. Friends, family, and his physicians were all urging more specialized treatment.

The family doctor suggested a sanatorium in the High Tatras for the mountain sun, and Franz, feeling worse and worse, bowed to pressure. He chose Villa Tatra at Matliary for the modest cost, promise of vegetarian meals and the opportunity to garden. The attending physician, Dr. Leopold Strelinger, was an affable Jewish man who advocated arsenic injections (which Franz rejected) and a diet of ample fresh cream and meat (which he reluctantly gave in to), along with the regular rest-cure regime. The parallels between Kafka's experience at Matliary and that of Mann's cast at Sanatorium Berghof in *The Magic Mountain* are striking: the high mountain locales reached by narrow-gauge train, carriage or sleigh; strict medical supervision, including temperature-measuring several times daily and rigorously enforced sun- and air-bathing on balcony lounge chairs; communal meals, and a pervasive chumminess. Franz was especially averse to the latter, but at Matliary he felt the first stirrings of solidarity with other lung patients, and soon fell under the spell of connectedness and affection that Mann treats thematically in his novel.

M. booked for us a room for the night at Hotel Kukučka—advertised online as "fabulous." It was a toss-up between Hotel Kukučka, Hotel Lomnica—billed as "exceptional," and the Grand Hotel Praha—a lookalike for the Grand Budapest Hotel in Wes Anderson's 2014 movie of the same name—billed as "superb." Villa Tatra, like Hotel Krone, is no longer standing, but I'd read that a monument to Kafka had been erected at the site, and with a Wagenbach photograph of the original buildings as guide, I figured the reception staff at the hotel would be able to direct us to the site of the former sanatorium.

The rain that accompanies us on the three-hour drive from Katowice to the Tatras lets up near the border. By the time we reach the Slovakian resort centre, the skies are clear enough for me to get a good drive-by shot of Grand Hotel Praha—its red roof, turrets and cupolas above the mountainside trees.

Within minutes we're at Hotel Kukučka. From the outside it looks quaint, in a faux-alpine way. There's a misty, moving view of the mountains from our balcony, but the room is cramped, there's no fridge, and no internet service. We end up walking over to Hotel Lomnica to get WiFi connection. As for locating the site of the former Villa Tatra, it doesn't help to tell reception that author Franz Kafka stayed there in 1920-21. None of the staff has heard of Villa Tatra, nor of Kafka. But mentioning Tatranské Matliary does the trick and we're told to "Go to Hotel Hutník."

Hotel Hutník is a four-minute drive in the direction we came from. We'd passed the turnoff on the way to Hotel Kukučka, without realizing it, and there's no sign announcing: Turn here to the site of the former sanatorium where author Franz Kafka stayed in 1920-21. The sign near the turnoff reads: Hotel Complex, Hutník 1 and Hutník 2. A long narrow road under a canopy of trees leads to Hutník 1—a squat, five-storey, ochre-brown building with parking and some sort of mini-golf course by the rear entrance.

The Hutník receptionist hasn't heard of Franz Kafka either, nor of any memorial monument. But I persist. I'm determined to find out if these are the grounds of the former sanatorium, and I want to see the monument. I ask to speak to the manager; I figure a manager would have to know about the sanatorium and the Kafka monument. The receptionist gives me an exasperated look but she places a call to someone and that someone tells her that the Kafka monument is "near the road." She can't be more specific than that.

There's only one way out, so we get back into the car and drive out slowly the way we came. This time I notice a sign showing two roosters and the place-name: Tatranské Matliary. M. parks the car and we get out to survey the lay of the land: the mountains, the woods, and the glade in which Hutník 1 and 2 are situated. The setting fits descriptions, also the backdrop of a photo of Franz sitting on sanatorium grounds with other patients, smiling his slightly embarrassed smile and looking too-dapper-by-half in a suit, white shirt and tie. Then I see the other sign: Pamätník Franza Kafku, and beyond it, on raised ground and partially circled by trees: a grouping of stones. A bronze plaque affixed to the largest stone features the face of Franz—a stern likeness—and an inscription in Slovak: Pražský Nemecký Spisovateľ Sa liečil v Sanatóriu OD18. XII 1920 DO 27 VIII 1921. "Franz Kafka, the Prague German writer was treated at the Sanatorium from December 18, 1920 until August 27, 1921."

The main sanatorium building, it now becomes clear, is where Hutník 1 now stands. Franz stayed at Villa Tatra, the smaller lodge—the site of Hutník 2. The Hutník hotels have none of the charm of the former sanatorium buildings and there's a bleakness to the stillness. I sit on the stone beside the memorial stone. The urgency of pursuit has drained away and M. and I are quiet. I recall Franz's words to his parents in a letter of March 1921: "On the whole I like it very well here." And to his sister Ottla, that same month: "I would gladly stay longer." The remoteness of the location suited him, the simple, rustic setting—the forest glade and mountain backdrop, most of all the quiet, though he moaned (characteristically) to Ottla that "the amount of quiet I need doesn't exist in the world." A loud caw suddenly breaks the stillness and M. and I both look up. There's a lone jackdaw, perched atop a nearby fir tree, a 'kavka', the very bird so emblematic of Franz. I laugh out loud: "He's here," and quickly grab the camera to capture his likeness.

In chapter five of Mann's sanatorium novel, the humanist Settembrini tells the hero Hans Castorp that "within a year at most of living 'up' in the magic mountain a person will never be able to take hold of any other sort of life." What was intended to be a visit of a few weeks with his ailing cousin, Joachim Ziemssen, stretches into months, then years, after Castorp himself is diagnosed as tubercular. The assistant sanatorium director, Dr. Krokowski, who lectures regularly on matters of the soul, deems the illness "a secondary phenomenon"—the primary phenomenon being "repressed desire." This psychological thread in the story loops into Castorp's impossible love for fellow patient Frau Clavdia Chauchat—the exotic femme fatale who bears a striking resemblance to a boy Castorp had likewise been impossibly drawn to in his youth. Before long, Castorp is musing to Settembrini: "I think I almost might want to stay feverish indefinitely and just sit right here." Castorp comes to revel in his status as one of the horizontal consumptives and Mann maintains a cool ambiguity as to how much of his hero's illness is genuine and how much of it the result of life and love at the heights. Settembrini holds that "illness is, if not entirely, then in large part of a moral nature." This line could have been a lifted directly from Kafka's own notes, for this was his view too—that the disease (though genuine in his case) was, at root, of a moral and mental / psychic / soul nature.

Despite his determination to resist sanatorium chumminess, Franz, like Hans Castorp, quickly came under the spell of affection. Soon after his arrival at Villa Tatra, he wrote to Max of a tablemate, a young Jewish patient named Arthur Szinay from Košice in Slovakia: "Charming in the Eastern Jewish sense. Full of irony, restlessness, moodiness, confidence, but also neediness. Everything is 'interesting, interesting' to him, but not in the usual sense. It means something like, 'It's burning, it's burning'." Franz called Szinay "a young man to fall in love with." Yet instead of Szinay, he drew close to another young Jewish man: a medical student named Robert Klopstock. In February he wrote to Max: "Yesterday, a 21-year-old student from Budapest was bothering me, but in a very friendly way. He is hardworking, smart, has a talent for literature despite his rough looks ... is very efficient, as though he was a doctor from birth." A month later, he wrote to Ottla: "He is young, big, broad-shouldered, strong, sturdy, unusually smart, real, unselfish and noble." Franz found Robert "positively handsome," "when he lay in bed in his nightshirt with tousled hair." In early May, he wrote to Max: "Actually, I associate only with the medical student, everything else is incidental." And instead of taking meals in the communal hall of the main building, he was having his meals brought to his room. The "medical student" became his main contact, go-between, even helping out with his medical treatment.

Kafka's friendship with Robert Klopstock deepened after Matliary. Klopstock was the person closest to Franz during his final weeks, along with Dora Diamant. Robert suspended his medical studies in April 1924, in order to care for his friend. He and Dora were Kafka's "little family," nursing him with total devotion at Hoffmann Sanatorium in Kierling, until the end.

During his stay at Villa Tatra, Franz received no visitors from home, and he wrote no fiction. But he did keep up regular correspondence with family and friends. For fear of collapse should he return to Prague, he extended his medical leave from the office beyond the original return-date of March 1921, to August. He was benefitting from the treatments, the company, and the sanatorium setting: "all that looks beautiful from the balcony in a villa at Tatra." In mid-April, he wrote to Max: "I can love only what I can place so high above me that I cannot reach it." Eight months later, he began writing *The Castle* at Spindelmühle in the Giant Mountains.

***

Back in Prague, near the end of our trip, I receive an email from Iveta Vošahlíková, the manager of Hotel Savoy, Špindleruv Mlýn. Attached to the mail are two photos: one of the old Hotel Savoy in 1963 and a second one of Iveta's mother and uncle, standing in front of the hotel in 1968. Iveta wasn't able to tell me when the former Hotel Savoy was torn down, only that the new Savoy was opened in 2008. I compare the photos of the former Hotel Savoy with Klaus Wagenbach's photo of Hotel Krone. Iveta was right: The two buildings, with different names, were one and the same. I thank her for getting back to me and for her kindness in sharing these personal pictures. For me, the slender link they tender—between then and now; person, place and creation—is immense.

At Planá

KAFKA ARRIVED IN Planá—a small resort town on the Lužnice River in south Bohemia—on Friday, June 23, 1922, a week before his official retirement from the Worker's Accident Insurance Institute in Prague. He'd been promoted to senior secretary in February 1922—in recognition of his fourteen years of valued civil service—despite several extended medical leaves following the diagnosis of tuberculosis in 1917. When it became clear that he would not be well enough again to return to work, he requested a disability pension and was approved for retirement with a monthly pension of 1,000 Czech crowns, effective July 1.

Kafka came by train—to spend his first months of retirement in the company of his sister Ottla, her husband Josef David, and their baby daughter Věra. Ottla had rented an apartment for the summer in the house of a local craftsman. Josef would be there on weekends only and Franz would be free to read, rest, and continue writing *The Castle*, begun in January while on leave from the Institute. Ottla would attend to her brother, as she had faithfully over the years. The two were close and she was sensitive to his needs and idiosyncrasies.

M. and I arrive by car: Friday, August 18, 2017. Our destination: Příčná 145. I want to see the place where Kafka wrote the bulk of his third, most ambitious novel before abruptly abandoning it, mid-sentence. Příčná is a narrow one-way street that connects to a slightly wider two-way street, Husova, that connects to the town's main thoroughfare, Čsla. In under two hours from Prague, we're almost there. M. parks the car on Husova and we step out.

In his first letter from retirement—to Max Brod—Franz wrote: "It's more peaceful in Planá than it's been at any previous summer resort … as far as I can see at present." This is our sense too. Planá is tranquil and flat. It has none of Prague's architectural elegance and less of the natural beauty of other Czech towns we've visited—at least on first impression. Husova Street is unremarkable … apart from the exposed side-wall of a house on a construction site next to where we've parked. I notice it as I get out of the car. The year the house was built —1908— is stamped into a panel on the exposed wall, which would have been concealed until the adjoining building was torn down. Kafka would have passed this house on his daily walks from Příčná to the other side of the Lužnice, but the year of its construction would have been hidden from him. The image of 'revealed concealment' strikes me as indicative: concealment, cover-up, obscuration and skewed disclosure being characteristic of Kafka, particularly in *The Castle*. I take out the camera to capture the exposure.

Příčná 145 is gated and fenced, barbed wire strung along the fence-top. A picture of a guard dog stands guard at the gate. There's no dog in sight, nor any sound of one. No people either. From our vantage point, outside the fence, there appear to be three buildings on the lot: a low, garage-like structure with a wood-panel door, and beyond it a tired-looking two-storey, greyish-white house with a gabled tile roof and thin brick chimney—like a smokestack. Both buildings look to be of Kafka's time and we're thinking the one with the chimney must be where Franz and the Davids stayed in the summer of 1922. If only we could get in and see it from up-close. The third building is newer: a two-storey, concrete and plaster house. There's no door on the street side, so the entrance must be on the other side. The absence of a 'front door' and three narrow windows on the gate-side of the house give the place a garrisoned look—augmented by a large lone casement window facing Příčná.

Windows figure prominently in a number of Kafka's works and the strangely placed windows in this house remind me of the many windows in *The Castle*: tiny windows, curtained windows, open windows, outer windows, upstairs windows, closed windows, peepholes, spy-windows, rooms without any windows. When land surveyor K. gets his first clear view of the eponymous castle, he sees that it is not a "knightly castle from the days of chivalry, nor a showy new structure, but a complex of buildings, a few of them with two storeys [with] small windows, shining in the sun … [There's] something crazed about the sight … as if drawn by an anxious or careless child." Windows set an edgy tone in the first chapter of the novel. In chapter three, "the window" assumes an active, intermediary role. When K. and his love-interest, Frieda, retire to his room at the Bridge Inn for the night, K.'s two assistants, Artur and Jeremias, follow in after them like tag-along children. "They were turned out," Kafka writes, "but they came back through the window," and "K. … lets them back in, to spend the night." (A strange 'ménage à quatre'.) In the absence of a 'front door' at Příčná 145, one can imagine having to enter the house, like Artur and Jeremias, through the large lone window facing the street. But the window is closed, the curtains drawn. The house is still; it admits no entry. The large garden on the east side of the house is quiet too, as is the street.

A few days into his stay at Planá, Franz was already complaining about the constant noise: "It would be lovely here if it were quiet," he wrote to Max, "there are a few hours of quiet but not nearly enough … a woodcutter has spent the whole day splitting wood for the landlady … On such a noisy day … I feel like someone expelled from the world." Noise was an anathema to Kafka and noise became topical in his letters from Planá: "… noise blasts sleep and shatters the head"; "If only there were not so much noise in the world"; "noise has something … narcotic about it." There were the neighbour's children, the horn-playing of a peasant youth, the saw mill—hammering, rumbling of logs, cries of the loaders, "the *gee* and *ho* of oxen attached to a winch." The whirr of the circular saw was especially distressing to Franz, even with the aid of Ohropax wool and cotton ear plugs, which he relied on day and night. "At the nearby railroad station," he wrote to Max mid-July, "timber is perpetually being loaded" … "The chain at the station clanks" and "for the past few days some two hundred Prague school children have been quartered here. A hellish noise, a scourge of humanity."

M. and I are struck by the general quiet here—the absence of children, animals, clanking; movement of any kind. I photograph the Příčná lot, the three buildings on the other side of the fence, the guard dog sign on the gate, the garden. We linger on the sidewalk, hoping someone will appear. No one does.

We head back to Husova Street, to look for the "nearby" train station. 250 meters up the street we see the station sign and platform— where Kafka must have disembarked on the Friday of his arrival in June 1922. And beside the station: the saw mill—heavy machinery, logs and planks stacked neatly between the warehouses and office buildings, the lot extending west. It's good to see the mill still in business—almost a hundred years after Kafka complained bitterly about the noise issuing from it. On this Friday, the day of our visit, it's silent. Not a worker or working animal to be seen—apart from a picture of a guard dog on a billboard inside the fence.

Kafka was hyper-excitable at Planá. Even with his sister's solicitousness, which he commended in letters to friends, he couldn't overcome the disquiet that dogged him here. "Ottla looks after me no less tenderly than after Věra, and that is saying a great deal," he wrote to Robert Klopstock. To Max he wrote: "I am given the use of the fine room ... where one has a magnificent view from the bed, with the woods in the distance ... while the family of three sleep in a tiny cubicle, with the view of the neighbour's yard and the chimney of the sawmill ... The lodgings themselves are very cleverly arranged ... Ottla looks after everything," yet "I have been dashing about or sitting as petrified as a desperate animal in his burrow. Enemies everywhere."

The enemies or fears, or ghosts as he often called them, were real to Franz, even if immaterial, and their power mounted during his stay at Planá—despite the close care of his sister, in the freedom of retirement, in a place he viewed as beautiful. "Ottla," he confided to his childhood friend Oskar Baum, "tries to explain the fear partly as springing from physical weakness ... but the physical weakness which surely does exist springs from psychic weakness." He used the term "mental disease" to refer to his lung condition. At the beginning of July, Oskar invited him to vacation in Georgental in Thuringia, Germany. Oskar had made the arrangements: "a fine quiet room with balcony, reclining chair, good food, and a garden view for 150 marks a day." Franz had only to take the train, but he couldn't bring himself to do it—for "fear of change" or "fear of attracting the attention of the gods," as he put it to Max. To Robert, he wrote that this "fear, which does not let me travel, is something I have known for a long time; it is more alive than I am and out to prove it." It was a kind of primordial fear, it seems, of an unknowable essentiality, from which a pervasive power and authority emanated.

Writing was the best defense against this "general fear"—but—and there was always a "but" with Kafka, it was distressed defense. "Writing sustains me," he wrote to Max in a long letter postmarked July 5, "By this I don't mean, of course, that my life is better when I don't write. Rather it is much worse then and wholly unbearable and has to end in madness ... I am a writer, which is actually true even when I am not writing, and a non-writing writer is a monster inviting madness ... Writing is a sweet and wonderful reward, but for what? In the night it became clear to me ... that it is the reward for serving the devil. This descent into the dark powers, this unshackling of spirits bound by nature ... and whatever else may take place in the nether parts ...

Perhaps there are other forms of writing, but I know only this kind; at night, when fear keeps me from sleeping."

"Grousing" to friends in letters eased the "repining" a bit. Walking provided a little relief. Of evenings, he would walk across the bridge over the Lužnice, through a neighbourhood of newly built villas, the landlady's dog his companion. The two would walk past the villas and up into the woods.

M. and I head south on Husova, cross Čsla—following Kafka's route—and pause on the Lužnice River Bridge. The view from here is beautiful, the river almost motionless, glassy in the noon shine, the foliage on both banks reflected impressionistically in the water. An old mill and weir lend the scene a painterly mien; a rowboat beneath a tree completes the picture. Franz did not mention rowing or swimming in his letters from Planá, though these were (and still are) popular summer activities here. He himself had been an avid swimmer and rower. But in Planá writing was his main engagement; walking, his diversion.

The villas he noted in letters are located on Ustrašícká Street, southeast of the bridge: large, well-kept homes with gabled red tile roofs and ornamented façades, big picture windows. He wrote of walking past the villas, of sitting on "a certain bench at the edge of the woods." M. and I walk along Ustrašícká Street, past the villas, toward the edge of the Bohemian Forest. I'm scanning discreetly for benches. M. picks up on my vigilance and asks me what I'm looking for. I don't mention the "certain bench." How can I even entertain the thought that it might still be here? "Nothing," I say, feeling suddenly sullen. "Let's go back to Čsla and see what's there." It's grown hot and a cool drink might bring me up.

On Čsla we stop in at a Cukrárna—a sweets shop—for ice-cream. The place is filled with families, children playing on the patio. Franz would have found the play noisy—a hindrance to writing. Yet despite all his complaints about children and their noisiness, his writing did advance at Planá, even if he considered it "less than average in quality, no more, and constantly endangered by noise." In a long letter from the end of July, he wrote to Max of the impact of children on his thinking: "Once I notice that they are here … it is as though I had pried up a stone and saw underneath the obvious, the expected, and the dreaded—the wood lice and all the creatures of the night. But this is obviously a transference. It is not the children who are the night's creatures, rather it is they who in the course of play pry up the stone from my head and 'favour' me with a glance into it."

I'm not so naïve as to suppose that Kafka's fiction can be directly, biographically, decoded. But a writer's imagination is not impersonal; novels are places where authors explore their subjectivity and Kafka was deeply attuned to the "tremendous world in his head," to how his inner and outer worlds could conflate and become enmeshed. I wonder how much of his professed "transference" makes its way into *The Castle*; how much of his daily life—as related in his letters from Planá—is mirrored or abstracted in the novel. Children and the qualities of childlikeness and childishness, figure so prominently in *The Castle*, just as they did in Kafka's life at Planá. For the most part, the children in *The Castle* are actual children: the schoolchildren at the schoolhouse where K. and Frieda take up temporary residence; Hans Brunswick, the "small boy" who befriends K., admires his "walking-stick" and looks down on K. as if he were the "younger boy." The lookalike assistants, Artur and Jeremias, are men but K. refers to them as children, and they often behave as such. I wonder if the two 'child-men' might represent a doubling of Kafka's shadow side—the dependent, infantilized Franz who required so much supervisory care at Planá. In a letter to Max from mid-September, he wrote that he "stood there like Gulliver listening to the giant women conversing"—meaning Ottla and the landlady, who took charge of him in his weakened state. Of course, one can search endlessly for parallels between Kafka's life and writing and be left guessing. Still the speculation remains irresistible, especially when there are so many clues in the 'private' writings.

After the ice-cream on Čsla, M. and I walk back to Příčná 145. I'm hoping there'll be someone there we can talk to, who may even invite us in to view the houses on the lot from inside the fence. I'm floating the idea that if we can see the rundown grey-white house up-close, it may reveal something about Kafka; and the more fanciful idea: something he might want us to know ... I linger at the fence, again awaiting a sign of life. "There's no one here," M. says. "Give it up. Let's go back to the car. We can drive around the block again on our way back to Prague, if you like."

Kafka stopped work on *The Castle* toward the end of August or beginning of September. In a long letter to Max, postmarked Sept 11, he wrote: "I will evidently have to drop work on the castle story forever, cannot pick it up again since the breakdown." Kafka names four "breakdowns" in the letter: The first one occurred on one of the days the neighbour's children were making noise, the second one when Oskar's letter regarding the Georgental trip arrived; the third when the possibility of Ottla's return to Prague for a month was raised, which would have entailed his taking meals at the town inn; and the fourth when the landlady invited him to stay on by himself as a boarder for the winter. He was afraid of "complete loneliness"—"loneliness among people." He described the paradox of this loneliness to Max: "Fundamentally, loneliness is my sole aim ... and it can be said that I have 'arranged' my life with the view that loneliness can fit comfortably in. And in spite of this, this fear of what I love so much."

The "breakdowns" are not described in symptomatic detail, but it was the last one—fear of being left to fend for himself alone—that apparently defeated Kafka's ability to proceed with *The Castle*. Or maybe the story itself had become too big and unwieldy, the strands of it too difficult to pull together, the intimations too close, the approach of the denouement too forbidding.

After he dropped "the castle story," he worked on a shorter piece, "Investigations of a Dog" ("Forschungen eines Hundes"). I can't help but wonder: Was this perhaps a nod to his faithful walking companion, the landlady's dog? "Investigations of a Dog" is a rambling, also unfinished story, in which Kafka writes of noise / music, a "strange dog ... brown, flecked here and there with white spots, a fine, strong, inquiring gaze ... and an awe-inspiring voice that made the forest fall silent." And this talking, singing dog tells the narrator: "'You must leave this place ... Walk away now, slowly.'" In fact, Kafka did go; he took the train back to Prague on Monday, Sept 18, 1922 after three months at Planá. Neither the office, nor any other obligation awaited him. On September 21, he wrote to Oskar that it would have been nice to stay on at Planá for the winter, but that he "would not have been able to bear it among the unleashed nature spirits."

M. and I return to Husova Street, get into the car, and drive along Příčná on our way to the highway. M. slows down at 145 so that I can have a last look before we head back to Prague. As we pass, an old woman walks out from behind the house and into the garden. "Look," I shout, "someone's here." M. brakes, pulls to the curb, and I leap out. "Excuse me," I call out to the woman. "I'm wondering if you can help me." She says something in Czech and I answer in English. She again says something in Czech and goes back behind the house. I stand there for a few moments waiting, then return to the car.

"What happened?" M. asks, pulling away. "I told her I understand that this is where the writer Franz Kafka stayed in the summer of 1922. She said something in Czech, then went back behind the house." "Maybe she understood you but couldn't answer in English," M. says. "Maybe she went back into the house to get someone who does speak English." "What are the chances of that?" I say. "She's an old woman, probably living alone, and she walked away because we couldn't communicate." "Well, maybe," M. says, "but maybe not. Let's drive around the block again and see." "Right," I say skeptically, "we've been past the lot twice, let's see if we get lucky on three." M. is usually the skeptical one, but here he offers me hope.

We come around the block again and this time I notice that the large window on the Příčná side of the house, facing the street, is open. And there's a young man in shorts and undershirt, sitting perched on the inside sill. I can hardly believe it. "Look, there is someone else here. You were right," I say to M. He pulls over and again I leap out of the car. It's almost comedic. "Excuse me," I call out again, this time to the young man. "I'm wondering if you can help me." "Maybe," he says in Czech-inflected English. "I understand that this is where the writer Franz Kafka stayed in the summer of 1922. Do you know anything about that?" I ask. "I've heard something about it," he replies, and waits to hear what I have to say next. "We're from Canada," I say, "and we would very much like to see the house where Kafka worked on his last novel, *The Castle*." "One moment," he says, and disappears from the window into the house.

I recall the first chapter of *The Castle*, the part where "the landlord was perched opposite K. on the edge of the windowsill." It's like a merger of life and literature. The young man reappears, together with the old woman, this time on the driveway inside the fence. The woman opens the gate and motions for us to enter. We are inside the gate; we've been admitted. I ask the young man, who, it turns out, is the woman's grandson, if I can photograph the grey-white house we've assumed is the house Kafka stayed in. "Yes," he says. I take several shots.

"But that is not the house where Kafka stayed," he says. "Kafka stayed here"— he indicates the newer house—"where my grandmother lives. The place where Kafka stayed was torn down and this house was built in its place. Kafka stayed there," he says, and the grandmother points to the south-facing window. "He wrote *The Castle* up there," she says, her grandson translating, "in the room with the view of the forest. But he didn't finish the story. He was bothered by the noise." "Yes," I say, "the noise," not knowing exactly what to add.

"Are we the only people who've come here to see where Kafka stayed?" I ask, collecting my thoughts. "No," the woman says, by way of her grandson. "Others have come, but they spoke German or English and I didn't understand them, so they went away." "Are we the first Kafka visitors you've invited in?" I ask. The grandson turns to check with his grandmother. "Yes," he says. "My grandmother invited you in because I am visiting and I know English." "What's your name?" I ask the young man. "Mira," he replies. "Thank you for being here, Mira, and please thank your grandmother for inviting us in." He does, she smiles, then motions for us to follow her. We walk past the back of the house, where the 'front door' is located, and come to the garden. Here M. and I are presented with a cluster of freshly picked ripe red tomatoes. "Thank you," I say. I'm too moved in the moment to think of saying much of anything else, and too shy to ask grandmother and grandson to pose for a picture.

It would have been nice to take away a face-shot of grandmother and grandson together, but it seems more fitting to have photos of the setting only. There are no photos of Franz at Planá either.

As for the ripe tomatoes, what could have been a more signal gift? Kafka was a gardener too, and a vegetarian. Prior to Planá, gardening had been an afternoon reprieve. Weeding, watering, and planting out were balm for the addled soul.

Graal-Müritz

GRAAL-MÜRITZ IS an old town on Germany's Baltic coast. It began as the medieval community of Müritz; grew to a hamlet with a nunnery and mill, then to a village with shops, restaurants, hotels, and a boardwalk and pier for its long sandy beach. Train service opened in July 1926. Müritz merged with the nearby village of Graal in 1938, and in 1960 the amalgamated town received official recognition as a coastal health spa.

M. and I arrive in Graal-Müritz mid-morning, July 12, 2016. We haven't come for the spas. We're here because Müritz was Kafka's last vacation destination, a significant one, and I've come to believe that every significant contact leaves a trace.

Kafka came to Müritz in the summer of 1923—with his sister Elli, nephew and two nieces—and stayed from July 10 till August 8. He'd just turned forty and was seriously ill. Retired in 1922 with a head secretary's pension from the Workers' Accident Insurance Institute, in Müritz he was "testing his transportability," as he put it, for a longer journey—to Palestine / Eretz Israel. His childhood friend, Hugo Bergmann, had moved to Jerusalem two years prior and the Bergmanns, visiting Prague that summer, were ready to take Franz back with them. He was sure Jerusalem didn't need a tubercular former civil-servant lawyer, but maybe he could garden there—he'd tried his hand at gardening, and that was part of the plan. If he grew stronger in Müritz, he told his friends, he would make the longer journey in the fall. The Bergmanns took another landsman back with them instead: Gerhard (Gershom) Scholem—the scholar credited with founding the modern study of Jewish mysticism. But in Müritz Kafka met a girl.

M. and I drive into town on Rostocker Strasse, turn on to Lange Strasse, which becomes Bahnhofstrasse, and park adjacent the train station. I photograph the shiny red Regio standing at the platform—number 642 184 of the Rostock S-Bahn—and imagine Franz arriving by carriage, before the expansion of rail service from the terminus at Rostock. We grab our bags from the trunk, walk back to the Tourist Information Center we'd passed on the way, and pick up a map of the town. Kafka, I'm surprised and pleased to see, is a main attraction, cited at No. 4 and No. 5 on the map—at Strandstrasse, on the other side of town. We take a roundabout route, along the gardened streets of the west end, through the woods of Rhododendron Park, down the ramp that leads to the beach: narrow between the dunes and sea.

The beach is long and wild. Wind brings tears to our eyes; ferries gull calls along the shore. The sea leaves bits of jelly-flesh, shell and plant in the sand. Bathers are back and forth—from the waves to their wicker chairs. These big roofed recliners, said to be ubiquitous on Baltic beaches, are all facing the grassy dunes—no doubt to shelter sitters from wind and surf. But it's an odd sight: chairs lined up like soldiers along the strand, all viewing the dunes. I photograph the beach, the chairs, the gulls in the wind—transfixed.

We walk, the beach repeats: sand and shore, what's washed up on it. I choose three small shells for the pillbox I'd purchased at Goethe's Garden House in Weimar the day before. Keepsakes for a keepsake. We pass the pier, a trampoline—caged and still as a relic; stop before a circular, swing-like ride— squealing children strung from its metal limbs, spinning at awkward angles. This looks more like punishment than fun to me. I'm reminded of Kafka's scratchy black-ink drawings of the execution machine in his story "In the Penal Colony"—the "peculiar apparatus" in his darkest story wherein "guilt is never to be doubted" and the sharp-toothed harrowing machine epitomizes the violence mobilized by the regime to imprint its codes of conduct into the bodies of the accused. The children spin and squeal happily as we pass.

Sand feeds gradually into grass and we come to the edge of a wood, a path named F.-Kafka-Weg. Formerly the Badeweg, this was the way that Kafka came, to and from the beach, during his stay here.

M. photographs me holding the pole with the sign that bears the name, the fingers of my right hand taut as a claw.

Elli chose, for her brother and her children, accommodations at Pension Glückauf—12 Strandstrasse: No. 4 on our map. The pension advertised comfortable, well-furnished rooms with balconies or glass verandahs, hot and cold running water, personally guided fine cuisine, central heat in the dining room, a view of the sea, and an "eight-minute walk to the beach."

M. clocks the walk through the woods—to check for the "eight-minute" match. I lag behind, snapping shots: the trees, the path, M. looking jaunty and boyish from behind. I imagine Franz on his way to the beach, his lean figure floating faintly toward me, wearing a summer jacket and straw boater hat. Formal for the sand, but Franz is a man of hats and fashion. He'll likely shed the jacket and shirt, bare his slender chest to the sun, resting in one of the wicker recliners. The figure fades and disappears before I can see if he's smiling, showing his teeth. (I want to see his teeth.)

We emerge from F.-Kafka-Weg and turn on to Strandstrasse. I photograph a clutch of hollyhocks, a typical Müritz thatched-roof house, Zur Goldenen Kugel restaurant with its half-timber frames and flower boxes. We've passed the "eight-minute" mark by the time we arrive at No. 4 on the map: a plexiglass-covered plaque on a metal stand. The text, translated, reads: "Here stood Pension Glückauf where Franz Kafka—born in Prague on July 3, 1883 and died of tuberculosis in Kierling, Austria on June 3, 1924—spent his last summer, from the beginning of July to August 8, 1923. From his window, he could see the former children's camp of the Jewish People's Home in Berlin, later Haus Huter. He met Dora Diamant at the camp on July 13, 1923. She travelled with him to Berlin and remained at his side till his death."—A distillation so reduced it hardly tells the truth. I photograph the plaque and the edge of the Rostocker Heath beyond: remnant of an ancient forest of mostly deciduous trees: birch, beech and oak.

Franz had a room with a forest view, on the third floor, at the back of the building. When he opened the balcony door, he could hear the voices of children singing in Yiddish. Their teacher, cook, and counsellor was Dora Diamant, a free-spirited woman of twenty-five who'd fled the strictures of her ultra-orthodox Eastern European Jewish family for the freedom and opportunity of Berlin, and was working for the summer at the Jewish children's camp. No. 5 on the map—

the building that housed the camp, was demolished, I learn, in 2007. The pension where Kafka stayed came down in 2002. A new building stands in its place.

I wonder if any stories were kindled in Kafka at Müritz. One can't know for sure. He wasn't keeping a diary by that time and there's no record of sketches. The last of his diary entries was written a month before his trip to Müritz—on June 12, 1923—in tiny spidery writing: "More and more fearful as I write … Every word twisted in the hands of the spirits—this twist of the hand is their characteristic gesture … a spear turned against the speaker." The language is conspiratorial, almost occult, and the entry seems to augur an end to his writing. Yet he did continue to write, and therefore to battle the spirits. Müritz was a fateful stay in an unexpected way.

It was Dora who first saw Franz. A tall, gaunt, dark-complexioned man, playing with three young children by the dunes. She was attracted at once, though assumed he was married to the woman he was with, vacationing with his family. She followed them from the beach through the woods, observing their interactions. Two days later, July 13, he appeared in the camp kitchen where she was cleaning fish for the Sabbath meals. He smiled, said something typically witty, tipped his hat and left. At mealtime they met again. He was the guest of honour: Dr. Kafka from Prague. A lawyer, retired high civil servant and author, visiting for Friday night dinner with his sister, nephew and nieces. Franz had never attended a Sabbath meal like this—in a communal hall filled with cheery Jewish children singing Hasidic songs. He'd brought a Hebrew prayer book along and verified which blessings would be read, so as not to show his lack of familiarity with the ritual.

There's no remnant of this to see, no original structures—apart from the path through the woods (now paved) and the canopied wicker recliners (updated models). Yet I do sense something of Kafka's presence in this place. It has nothing to do with structures. He tapped into connection here—general and Jewish—and felt the gladness that came of that. From Müritz he wrote to Hugo Bergmann: "It's not that I am happy … but I am at the threshold of happiness."

In addition to letters to friends, fragments of the story of Kafka's stay in Müritz are told—most personally in *Kafka's Last Love: The*

Mystery of Dora Diamant, a pioneering work by Kathi Diamant (no relation to Dora) and in *Kafka: The Years of Insight*, the third volume of Reiner's Stach's formidable biography. By Kathi Diamant's report, not a single day passed after their first Sabbath meeting on Friday, July 13, that the two did not spend some time together here. Franz was no doubt drawn to Dora's youth and independence, impressed by her knowledge of Yiddish, Hebrew and scripture, Hasidic music, lore and tradition.

Dora was born in a town near Lódź, Poland. She was of the *Ostjuden*—Eastern European Jewry that Kafka regarded as embodying the authentic spirit of Judaism. The element of authenticity had attracted him to other friendships as well—to Yitzchak Löwy, the Yiddish-speaking actor from Galicia who'd performed with his troupe in Prague from 1911 to 1913. And to the eccentric Prague-born writer, Hebrew teacher and Zionist, Georg Langer, "the Western Jew who assimilated to the Hasidim," as Kafka describes him in his diary entry of March 25, 1915. Dora loved the theatre, too, and had acted in plays. She was also an avowed Zionist, with practical plans.

Kafka and Dora met as often as her duties permitted—to walk, talk, and sit on the beach reading Hebrew. Dora had knowledge Kafka wanted and he was an eager learner. She, for her part, was fully enthralled—by his voice, the stories of his work, his being, and his interest in her. They shared their dreams of immigrating to Eretz Israel and spoke of what they might do as pioneers. Maybe open a restaurant—Dora would be the cook and Franz the waiter. They had to have laughed at that.

Franz's spirits were lifted in Müritz but his physical health declined. He lost weight, suffered headaches, was weak and fatigued. He knew he wasn't well enough for the rigors of the longed-for longer trip, even with Dora by his side. But she had entered his life and revived another possibility. With Dora, his vision turned to Berlin, the city that had long held liberation allure. "Berlin is the best medicine against Prague," he wrote in a letter to Robert Klopstock in 1922. Dora lived there, and she was keen to facilitate Franz's move to the city, to help make his life there as liveable as possible, to keep him close.

On August 10, Kafka left Müritz for a three-day stay in Berlin. He scouted the housing in the neighbourhoods recommended by Dora;

she stayed on at the camp to complete her work obligations, praying Franz would join her in Berlin. On August 16, back in Prague, he was visited at his parents' home by Max Brod. Brod noted that his friend had taken up praying and wanted a set of *tefillin*. Wheels of change were in motion, the tight "crone claws"—as Franz had once described the grip his hometown had on him—were easing their hold. Dora arranged a room for him at Miquelstrasse 8 in the suburb of Steglitz. Hesitant, then with conviction, he left his parents' apartment and boarded the train; he lived in Berlin from September 23, 1923 till March 17, 1924.

But Berlin is another stop on the itinerary, and M. and I are standing before the Kafka memorial plaque on Strandstrasse. This is the point we've come to. My photos of the plaque and its backdrop look flat. I'm feeling a little deflated—wrangling with the idea that the purpose of a quest is not to reach a particular point. It's not about the thrill of a peak experience, but about the experience of the journey as a whole. It's the path that sacralizes any given point; the journey is the metonym for the point. I read that somewhere, can't remember where. But I'm trying to take it up—for the sake of assuagement.

Strandstrasse turns into Ribnitzer Strasse. M. and I are silent as we walk along the wooded side of the street, heading back to the centre of town. We've visited the Kafka sites on the map, admired the bright gardens and architectural charm of Graal-Müritz, the wild beauty of the Baltic beach. Randomly, it seems, at a certain point, we stop and both look down. We're startled by what we see. Turning in the grass at the side of the path is a large black beetle, its iridescent carapace bright in the noon sun. "Gregor!" we both exclaim—meaning Gregor Samsa, the human insect protagonist of *The Metamorphosis*; the creature Gregor wakes up as, in the first fantastical sentence of the novella. The beetle before us circles in the clover, as if to show off his shiny coat, not trying at all to elude us. I pull up the camera and snap and snap. The digits on his right foreleg look almost like little fingers—skillful at gripping. I can't remember ever thinking I'd seen a lovelier bug. He feels like a peak to me, a point.

We mull the encounter over lunch. M. is generally skeptical. But the sudden sighting of the beetle, out of the blue, strikes us both as remarkable. And we'd sensed his presence together, stopped spontaneously, both looked down. We'd called out "Gregor" simultaneously, and Gregor, for his part, did not abscond. He let himself be seen, homed in on, photographed—for confirmation, as proof. I'm feeling we've been paid a visitation, given an affirmation, a tangible trace of Kafka's presence, in a place where he himself had felt kinship and connection. As usual, M. is less effusive than I am. He can only take so much of this exalted kind of talk, even if he's in basic agreement. And he wants to get back on the road. He googles our next destination: Lübeck. "West-southwest on Highway 20," he says, "ninety minutes, if the way is clear."

Until he came to Müritz, Kafka had not been to the seaside for years. Not since July 1914, when he travelled to Lübeck after the "tribunal" at the Askanischer Hof Hotel in Berlin where his first engagement to Felice Bauer was dissolved. Lübeck was a consolation vacation. Franz needed to get away and decompress. He left Berlin from the Lehrter Station (now the Hauptbahnhof), arrived in Lübeck the next day, checked into a railway hotel, Hotel Schützenhuas, which he found "dreadful," and switched to the Hotel Kaiserhof by the Trave River. He recorded this in his diary, without a hint of post-tribunal contrition or sadness. He went for a walk on the Old City Wall, ate at the Hansa dairy, visited Travemünde on Lübeck Bay—with its "view of the beach" and "mixed bathing." "My bare feet struck people as indecent," he said, projecting his self-consciousness.

Hotel Kaiserhof, built in 1898, is still standing—restored yet faded—and I'd booked us a room for the night of July 12.

We check in, late afternoon, and set out to explore; we cross the bridge over the Trave and enter the Old City. We visit the great two-turreted Holstentor (Holsten Gate)—emblem of Lübeck, built in 1477; Gothic Marienkirche (St. Mary's Church) with its high brick vault—tallest in the world; and view the lay of the land from the tower of Petrikirche (St. Peter's Church). The Hansa dairy is no longer extant. From what we're told at the Tourist Information Center, McDonald's has taken its place. Lübeck, a Hanseatic port, is a stately place. Kafka came, then went from here, by ferry, to Falster Island, Denmark—to continue vacationing with his writer friend, Ernst Weiss and Weiss's girlfriend, at Marielyst, a resort with a sandy beach. Lübeck, it seems, does not remember Franz. His stay was too brief. There's no commemorative wall plaque, no bronze bust on a stand in the foyer. No literary or fateful traces either. If not for his 'private writings', we would not know he'd been here. His intersection with the city was evanescent, and washed away.

We pack up early morning, July 13. It occurs to me that this is the same day that Franz and Dora met in Müritz, ninety-three years ago. I'm warmed by the thought of this little convergence. It feels like a checkpoint on the course I'm on. We leave Hotel Kaiserhof and Lübeck before the sun is up. We're heading south to Berlin, the inland city that Kafka called the antidote to Prague.

A Circle

KAFKA LIVED IN Berlin from September 1923 till March 1924—the twilight of his life; a time of hyperinflation and general upheaval in Germany. Dora Diamant came daily to attend to him, first on Miquelstrasse, then on Grunewaldstrasse. By the end of January 1924, financial constraints and Kafka's deteriorating health necessitated their living under one roof and they moved into two rooms on the ground floor of a house at Heidestrasse 25-6, subsisting for the most part on Kafka's modest pension.

Franz was striving to live out his dream of freedom in the city he'd longed to reach: studying and reading Hebrew, receiving visitors, taking the tram from the suburbs to the Academy for the Study of Judaism (*Hochschule für die Wissenschaft des Judentums*) to take classes in Jewish history and scripture; also writing: stories and letters. Only a few of these stories have survived. The tone in the letters is mostly more hopeful than circumstances warranted. By winter of 1924, his health was in rapid decline.

Early in March Dr. Siegfried Löwy made the trip from Triesch in Moravia to check on his nephew's condition. Franz wrote to Robert Klopstock to report that he'd soon be returning to his parents' apartment in Prague and from there would likely relocate to a sanatorium in the Vienna Woods: "A temperature of 100.4 has become my daily bread and on account of the fever I have not been out of the house for weeks." Uncle Siegfried advised going directly to a sanatorium in Vienna or Davos. It was Franz who insisted on first going home to his parents, and Max Brod who brought him from Berlin to Prague, where he stayed for three weeks.

On April 7 Franz and Dora travelled from Prague to Wienerwald Sanatorium, 40 km southwest of Vienna. There he was tentatively diagnosed with laryngeal tuberculosis. Wienerwald was not set up to treat the condition and he was transferred to the university clinic in Vienna where the diagnosis of tuberculosis of the larynx was made official. On April 19 he was brought to Hoffmann Sanatorium in Kierling, northwest of the capital, and cared for by Robert Klopstock (who deferred his medical studies to attend to his friend), and Dora, in whose arms he succumbed. On May 11 Max Brod visited his best friend for the last time. Franz discouraged his parents from making the journey: "I am not at all a sight worth seeing," he wrote to them … "If you count in the fact that I am only allowed to speak in whispers and even that not too often, you will gladly postpone the visit." That he wrote "postpone" was likely not an indication that he expected to get better.

During the three-week layover at his parents' apartment, Kafka wrote his final story, "Josephine the Singer, or the Mouse Folk" ("Josefine die Sängerin, oder das Volk die Mäuse"). He asked Max to look into getting the story published. Brod gave the story to their mutual friend Otto Pick who used his influence with the editor-in-chief at *Prager Presse*, Prague's German language press, and the piece appeared in the Easter supplement on April 20, 1924. Josephine helped out a little in defraying costs at the Hoffmann Sanatorium.

The story of Josephine features a female protagonist (one of only two Kafka stories to do so) and an unnamed narrator who introduces the singer in the first sentence. Both are members of the mouse folk and although Josephine is the focus of the story, she doesn't have a speaking part. It is the narrator who speaks and he's full of contradictions. "Josephine the Singer …" recalls Franz Grillparzer's novella *The Poor Fiddler*—a story that had once meant a great deal to Kafka, though he also wrote of being "ashamed of it" … "for its defects" … "as though he had written it [himself]." In "Josephine," the narrator relates that the singer doesn't actually sing, but rather "pipes" or whistles and yet is able to turn this 'mere' piping or whistling into art through her unwavering faith in her artistry. The mouse singer, like Grillparzer's poor fiddler, are both defined by unwavering faith and love for their art, though in the assessment of the narrators in both stories their talent is questionable. Both stories also feature doubling: two protagonists who have something in common, like two sides of the same coin. And in both stories the artists are frail: The singer is little and weak; the fiddler is old, his instrument cracked. He's also branded with womanish weakness by the tough woman he loves, who calls him an "effeminate man." The poor fiddler and the mouse singer, as well as the narrators in the two stories, all parallel aspects of Franz as he saw himself.

Kafka's high standards for art, his ambivalence concerning the merit of much of his own, and his professed weaknesses and lack of musicality, are represented in his waffling throughout the story. Little Josephine is admired by her people, considered a treasure. With her rare singing ability, which no others in her community have displayed, she helps the mouse people tolerate their hard lives. Yet some of her people do not like her, and do not believe she's truly singing. As for Josephine herself, only a particular kind of audience appreciation is gratifying. 'Mere' admiration for her artistry is insufficient.

In "Josephine" Kafka also broaches the matter of the artist's responsibility for earning a living, a matter he likewise addresses in a short, dense, largely unknown, untitled piece he wrote not long before the mouse story—perhaps in a vein of exploration leading to the longer tale. Both pieces appear at the end of volume two of *Nachgelassene Schriften und Fragmente* (*Writings and Fragments from the Estate*) published by S. Fischer Verlag in 1992. The burden of earning a living, which preoccupied Kafka throughout his adult life, was only brought to fictional expression at the end of his life, in the perambulating tale of "Josephine," which he felt impelled to publish in order to cover costs at the sanatorium.

Josephine—as Kafka's mouthpiece—believes that she should not bear any responsibility for earning her keep: As an artist, she should be provided for, supported by her people. The mouse folk think differently, and refuse to exempt her from the work of earning a living: singing doesn't count as work. In retaliation for her people's contraposition, Josephine disappears just when she's set to perform. And this time, the narrator relates, she disappears for good.

At the end of the story, we're told that Josephine will soon be freed of her earthly torments: She will lose herself happily among the numberless host of her people's heroes, and, in the last line—redeemed and transfigured—will be forgotten, like all her brethren. This seems to be Kafka's pronouncement on the fate of the mouse artist, himself included, as he lay dying. In the penultimate paragraph, however, the narrator (wishfully or presciently) offers an alternate possibility: Perhaps, the mouse people, *in their wisdom, have placed Josephine's song on such a high pedestal, because in this way it could never be lost*; not forgotten.

In his final story, written when he, like Josephine, could hardly more than whistle or whisper, Kafka presented, in thick dialectical mode, through the dual-voices of Josephine and the narrator— questions about the life and work of the artist. What makes an artist? What constitutes art? Who is it for? How does it serve? What is the relationship of art to audience, art to legacy? What is the role of the nation in art, the relationship of the individual artist to his or her people / folk / nation / brethren? What is indicated by redemption / salvation / transcendent freedom / transfiguration? These words— chosen by different translators for last words ("gersteigerter Erlösung") in the last lines of Kafka's last story—sit like Gordian knots.

***

The story of Josephine has a personal resonance. In 2012, a year after I presented 'dead mentor' Franz Kafka's life and work for the final assignment in the Biography as Art course I was enrolled in, director Regine Kurek—artist and teacher par excellence—brought for me a gift from her summer vacation with her husband Jef. She looked slightly sheepish in handing me a thick, gold-foil-wrapped, circular piece of chocolate with *KAFKA* written on it in diagonal block letters, the grave face of the author stamped into a small *vesica piscis* shape on the side of the wrapper.

"This is for you," she said, "a souvenir from Prague. But somewhere along the way, probably while we were still in Prague, it seems to have been bitten into by a mouse! I only noticed when we got home and unpacked. I was considering *not* giving it to you—who wants to get a piece of chocolate that's been bitten into by a mouse?! But then I thought, better to give it anyway. It's the thought that counts. So here it is, mouse nibble and all." She laughed, handing me the bitten-into gift; I couldn't contain my surprise and delight.

"Regine," I exclaimed. "Thank you *so* much! This is amazing. Totally amazing. The last story Kafka wrote, at his parents' apartment in Prague, only a few months before he died, was 'Josefine die Sängerin, oder das Volk die Mäuse'—'Josephine the Singer, or the Mouse Folk.' A *mouse* story!" (Regine was not familiar with the story.) "This chocolate, bitten into by a mouse, feels like a gift personalized by Franz!"

"Well, so it is then," Regine said, looking pleased to see me pleased. "It's an almost perfect circle."

I didn't ask her what she meant by that. Regine, whose mother tongue is German, has a distinctive way of expressing things, and sometimes it's better to accept what a person says than to ask what is meant by it. And I was just happy in the moment to have a *KAFKA*-stamped gift of chocolate with a mouse nibble in it. I brought it home and put it in the vitrine in the kitchen: a keepsake, not to be eaten. The nibble has crumbled a bit over the years, but it's still there.

I've thought about Regine's words: "almost perfect circle." The circle is the perfect figure—seamless—a symbol for total symmetry, the soul, the divine. And if it's less than seamless, less than wholly circular—as in a round piece of chocolate that's been nibbled into by a mouse, it then becomes a whimsical indication of connection. A personalized blessing for an ongoing quest. Perfectly imperfect. Imperfectly perfect. I like to think that that's what Regine (and Kafka) meant.

Trumpeldor Cemetery

Tel Aviv

Two graves away from the resting
place of beloved Israeli singer,

Arik Einstein,
lies the grave of Kafka's lifelong

bosom-friend, Max Brod.
The singer's grave is easy to spot—

the monument is raised, its plinth
the site of gifts and votives.

A palm has risen from the foot
of Max Brod's resting place—

a tree that half-conceals the grave,
as if in close devotion.

What could be more naturally apt
for a friend like Max was to Franz?

The sky is stripped of wind today,
of everything but sheer blue sweep.

The scene: a palm and stone,
the rows, and we the only living

souls in sight. You're measuring
the steps between the singer's grave

and Brod's. After I recite a psalm,
I place a stone on the grave. In

your photo of me by the tree,
placing the stone beneath the name,

your shadow in the foreground
is a trace.

Rereading "Conversation with the Supplicant" in the Pandemic

DURING THE EARLY weeks of the COVID-19 lockdown, newly anxious and with extra at-home time to myself, I turned—for fictional reassurance—to my raft of favourite rereads. Among them: Joyce's *Dubliners*, (especially "Araby" and "The Dead"), Mann's *The Magic Mountain* (John E. Woods translation), and W.G. Sebald's *Vertigo*, a beguiling 'nonfiction-fiction' of interconnected stories told by an unnamed narrator, who, beset by a mysterious ailment, travels across Europe in the footsteps of Stendhal, Casanova, and Franz Kafka, finally to arrive at his own childhood home in the Bavarian Alps.

I was captivated yet again, by Sebald's wondrous way of obliquely weaving a story—in long, haunting, meticulously built sentences—particularly the chapter, "Dr. K. Takes the Waters at Riva," a poeticized retelling of Kafka's real-life trip to northern Italy in the fall of 1913. A trip that M. and I have retraced.

A stiff wind must have sprung up as I was reading—sequestered in the backyard—at the part where Dr. K., in Verona, enters the Church of Sant' Anastasia, and after resting in the cool shadowy interior, sets off again with conflicting feelings: both gratitude and distaste. My hair strafed the page at this specific passage and my thoughts shifted to an early Kafka story, also set in a church, also shadowed in distaste: "Conversation with the Supplicant"—a text I've found difficult, off-putting, and repeatedly set aside. So it struck me as strange that I set Sebald aside, mid-sentence, and went down to the basement to look for the supplicant story on my shelves. Stranger still, that in the following hour, my distaste for the story gave way, in concentrated rereading, to unexpected appreciation.

The story starts in a church, where the narrator goes—not to pray—but to watch a girl he's said to be in love with, from a distance, undisturbed. One day when the girl does not arrive, the narrator's attention turns to a young man—the supplicant of the title—who has thrown himself down and is clutching his head, sighing and beating his upturned palms noisily on the flagstone. The narrator is irritated by the outburst, at every point of his bodily compass, but only after hesitation, on several occasions of witnessing this same behaviour, does he bring himself to confront the young man. At this point, a conversation ensues.

The supplicant admits that he prays this way, ostentatiously, because he needs to make people look at him. He claims that he has only a fugitive awareness of things around him, and longs to catch a glimpse of things as they may have been before they showed themselves to him—a person full of constant and lonely dread. Through the strange, disjunctive roundabout of the conversation, the narrator comes to realize that he actually sympathizes with the supplicant's perception of a disjointed, unstable, and unsettling world. He comes to recognize in the supplicant a facet of his own unsettled self.

But—and this is the twist—the narrator's sympathy is only fully expressed, and then only received by the supplicant, when it's reversed. In other words, the narrator's true sentiment—his agreement with the other—is only affirmed through his denial of agreement. A kind of backward logic, or reverse psychology. This is the force of the story's closing pronouncement: *Admissions become most clear and unequivocal when one withdraws them.* Once the narrator withdraws his admission of fellow-feeling with the supplicant, the latter feels 'seen', and is pleased. He compliments the other on his fine complexion and nice tie (Kafka was something of a dandy), and goes on his way affirmed.

I closed the book on the story, which, this time, surprisingly (though perhaps not so surprisingly), I was able to read attentively to the end. And in the shadowy dankness of the basement, I experienced a sense of quiescence, not to say inertia. I felt somehow buoyed by a sense of the *possibility of contradiction*—elicited through being brought, by way of Sebald, to this early, convoluted, experimentally odd piece by Kafka.

Amid the strange turns and uncertainties of the pandemic—the restrictions, flattening curves, surges, waves and variants; the declarations, equivocations, scientific breakthroughs, and proliferation of conspiracy theories, I found myself enlivened by what Kafka's text now suggested to me across the decades; namely, that rupture can be revelatory in paradoxical ways; that individuals can catch slant glimpses of things as they might be/come; that adversity can be productively confronted through difficult conversation—when pursued. I found in Kafka's eccentric story: a backward clarity, fierce firmness, and stubborn hopefulness in the dialectics of reversals. A useful kind of thinking for the times.

Notes on Questing

Questing inhabits the realm of transformation. Humans might appear as birds, mammals, insects, even inanimate objects. Humans appear as humans too, and disappear.

The visible withdraws into the invisible, the unrevealed—into spaces of outward pause. This doesn't mean the quest is done.

The quester has a passion for the visible, for outlines and traces—in the light and in the dark. A passion for presence.

The quest is always returnable or retrievable, if not the field, then in the vat of imagination.

Questing is a form of hunting—beings pursuing being/s. Insatiably.

The quested can be alive or dead, living or enlivened. The enlivened are similar to the living, only more holy.

The quested dead can communicate, but prefer silence. Silence is communication by means other than speech.

Questing is purifiable, distillable. For what is purity but separating out—

Questers perform acts of devotion, often under cover.

Questing is both physical and metaphysical, personal and transpersonal. (This might seem obvious, but for the sake of clarity must be iterated.)

The quester who addresses the quested by name offers promise that neither will come to ill. Though no one can foretell what will happen upon meeting face-to-face, or face-to-trace.

A degree of guilt seems to be unavoidable for the serious quester: guilt of transgression, transference, appropriation, procrastination, vanity, excess, inadequacy.

On Translation

> *"Have you read Kafka?" Milan Kundera asks Carlos Fuentes.*
> *"Of course," Fuentes replies. "Kafka is the essential writer of the*
> *twentieth century. Without Kafka, we could never understand the*
> *age we live in."*
> *"Have you read him in German?" Kundera asks.*
> *"No," Fuentes says. "Only in Spanish."*
> *"Then you have not read Kafka."*

KUNDERA'S QUIP—INCLUDED in the K entry of Fuentes' entertaining
and provocative work, *This I Believe: An A to Z of Life*—is (of course)
an ironic verdict on the untranslatability of Kafka. Fuentes, not to
be topped by his friend's facetiousness, advances an exception, *Franz
Kafka, Obras Completas*, Galaxia Gutenberg / Cículo de Lectores,
Barcelonas—a translation by Miguel Saènz that Fuentes holds to be so
very splendid he doubts it could offend the excellence of Kafka in the
original, even Kundera himself.

There are better and lesser translations (of course), just as there are
better and lesser originals. Most readers of Kafka, possibly of Fuentes,
most likely of Kundera too, have to rely on translations in order to
read the authors' works. Without translations, and the essential work
of translators, the great (and lesser) works of literature would simply
not be available to the world of readers—a truism I bring to poke at
Kundera's drollery. Reading originals is the ideal, if one has the language.

My reading of Kafka is for the most part in English, in various
translations. I'm able to read the German, but I require the English
to properly negotiate Kafka's long, often breathless sentences,
complex syntax and layered indications. Translations bridge languages
and cultures, enrich sensibilities, make possible the broadening of
imagination—the very ground of empathy. Translating works and
reading works in translation are vital, vibrant connective engagements.
For many readers and writers—myself included—translations have
formed, transformed, and continue to form and transform, my frames
of literary reference, intimately, and at large.

Much has been made of the superiority of one translation over another. Michelle Woods, in *Kafka Translated: How Translators Have Shaped our Reading of Kafka*, devotes nearly 300 pages to focusing on four of Kafka's translators: the earliest translators, Milena Jesenská and Willa Muir (wife and partner-in-translation of Edwin Muir), and contemporary translators, Mark Harman and Michael Hofmann. Rather than adjudicating worth or superiority, however, Woods advocates a practice of "transreading": looking at how different translators approach the text, and how these differences point the reader to what is difficult, interesting and unusual in the author's use of language.

Margaret Jull Costa, British translator of Portuguese- and Spanish-language fiction and poetry—including works of José Saramago, Fernando Pessoa, Paulo Coelho and Javier Marías—takes a similar tack. In an interview with *The Paris Review* (Summer 2020, Issue 233), she alleges it's tricky to assert that translations need be renewed every generation or so, on grounds that language changes; that it's even vaguely insulting to hold, as some do, that translations grow obsolete, and best be replaced. We may have our preferences—Costa herself admits a preference for many older translations, including Helen Lowe-Porter's much maligned translations of Thomas Mann—but maintains that translations can co-exist. And by extrapolation, that a practice of what Woods has termed "transreading" can deepen appreciation of what is thorny, distinctive and extraordinary in favourite works. This I've found to be true in "transreading" Kafka.

Costa makes no distinction between writing and translating, and holds that translating is the closest possible praxis to textual analysis. Despite my modest experience, this rings true to me as well, having worked collaboratively with M. in translating Georg Mordechai Langer's poetry from Hebrew, a late Kafka text—via the lens of Hebrew—from German, and other assorted pieces.

In translating Langer's poems, the challenge was to be faithful to the tone, register, diction and content of the Hebrew originals while creating pieces that read as poems—not interlinear translations—in English. Achieving a poem in English sometimes required being slightly unfaithful to the Hebrew originals. Faithfulness is a struggle; although one wants the spaces between languages to be as small as possible, a translation creates a new text, a work that cannot be equivalent to the original. It's a bonus that we have a bilingual edition of Langer's poetry (*Songs and Poems of Love*, Guernica Editions, 2014; 2015). For those who can read both versions, the parallel presentation permits transparency, a certain intimacy, and shows that the translation of the poems is a close dialogue between the translators and the poet.

Prose translation is obviously also a dialogue between writer and translator, though perhaps a little less intimate, as attentiveness to sound and inner / metrical workings are less crucial to prose than to poetry. In translating Kafka's short late text, the starting point was Ilana Hammerman's translation of the original German into Hebrew; there was no English translation available (at the time) to refer to (had we wanted to). Every effort was made to maintain fidelity to Kafka's personal style—his transgressions, as Kundera would call them (in *Testaments Betrayed*): shifts in tense and mood, long sentences, abrupt turns and interpolations. I avoided eliding, simplifying, 'normalizing' for the sake of making the piece more 'readerly', more idiomatic in English. In Kafka it seems that ironic acknowledgement of non-understanding and/or misunderstanding are built in to the work.

In translating Langer's poems, M. and I collaborated closely, and through the work, experienced a kind of communion of spirit. We absorbed Langer's language—his tone, his voice, the difficult intimacy of his longing, and we empathized. Translating is reading as close as it gets. A translator might even feel 'twinned' with the writer. As close co-translators, M. and I also came to a fresh understanding of each other—how we approach a linguistic difficulty, where we converge, where we differ, how we complement each other in difference as well as similarity.

I rely on the work of various translators in reading Kafka: Willa and Edwin Muir, Eithne Wilkins and Ernst Kaiser, Mark Harman, Michael Hofmann, Breon Mitchell, Anthea Bell, Joyce Crick, Richard and Clara Winston, Malcolm Pasley, Joseph Kresh, Martin Greenberg and Hannah Arendt; my colleague Thor Polson, and others. At nineteen, Kafka famously wrote in a letter to his school friend Oskar Pollak that "a book must be the axe for the frozen sea within us"; not what we already know, not what fits into a preordained category and reinforces held beliefs, but that which arouses or jolts us into looking, thinking and feeling something different, unexpected, new. Kafka demanded, and created, the kind of work that is angled, edgy, atypical, penetrating, transformative.

A transformative experience that comes through reading an exceptional text in the original language may be the ideal. But without translations, the transformative experience would not be possible for readers who can't access the original. I cast back to my first reading of *The Metamorphosis*; I was slightly younger than Kafka when he wrote his "frozen sea" words to Oscar Pollak; an uninitiated teen, journeying on my own into world literature. The experience of reading Kafka's novella was mind-altering. I felt a zap of awe, astonishment, something akin to recognition that I could not articulate at the time, only feel—deeply. A powerful, enigmatic sense of truth piercing the fantastical real, and I was transported. Thanks to translation.

K. Under Erasure

He came to me and said
                    caw is

more than up-and-down
        unmusical
            movement

                Less absurd
                than
                gyre

        mind
    unwinding

its own desire.
        Don't we believe that

apprehending
a detail
                    is sufficient?

                economical also

Therefore once

            we apprehend
        the caw-caw,   then

Later

IN HIS ESSAY "The Composite Artist," included in *Language of Truth: Essays 2003-2020*, Salman Rushdie writes that the overcoming of monsters, desire for an idea of nobility, love of magic, need for quest, and addiction to story are perhaps what human beings have most in common. I can concur—especially on the points of love of magic (which I'd prefer to call love of stealth and timing), need for quest (particularly a quest that ventures beyond the limits of ordinary experience), and delight in story ("addiction" may be a stark designation, but it does capture the insatiable aspect of questing).

It is delight in story that connects us as language animals. And story, as pursuit, is as ongoing as human history, as unfinished, and for as long as we're on this planet, probably unfinishable. Kafka was acclimated to the latter—the unfinished, the unfinishable, the fragmentary. One can argue—as does Reiner Stach in the afterword to his selection of late Kafka fragments, *The Lost Writings*—that Kafka was a master fragmentarian who elevated the fragment to a bona fide literary form: in three unfinished novels, a number of nearly achieved stories, and scores of sketches, flashes and one-liners. Kafka often despaired of endings, even when he achieved them. He expressed displeasure with the endings of two of his most iconic stories, *The Metamorphosis* ("unreadable ending"), and *In the Penal Colony*, which he attempted to revise time and again, and gave up trying.

I empathize. What if a core question or conflict cannot be resolved satisfactorily, unsatisfactorily, or at all? What if the work itself resists? (Let's give it some autonomy.) 'Un-endedness' may be its way of saying, take me as I am, leave me be. Or leave me for later, which is where I've felt poised in the travel / pilgrimage part of my search for Franz: not finished and not in position to finish, though prepped with projections, questions, and a few contextual storyboards:

> **E. and M. later resume pursuit:** They visit K. places in the Czech Republic—that beautiful and gentle country. They travel to Hungary, Denmark, Switzerland, and return to Germany.

There's faith, after all, that the field can deepen the yield.

E. and M. stage a re-enactment (re-enactment implying identification)**:** E. reads K.'s parabolic story "Before the Law" aloud to M. at a hotel in Bodenbach-Tetschen (Podmokly-Děčín) on the Elbe (Labe), as in January 1915 Franz read the piece (to no great avail) to Felice. What might come of a gender role switch; E. taking the part of K. and M. taking the part of F.? Of revisiting hi/s/tory *in situ*—with a woman voicing "the Law"? And upon intoning the near-closing words, "a radiance streaming immortally from the door," what might transpire? Real and imaginary events merge libertinely in the human mind, including E.'s, and experience has led her to side with possibility for radical surprise.

E. visits the kibbutz that Kafka wrote to in the last months of his life, offering his services as an accountant. E. is certain she read this somewhere, but can't recall where … Perhaps this was the same kibbutz where she lived and worked as a teen during her gap year, where she read lines from *The Trial* aloud to the wide-eyed, blank-faced goats. Quite possibly, it was. A coincidence? How E. loves the scintillation of coincidence, its animating strangeness. Dora Diamant had connections to the Maletz family at the kibbutz. She visited them there after Kafka's death and left with them his hard-bristled hairbrush, intending to return, to retrieve it. She never did. What might come of reaching and touching the brush—one of Kafka's only personal items known to exist … Of holding it in hand and picturing the path to its past … What might a relic reveal …

When seeking in the field was interrupted by COVID-19, reading became the destination, a sort of dwelling place in and of itself. Reading had to suffice, and it does. "Art," after all, as James Woods puts it, instructively, in *How Fiction Works*, "is close to life," and "in certain art works [Kafka's among them] the otherness of the fictionalized form … has 'reality-power.'" Reading Kafka has always been real for me, always powerful, even when difficult. Probably especially then—when it challenges. Reading Kafka has a perpetual power—to move, provoke, penetrate, inspire—break, make and remake—into, and after, innumerable readings.

Yet having taken steps the author took; steps his ciphers, stand-ins, and characters also took; in seeing and feeling convergences of life and art on location, in company with M., in triangulation with 'atemporal-aspatial' Kafka, through signs, signals, messages, indications and 'visitations'—through these, the experience of reading has become heightened, deepened, 'lived into'. Questing has whetted the appetite for more. I've become compulsively recursive in my search. I can't settle.

On Falster

THE DAY AFTER the dissolution of his first engagement to Felice Bauer at the Askanischer Hof Hotel "tribunal" in Berlin, Franz Kafka travelled to Lübeck to unwind. He'd planned to continue his summer vacation in Gleschendorf by Lake Pönizter, 20 km northwest. Instead, he was persuaded by Ernst Weiss to join Weiss and his girlfriend, Hanni Bleschke (later the actress and writer Rahel Sansara), at a guesthouse in Marielyst on the Danish island of Falster. Weiss had advised Franz against Felice, whom he deemed had only business efficacy to recommend her, and was relieved to hear of the breakup. A physician, he might have been concerned for Kafka's emotional health in the wake of the costly split, but he was also a writer and could count on his friend's editorial help with the novel he was writing, *Der Kampf* (*The Struggle*), first published in 1916 and retitled *Franziska* in 1919—a title that bears Kafka's stamp.

Franz met up with Ernst and Hanni in Lübeck and the three travelled by ferry to Falster Island on July 13, 1914. He wrote in his diary of a "despairing first impression, the barrenness, the miserable house, the bad food with neither fruit nor vegetable, the quarrels between Weiss and Hanni," and impulsively gave notice that he'd be leaving the next day. In his characteristic flip-flop fashion, he "nevertheless stayed: I have put aside my apparent stubbornness," he wrote to Max Brod, "and eat almost nothing but meat (Kafka was largely committed to a vegetarian diet) … after terrible nights I wake early with open mouth and feeling my abused and punished body in the bed like something alien and disgusting" (a veritable Gregor Samsa). Despite the grumblings, he stayed on at Marielyst for ten days, the full duration of his vacation.

During his stay, he managed not only to help Weiss "correct" *Der Kampf,* but also to pen a sketch in his diary that seems to anticipate *The Trial* (which he began writing soon after returning to Prague); a long letter to his parents outlining his plans for his future in Berlin, sans Felice; and a postcard to Ottla in which he admitted to doing "fairly well. Every day the same lovely weather and the same swim on the same lovely beach." All in all, aside from the "abominable food, nothing but meat" and the bickering between Ernst and Hanni, Kafka must have enjoyed the stay on Falster, at least enough to be distracted from his recent tribulations.

In June 2022, after a two-year hiatus due to the coronavirus, M. and I resume the travel component of my Kafka quest—picking up from our 2016-trip to Germany, when our trek included a visit to Lübeck. Had we been able to take the ferry from Lübeck to Falster Island, I would have considered it—one of the pleasures of questing is retracing an actual path—but the Travemunde-Lübeck route to Denmark has long been discontinued. We opt to fly in to Copenhagen, take in a bit of the city, drive south to Falster Island, then return to Copenhagen for the night before continuing on to Tel Aviv.

Kafka wrote little of his passage to Marielyst Østersøbad—the name of the guesthouse on Falster. A diary entry reads: "Mysterious disappearance of a young man wearing a raincoat and hat and his mysterious reappearance in the carriage ride from Vaeggerloese to Marielyst." The young man in the raincoat was evidently more interesting to Franz than the passage itself, and Vaeggerloese, a transfer-point, is mentioned only by the way. A glance at a map shows Vaeggerloese to be an inland town, with no port. So the travellers had to have docked elsewhere on the island. Tracking the route will be part of our search.

A photo, likely taken by Hanni, shows Ernst and Franz in swim trunks, sitting side by side in front of the guesthouse—Ernst upright, beaming for the camera; Franz, hunched forward, smiling shyly. I'm hoping, as always, to experience the sensory reward of staying at the same place as Kafka, perhaps of tapping into some remnant of his presence there. But all I find of Marielyst Østersøbad is a brief Wikipedia entry (here paraphrased):

In 1872, a farmer by the name of Hans Jørgensen succeeded in draining his land following disastrous flooding on the island and built a new farmhouse that he named Marielyst for his wife Marie. In 1906, a lawyer named Frederik Graae bought the farmhouse and converted it into a guesthouse with twelve rooms. Pitched as a new beachside resort, Marielyst Østersøbad opened on July 28, 1906. Due to its popularity with national and international

*celebrities, additional accommodations were made available in
another nearby farmhouse, called Nørrevang.*

Marielyst Østersøbad may no longer be standing but Nørrevang
I do find online. The website shows a quaint inn with half-timber
accents and a thatched roof. Kafka mentions the "thatch" in his letter
to Max, so I'm feeling on-track. An email to the booking manager
confirms that Nørrevang, newly renovated earlier in 2022, stands on
the same ground as the original building. Expanded and renovated to
twenty-first century standards, she writes, it's essentially a replica. She
knows nothing of Franz Kafka's stay on Falster; in fact, she hasn't heard
of the author at all. No matter, I reserve a room at Nørrevang for the
night of June 28. From all indications, this is not where Kafka and
company stayed, but it has to be close by, and I'm confident more will
be revealed on location.

M. and I are scheduled to depart Toronto for Zürich—our transfer-
point to Copenhagen—on Sunday, June 26 at 6:20 pm. We arrive at the
airport four hours before departure, given 'post-pandemic' disruptions,
and don't end up departing until 9 pm—after having sat in the plane
for two hours, assured by the flight staff that the pilots will make up for
lost time and that we'll all be able to reach our connecting flights. This
sounds like passenger management to us. We don't expect the pilots
to make up for lost time, and they don't. We arrive in Zürich the next
morning too late to make our SAS connection and are rerouted to a
Swiss Air flight. A Swiss Air attendant assures us our luggage is "in the
system" and will arrive, with us, in Copenhagen.

In Copenhagen we stand for an hour and a half at the baggage
carousel, eyes on the chute, hoping against hope that our two big bags,
packed mostly with valuables for bringing to Tel Aviv, will soon tumble
into view. They don't, and we join the line of disgruntled others at the
Aviator baggage handling counter, submit a missing baggage report
form, and are told that we'll be notified of the delivery of our bags
to our hotel within 24-48 hours. We'll only be in Denmark for three
nights, and at three different hotels, one, the Nørrevang, on Falster. We
figure the best chance of a delivery will be on Wednesday the 29th, at
Hotel Admiral, after we return to Copenhagen. But seeing the scores

of unclaimed bags—many tagged *Rush* and *Priority*—stacked on the floor and on wagons and racks throughout the hall we're not feeling particularly optimistic.

I'm getting that vertiginous Kafkaesque feeling that our bags may have entered the oblivion of "the system," along with hundreds and hundreds of brethren bags. I try not to give in to the feeling—not to be disheartened at the very start of our first Kafka trip in over two years. I shut out worst-case-scenario thoughts as we exit the airport without our bags, and refrain from grumbling. M. is apparently feeling the same way. Silent and solemn, we walk over to the airport shuttle stop and board the complimentary shuttle to the car rental park where the kind folks at the Avis counter, who have also not heard of Kafka, brighten my spirits a little by informing us that he probably arrived on Falster at Gedser (which we learn is properly pronounced Gayzuh), or else Nykøbing. These are the only two ports on the island—Gedser, in the south, is closer to Germany; Nykøbing is bigger. I note the locations in my notebook, we collect the keys to our black VW T-Roc—a medium-sized hatchback that M. chose over a smaller model in order to accommodate our two large suitcases—and we begin our sojourn in Denmark with only our carry-ons, backpacks, the camera, and my computer in tow.

Fortunately, we've brought a change of clothes (including underwear) for just this eventuality. One has to count the small mercies. And the weather is lovely, Copenhagen more delightful than we've imagined: bright townhouses, cobblestone streets (more cyclists than drivers), canal-side restaurants and pubs buzzing with tourists and locals—no one wearing a COVID mask. The modern and postmodern, baroque and nouveau side by side, and an air of Nordic warmth. We take an evening walk in the historic harbour district of Nyhavn (which we learn is properly pronounced Newhaun), then retire to our slant-ceilinged hotel room overlooking the water. The slant reminds me of the attic room we had for our first stay at Hotel Gabrielli-Sandwirth during our Kafka-trip to Venice in 2019. The ceiling in that room had an even more angled slant, also a watery view from an awning window.

Next morning I'm feeling wonky. The toilet started flushing in the middle of the night and wouldn't be stopped. I let M. sleep, tried to fix it myself, failed, and lay there staring at the slanted ceiling in the dimness, listening to the water swirl. Again, I'm reminded of Hotel Gabrielli-Sandwirth—the night, on our second stay at the hotel, that we slept in the same room Kafka had slept in during his 1913-visit to Venice. I was awakened in the middle of the night there too, but by the sensation of breath in my face. Then a shadow, like a spectre listing above me near the ceiling. One doesn't imagine these things …

I tank up on coffee at breakfast, we stroll the streets beyond the harbour until the shops open at 9, make some necessary purchases at the NORMAL—which strikes us an odd name for a store that sells personal care products—then check out of the hotel and set off for Falster in our black VW T-Roc. We've resolved to embrace the way, enjoy the warm weather, and not mention the suitcases—at least not today.

Denmark is a country of islands, water and bridges. The under-two-hour drive south to Vaeggerloese—our stop on the way to Marielyst—is scenic, breathtaking in spots. Crossing the high cable-stayed bridge that spans Storstrømmen Sound and connects the small island of Farø to Falster is giddying for me. The bridge, I read on my cellphone, is 1,726 metres long, with suspension towers 95 meters high. The two diamond-shaped towers supporting the span rise and combine to a single point above the centre of the bridge. Gazing up from the passenger seat at the row of suspension cables as we pass under them, I have the swirling sensation of being flipped outside-in and out again—a kind of carry-over from the water episode of the night before. "Don't you dare look up," I warn M. "Keep your eyes on the road." He's doing just that.

We reach Vaeggerloese—a small sleepy burg—in the early afternoon. There's always a tingle of anticipation in approaching a K. location, even a place like Vaeggerloese that Kafka mentions only as passing through. I'm hoping to see the spot where he, Ernst, Hanni and the "mysterious young man in the raincoat" boarded the carriage to Marielyst Østersøbad. A station, a depot, or the remnant of one. But I've learned to temper my expectations, and M. has learned to be patient. He drives around the town, the neat residential streets. No downtown, no main street. No sign of a station or remnant of one, and no one to ask. A Romanesque Church towering like a fortress on the hilltop is the standout feature of the town.

It brings to mind the cathedral in the penultimate chapter of *The Trial*—how deserted it appeared to Josef K. upon entering, ostensibly to meet with a business associate, who doesn't show up. "Why don't we continue on to Marielyst, check in to the Nørrevang and have some lunch," M. says. "We'll feel better on a full stomach, and we can always come back." He's right, of course.

Marielyst is under four km from Vaeggerloese, a five-minute drive. It probably took half an hour or more to make the trip by carriage in 1914. We check in to Nørrevang—a three-star inn with five-star appeal. For me it's enough that the newly thatched roof matches the "thatch" that Kafka mentions in his letter to Max. It gives the place authentic country charm, stirs a little nostalgia for a past that might have been mine, if one thinks in those terms. Our room is basic—functional and spotless. We drop off our carry-ons and step out to explore. Everything about the Nørrevang is spotless—new, orderly and spanking clean. The giant beech tree bordering the street has to be the oldest living being on the grounds. Under its shade in the heat of the day, one almost feels its world weariness.

We get no sense of history in walking down Marielyst Strandvej— the main street in Marielyst. Most of the buildings are nondescript single-storey structures—clothing stores, a supermarket, a few restaurants and real estate offices—that all look to be of late twentieth century construction, or newer. We stop in at one of the restaurants, Larsen's Plads, hoping we'll be able to order a meal-size salad. The young woman at the bar kindly agrees to customize a salad for us and I ask her about the history of the town. Larsen's Plads, she tells us, dates back to 1919 (it doesn't look that old), but there are older buildings in town. She mentions a farmhouse on the strand road. I ask her if she knows how visitors from Germany came to Marielyst back in 1914. "Back then," she says, "they could only arrive by water. My grandmother grew up on the island and in her time visitors from Germany came by ferry to Gedser. From Gedser they took the train to Vaeggerloese and from Vaeggerloese they came to Marielyst by cart." Kafka called the "cart" a "carriage," but this is probably a matter of perception, or translation.

I'm feeling lucky to have met up with this young woman. She's helped us, just as we've been helped by women on trips past. She accommodates our salad request—Kafka himself didn't get a salad on Falster—and verifies the 1914 travel route. We'll be looking for the train station at Gedser and returning to Vaeggerloese. I thank her and ask her name. Names, I've found, have been indicative on this quest. "Julie," she says, and I smile. Another one of those little convergences that might not mean much yet brightens the way. Julie was Kafka's mother's name, also the name of his second fiancée. Two women who abided Franz, despite his eccentricities, contradictions and transgressions.

After lunch we walk down to Marielyst strand—touted for its white sands and virginal beauty. It's reminiscent of the strand at Graal-Müritz on the other shore of the Baltic, in Germany, where Kafka took his last vacation in 1923, and where we visited in 2016 on our way to Lübeck. The beach here is wilder and emptier than at Graal-Müritz. There are no big wicker recliners, no long pier, and no rides set up for children. Bathers have brought their own ground-covers, and are back and forth from beach to sea, everyone wearing a bathing suit. Unlike at Graal-Müritz where, in 2016, many of the bathers—parents and children alike—were suitless.

We find no farmhouse by the strand. Back at Nørrevang we ask the concierge if he knows anything about it. He's new to Marielyst and can't tell us anything about the history of the town. But he's keen to help and pulls up a Danish website that supplements the information I already have: *Marielyst Folk High School is an old half-timbered house that forms the beautiful foundation of the folk high school ... a little more than 200 metres from the Baltic Sea at one of Denmark's best beaches. In 1906 a farm was converted into a seaside hotel. The hotel closed in 1968 and from 1971 there has been a folk high school for senior citizens at Marielyst. In the 70s, a four-room wing was built, so that the school has a total of 60 rooms, all with their own shower and toilet. (A folk* high school, we learn, is a non-formal residential school that offers learning programs in almost any subject.) Marielyst Østersøbad is not mentioned by name, but the year 1906—when the farm was converted into a summer boarding house—indicates that the guesthouse where Kafka et al. stayed, and what is now the folk school building, are one and the same. This is probably the farmhouse that Julie referred to as well. The building, repurposed, is at Bøtøvej 2—an eight-minute walk from Hotel Nørrevang.

The street sign at Bøtøvej 2 reads Højskolen Marielyst and an arrow points the way to the former Marielyst Østersøbad. There's a paved road to a car park in front of the building now called just Marielyst, and the roof is no longer "thatch." But this is it.

The front door is unlocked. We enter and come to a small foyer. A large group of seniors are gathered in a dining hall to our left. "This is an old folks home now," M. says. "People live here. What do you expect to find?" "One never knows," I reply. "Let's go in and explore." M. is uneasy about exploring in what appears to be more of a home than a school and opts to wait in the foyer. I go in on my own. There's no front desk or concierge, no one to ask for information. I pass through a library and come to a long hallway displaying art that looks to be the work of the residents. I come to a small exercise room, then an anteroom that connects to the other end of the dining hall. There are old photos mounted on the wall; each one contributes a piece to the bigger picture. There's a photo of the farmer Hans Jørgensen sitting beside his wife Marie (a stalwart pair) and four others in front of their Marielyst farmhouse. There are photos of the guesthouse, Marielyst Østersøbad, photos of the strand, of Vaeggerloese, and a photo of Vaeggerloese station with a vehicle parked out front. It looks to be an early model car, not a carriage or cart as described by Kafka and Julie. But all three vehicles might have been in use. I'm feeling affirmed.

I bring M. in from the foyer to show him the photos: my findings. So he can't say we came here for nothing. And he wouldn't, not at this stage. We won't be locating a room that Kafka and Ernst and Hanni might have slept in, and the dining hall where too much meat was consumed for Franz's vegetarian palate is probably not the same room where the large group of seniors are now gathered. Or maybe it is. No matter. Wherever there's a building, there's a mash-up of the unsettled present and a multifarious past that's not fully gone. We've entered a place that belonged to Kafka's post-disengagement vacation—where he helped Ernst Weiss with his Franz-inflected novel; where he felt guilty enough at the "tribunal" in his breakup from Felice that the feeling became the amorphous nub of the novel he would soon start writing; where he wrote to friends, his sister, and his parents—sharing with the latter his plans for moving ahead with his life as a writer, on his own, in Berlin. That he seemed oblivious to the storm of imminent war is indicative of his general inwardness, his preoccupation with his own art and life above and beyond other realities. On August 2, a few hours into what would become the Great War, he wrote in his diary, "Germany has declared war on Russia.—Swimming in the afternoon." Soon enough he'd realize he'd have to regroup. He wouldn't be leaving his position at the Workers' Accident Insurance Institute; he wouldn't soon be relocating to Berlin, as planned on Falster.

No one sees us enter the Folk School and no one sees us leave. We head back to Nørrevang, get into the car and head south to Gedser—18 km on highway E55. Driving along the open road, fallow fields to the east and west, a large crow suddenly swoops down on my side of the car—hops, leaps and almost somersaults across the road in front of us. M. doesn't have time to think of braking or swerving. And I don't have time to pull up the camera. "A 'kavka'," we both shout out, meaning Kafka's avian namesake, but we've already passed him. Out of the blue and into the blue; we don't see where he's flown. "Wow," I say, "what do you make of that?" "It was weird," M. says, though he's not one to label a thing weird—with its suggestion of otherworldliness and etymology of destiny. "Maybe it was just a little comical hello," I say, and we leave it at that.

At Gedser—a burg even sleepier than Vaeggerloese—we park and get out to explore. I walk in the direction of the sign, Gedser Remise

(Gedser Depot), toward the port area. M. stays behind. The port, like the rest of the town, is quiet. There's no sign of any activity, though a company called Scandlines advertises ferry service between Gedser and Rostock, Germany. I walk north in the area and arrive at Gedser Remise, the site of the old train station, locked behind a chain-link fence. Train service, I learn, was closed in 2009 and Gedser Remise is a museum now. Opening hours are listed as Tuesday to Sunday, 11 - 16. It's Tuesday, close to 4 pm for our visit, but the place is deserted. I take photos through the fence, the glare of the sun in my face. Not one of the shots is great. I'm sorry we've missed the opportunity to see the museum pieces, also the opportunity to ride to Vaeggerloese; excursions by rail bus are offered on some days. Bus service apparently now connects Gedser with the main train station in Nykøbing. But I don't see any buses, or people waiting. Maybe services have been reduced for the summer. Gedser has the air of a place that was once a little greater.

We return to Vaeggerloese. This time round we see what we didn't see the first time: the level crossing signs and the train tracks— overgrown now with grass in spots.

We see the street sign Stationsvej and get out of the car to look for the station, but there's no station on 'Stationway Street'. "The station must have been taken down," M. says. "Otherwise this is where it would be." I'm not convinced. Things are not always as they appear where Kafka is involved, even peripherally. But there's no one out and about to ask. I see a woman through a large living room window, puttering about inside the house. We've had luck with windows before. I take a chance, approach the window, wave to get the woman's attention. She waves back, leaves the room and comes out a door on the side of the house.

"Hello," I say. "We're wondering if the Vaeggerloese train station is still standing." "It is," she says, but it's not a station anymore." "I thought so," I say. "There's a "Stationvej" road sign here, but no sign of a station building." "That's because the station is not on station street," she says, laughing. "It's down the road behind those trees." She points. "But it's a private house, a family live there now." "I understand," I say. "We just want to see the building." "If you like train stations," she says, "you can ride a rail bus from the station at Gedser. The station is a museum now but there are rail bus rides between Gedser and Vaerggerloese." She sounds pleased to inform me. "Yes, thank you," I say. "Thank you for letting us know." (There's no point in mentioning that I already know.) She nods, goes back into her house and I quickly scoot down the road behind the trees as M. watches on. I feel a bit like a trespasser and I'm hoping no one will come out of the former station building just as I'm snapping photos from the side. The building is a shadow of the station pictured in sepia on the wall at the Folk School. But there's a cart out front of what is now a family home that completes the connection.

It's been a full day. The sun will soon be setting; its minutes are flying into the dimming trees. "Let's turn in early tonight," I say as we get back in the car. "And get up early too. Let's watch the sun rise from the beach, walk with our feet in the sea. It'll be only us." "Maybe," M. says, "if the ghost of Kafka doesn't arrive in swim trunks." I smile. "What are the chances of that," I say.

We don't make it up before the sun. But we're at the strand by 5:15. The day is clear, already warm. And windy. We shed our shoes for beauty and walk in the water, in quiet. Not even the birds are out. The only structure on the beach is a retro-looking lookout booth—like something out of a screen-set in a Wes Anderson film. I photograph our long shadows on the strand. It seems to me no less pristine than it would have looked to Franz. He called it "lovely" in his letter to Ottla. I snap a shot of a little jelly sea creature, goggling at me out of his watery ghost face.

"Let's walk to the Folk School building from here," M. says. "The way Kafka would have walked. We'll trail him." That's what we do. One gets the sense that the sea and the beach and the warm summer air here did him some good. From the Folk School we walk back to Nørrevang, have breakfast, check out, and head back to Copenhagen.

Our last day in Denmark, at the fine Admiral Hotel, is overshadowed by the suitcases, which have not been delivered to us. We manage to get through to the Aviator baggage handling people and are invited to come to the airport at 4 p.m. to be met by an Aviator representative and admitted, by back passage, to the baggage claim hall to look for our bags. We arrive early and join a group of other travellers on the same mission. The others are luckier. We spend two hours in the baggage claim hall walking from pile to rack and back room to back room looking for our two suitcases—to no avail. The representative is kind, she tries to be helpful. "It would be good to purchase pink suitcases for your next flight," she says, "or a leopard skin design. That way your bags will stand out among the others in case they go missing again. Black is just too common." She's speaking only slightly tongue-in-cheek. "The post-COVID situation at airports, worldwide, is terrible.

Not only here in Copenhagen." This isn't much of a consolation. "It seems your suitcases never left Zürich," she says. "They will now be rerouted to Tel Aviv. You are in the system." And with these words I feel the hovering presence of Franz.

I've been finding my form as we go—by rite of passage, trial and error, serendipitous encounter, hunch and imagination. Things are indeterminate, inevitably incomplete. Events and objects are not so much events and objects, in and of themselves, but rather concatenations. One event or thing leading to, linking, and becoming another. Everything in process. Questing, like writing, a matter of becoming.

We arrive in Tel Aviv on June 30, without our two suitcases. I've been wearing the same black jumper for four days, washing and changing my T-shirts and underwear as we go. M. has more tolerance for wearing the same garment day in and out than I do. It'll be a while before I wear that black jumper again, though it bears the air of a Kafkaesque adventure. Two weeks into our stay in Tel Aviv, we find out that we are no longer "in the system" and we have no idea where our bags have gone to. I buy a few new pieces of clothing. M. is holding out with the few pieces he's brought. Out of desperation more than anything else, he decides to go to the airport and look to see if our suitcases were rerouted to Tel Aviv after all, though we've received no word to this effect.

At the airport he meets up with a similar scene to the one in Copenhagen. Hundreds and hundreds of unclaimed bags stacked in the baggage claim hall. He phones me from the taxi on the way back. I'm leery of asking him if he found our bags but he waits to let me ask. "Were they there?" "Yes," he says, "both of them, together and intact, waiting for me to arrive." "A miracle," I say. "Yes," he says, "I guess you could call it that, and Kafka probably had nothing to do with it." I'm not so sure about that. What do we know about the way these things work …

Josef K.'s Mother Submits Her Report on the Trial

"MY DEAR ONE has been arrested on suspicion of something criminal—how can that be? Josef was always an excellent son, a model student, upright citizen, much-respected at the bank … Hasn't he been the president there for years? His guardian, Karl, brother of my late dear husband Herman, rang to tell me the shocking news, said he'd never known the court to be this unforthcoming. Secretive was the word. Karl, I responded, you've resided in the countryside for over twenty years! How could you know the ways of the city courts? And if this is a criminal case, how can it be that Josef is free to come and go and work and live at home—although he's under surveillance by the Office of Prosecution and has to appear before a court commission? But not at the Palace of Justice, no! At some dark room in the suburbs! "It all sounds laughable," Karl said. "It would be, if it weren't the truth. And Josef wanted to represent himself, imagine that!" Karl advised good legal help and recommended his old friend Huld, *a poor man's lawyer* he hadn't seen in years. "*One can't assume the best in trials like these,*" he added gravely.

"Good Lord, dear Karl," I said. "How can you be so leery? Josef is surely guiltless, this is all a great mistake!" "Well," Karl said, "it seems that way, but what do we really know … of the company Josef keeps these days, how he spends his hours after work … He could, dear Sister, have another side. And when did he visit you last?" he asked, as if to press a point. "Didn't he promise to come each year for his birthday? It must be three years now since he gave his word." "Yes," I said, "that's true but he's been so busy these many months, and being the president at the bank, has had to travel for work." Karl corrected me here, saying: "Dear Sister, you're mistaken. Josef was never president. It was the president himself who told me yesterday, in confidence, that he'd spoken with Josef the day before in the course of a business meeting. That took our lad off-guard. The president said he thought he'd seen our Josef the night before—with public prosecutor Hasterer—the two in close-knit conversation *walking arm in arm*! And to make it hard to refute, he named the location—*near the fountain by the church.* Seriously, he told me, had he come upon a *mirage, he couldn't have been more astonished.* Josef, unprepared for this, attested to a *friendship.* Even going so far as to call it a *pledge of brotherhood!* I must admit I never thought of Josef in that light, but one can understand—in light of the Law and societal norms, why he was arrested in his bed and put on trial. A high financial officer at the bank must be above reproach, not only in matters of finance. He should have married that nice young woman—Frieda, was it? Felice? That would have stanched the doubts, or at least reduced them. He might have averted this dreadful mess, which doesn't augur well for the family either!"

"Karl," I said. "What are you saying? What do you mean?" "I might have attempted to intervene," he said, ignoring my questions, "but *trials like this are lost from the start.* It may be unjust, I know, but it is what it is." Just then as I wanted to hear no more, as I yearned to give dear Karl *two loud slaps on his pale round cheeks, a sound like breaking china came from the hall* outside the door. "What a lucky break," I said to myself and slammed the receiver down. How could I, a mother, bear another word of that *slander.* "Oh, Karl," I said to myself alone, "such muck. Oh, Josef, Oh, Josef …"

Concern for Soul Consumes Me

In the northern garden
dwell two tall
catalpa trees.
Their large and heart-
shaped pointy leaves, downy
undersides—soft as fontanelles.
They've let the spotted
red-capped woodpecker in.

Form is the polar opposite of chaos,
wrote Roberto B.
I take release from this and that

the dead, he said, yes even *the dead*
are being developed.
Eventually, by this conception, everyone
will be among the co-
developed dead.

Concern for soul consumes me.
I sit in the northern garden—
in the hazy
shady shape of it
and follow my steady breath—born
as it's being breathed, it seems. Streaming
so organically,
it can't be pre-constructed.

Invisible and thin and free,
as baffling as Kafka—
whose rendering of difficult things
was easier for him, it seems to me,
than birthing breath.
   Will teachers of any persuasion contravene me?

Not the two catalpa trees.
Not the spotted woodpecker. Not his crimson cap.

Notes

Before the Door: riffs on Kafka's short story "Before the Law" ("Vor dem Gesetz"), written in December 1914; first published in the 1915 New Year's edition of the independent Jewish weekly *Selbstwehr*, then in 1919 as part of the collection *A Country Doctor* and posthumously in 1925 as part of the penultimate chapter of *The Trial*.

Kafka's Death House: Pg. 18, "The old apparatus reportedly made a huge racket and drained the village's electrical reserves ..."; Kathi Diamant (no relation to Dora) relates this anecdote in her biography of Dora Diamant, *Kafka's Last Love* (2003:101).
Pg. 19 and 20, "Kill me," he's said to have commanded his friend, "or you're a murderer." Kafka's words to Robert Klopstock told to Max Brod are related in *Franz Kafka: A Biography* (1995:210); as is the astonishing item: "When we got back to the house of mourning in Franz's home on Old Town Square, we saw that the great clock on the Town Hall had stopped at four o'clock"; the hour that Kafka's coffin was placed in the grave (1995:209).

Paging Kafka's Elegist: Pg. 36, "So he was trying me out when he asked me some time ago, with every appearance of innocence, how do you count in Hebrew..." Max Brod notes Kafka's penchant for secretiveness in *Franz Kafka: A Biography* (1995:163).
Pg. 37, "In 1939 Jiří escaped Prague for Palestine along the Danube-to-Istanbul route. (Max Brod also escaped Prague for Palestine—on March 15, 1939, on the last train before the borders were closed—carrying most of Kafka's manuscripts in his suitcase.)" He settled in Tel Aviv where he kept the collection in his apartment, as well as in safe deposit boxes in Israel and Switzerland. In a 1961 will, he bequeathed the collection to his long-time secretary Esther Hoffe, asking that his literary estate be placed, "at Esther's discretion with the library of the Hebrew University of Jerusalem (renamed the National Library of Israel), or at the Municipal Library in Tel Aviv, or another public archive in Israel or abroad." It appears that Brod intended Esther to have the papers (where he could access them)

in his lifetime and upon his death that they be deposited in a public archive, preferably in Israel. After Brod died in 1968, Esther Hoffe chose not to carry out the terms of his will and in 1988 sold the manuscript of *The Trial*. It was auctioned at Sotheby's for 3.5 million German marks and is held in a bunker at the German Literature Archive in Marbach, Germany. Esther willed the rest of the collection to her daughters, Eva and Ruth, and when she died in 2007, the National Library of Israel, represented by lawyer Meir Heller, sued the Hoffes for possession of the manuscripts, contesting that they had betrayed Max Brod's will. Heller, on behalf of the National Library, maintained that the Kafka papers, in accordance with Brod's will, and in accordance with his judgement that Kafka's writings are treasures of Jewish culture and knowledge, must be bequeathed to the National Library of Israel, and without a shekel of compensation to the Hoffes. The legal battle raged for nine years, locally—at family and district courts, nationally, at the Supreme Court, and internationally, with a powerful bid for the installation of the Kafka manuscripts at the German Literature Archive in Marbach, Germany. On August 7, 2016, Israel's Supreme Court issued its unappealable decision: The Brod literary estate, including Kafka's manuscripts, would be deposited at the National Library of Israel, and Eva Hoffe (Ruth had passed) would not receive a shekel in return. On May 21, 2019, following extensive cataloguing, restoration and digitization, the National Library of Israel announced the Franz Kafka Collection online: including three different draft versions of the early story, "Wedding Preparations in the Country," travel journals, notebooks, letters, drawings, and a notebook in which Kafka practised Hebrew: https://www.nli.org.il/en/discover/literature-and-poetry/authors/franz-kafka.

The Bodleian Library in Oxford holds the majority of Franz Kafka's papers, including the manuscripts of *The Castle*, *Amerika*, "The Judgement," *The Metamorphosis*, "A Hunger Artist," and others. Following an appeal by Kafka's heirs, Max Brod was forced to hand over most of the materials to them in 1962; they thus found their way to England. The long legal saga surrounding the fate of Brod's literary estate, including Kafka's works, is grippingly told by Benjamin Balint in his 2018 book, *Kafka's Last Trial: The Strange Case of a Literary Legacy*. Pg. 38, "It soon became plain that these were intensely personal pieces.

Poems of passion, spirituality, longing, loneliness, and unreciprocated homo-romantic love; written male to male." In an essay titled "Coming Out of the Hasidic Closet: Jiří Mordechai Langer (1894-1943) and the Fashioning of Homosexual-Jewish Identity," published in the *Jewish Quarterly Review*, Vol. 101, No. 2 (Spring 2011:189-201), pioneering LGBT historian Shaun Jacob Halper takes up the question of how Langer used sexological and psychological knowledge to articulate a specific Jewish identity; also the question of why homosexuality became for Langer a Jewish question. Halper focuses predominantly on *Die Erotik der Kabbala* (reissued by Neu Isenberg, 2006; available only in German), Langer's first book and comprehensive personal statement on sexuality and Judaism, yet notes that the evidence for Langer's homosexuality, in addition to *Die Erotik der Kabbala*, comes from his Hebrew poetry and correspondence. Halper's findings, in some ways, dovetail with M.'s and mine, but I did not come across Halper's article until fall of 2012, a full year after M. and I had taken up our own translation of Langer's poems, by which time the discovery of the homo-romantic content was long behind us.

Pg. 44, "Michael Mirolla, himself a Kafka enthusiast, was keen on having the first English translation of Langer's elegy to Kafka and Langer's prose piece, "Something about Kafka," published with Guernica." Reiner Stach's collection of short pieces on Kafka, *Is that Kafka? 99 Finds*, contains an alternate translation of Langer's "Something about Kafka," but it was published in 2016 (pages 243-246); that is, after M.'s and mine, and with no credit to the translator from the original Hebrew.

Kafka-in-Between: Pg. 50, "… tap the veiled 'tremendous world' he said he had in his head." Kafka writes of the "tremendous world" he has in his head in his diary entry of June 21, 1913. "Kafka, if he knew, would be aggrieved: "'I can believe that.'" I am mimicking Kafka's repeated use of this expression in *The Castle*—in Chapter 2, titled Barnabas; in Chapter 6, titled Second Conversation with the Landlady; and in Chapter 23 in Bürgel's speech.

Pg. 51, "Biographer Rainer Stach has deemed the work 'no more than a footnote in literary history'"; in *Kafka: The Early Years* (2017:289).

Two Short Talks: Pg. 69, "They look like prose—set in narrow, justified columns …" My reading of *Short Talks* is based on the 1992 edition of Anne Carson's first book of poems, in which the prose poems are all fully justified. The 2014 edition, issued on the occasion of Brick Books 40th anniversary, does not preserve the original fully justified format, as noted by then-editor Kitty Lewis on the Brick Books website, where this essay first appeared.

What More Is There to Say of Hearts: Pg 84, inspired by *Sculpture Garden at Chotek Park*, gouache on black art paper, 10" x 12", by Women's Association of Canada studio artist, Barbara Feith (1927-2021).

Back at the Office: Pg. 86, "I was thrilled to be staying in the room where Kafka had worked as a respected civil servant for fourteen years—longer than he lived and wrote in any of his many dwelling places around town." The Kafka family moved frequently, as their financial circumstances improved.
1883 - 1885: Franz Kafka was born in a two-storey house at the corner of Maiselgasse (Maislova) and Karpfergasse (Karpova), bordering the then-existant Jewish ghetto. Only the portal is now remaining at what is now Náměstí Franze Kafky 3, Staré Město.
1885 - 1887: The Kafkas lived at 56 Wenceslas Square (Václavské Náměsti); the building was destroyed by fire in 1897.
1887 - 1889: The Kafkas lived at the Sixt-House, 2 Zeltnergasse (Celetná 2, Staré Město).
1889 - 1896: The Kafkas lived at the gabled and graffitied House Zur Minute (Staroměstské Náměsti 2, Staré Město).
1896 - 1907: The Kafkas lived at the House of the Three Kings (Zu den drei Königen), 3 Zeltnergasse (Celetná 3, Staré Město).
1907 - 1913: The Kafkas lived at the House "Of the Ship" (Zum Schiff) on the former Niklasstrasse (36 Pařížka, Staré Město); the building was destroyed at the end of World War Two. The InterContinental Hotel now stands at this location.
From November 1913: The Kafkas lived on the top floor of the Oppelt House on Old Town Square (Staroměstské Náměsti 5, Staré Město); the

building was heavily damaged in World War Two and restored after the war but without the top floor, which had housed the Kafkas' apartment.

From summer of 1914 - March 1915: Franz rented an apartment at 10 Bilekgasse (Bilkóva 10).

From March 1915 - February 1917: Franz rented an apartment at 16 Langegasse (Dlouhá16).

From autumn of 1916 - spring 1917: Franz used his sister Ottla's rented house at 22 Alchemistengasse in the Prague Castle-complex (Zlatá Ulička 22) as a retreat for writing. Now Staroměstské Náměsti 2, Staré Město.

From March - August 1917: Franz rented a two-room flat at the Schönborn Palace on the Kleinseitner / Narrow Embankment. Now the American Embassy building (Tržiště15, Malá Strana).

Pg. 87, "… writing and the office cannot be reconciled." Kafka writes this in a letter to Felice, June 26, 1913.

In Berlin: Pg. 96, "… he 'hated Vienna,' that 'decaying mammoth village'—as he put it in a letter of April 8, 1914"; to Grete Bloch.

Pg. 104, "… the self-knowledge of a man of thirty who for deep-seated reasons (he cannot specify what they are) has several times been close to madness." In his long letter of February 23-24, 1913 to Felice, Kafka points to a "deep-seated reason" in revealing his 'inexplicable' attraction to a Jewish man he has known from his youth, son of a local shopkeeper, once married but no longer, who works in his parents' shop and "when it's cold he stands behind the book-covered door, and through the gaps in the books, mostly obscene, he gazes out onto the street." At length, he builds up to a telling question: "He walked along ahead of me just as I remember him as a young man … His back is remarkably broad, and his walk so peculiar and stiff that one cannot tell whether he is merely stiff or actually deformed; in any case, he is very bony and his lower jaw is enormous. Well, can you imagine, dearest [Franz dares Felice to imagine], *tell me!* [he accentuates the imperative with italics], what made me follow this man greedily along Zeltnergasse, turn off behind him into the Graben, and with infinite pleasure watch him?" Kafka comes daringly close in this passage to disclosing to Felice the secret of his "greedy … infinite pleasure"—his dangerous (at the time) homoerotic attraction. Unfortunately, most of Felice's letters to Franz, including her response to this one, were not preserved. She may have understood the intimation, but it's fairly safe to surmise that she waved it off. Despite any doubts she had concerning her suitor, and she did have doubts, she was clearly enamoured enough to keep up the connection.

In his poeticized version of Kafka's 1913-trip to northern Italy, "Dr K. Takes the Waters at Riva," in his novel *Vertigo*, W.G. Sebald's narrator intimates that Kafka's "deep-seated" problem with love was due to a secret desire for men. Carol Angier, in her biography of Sebald, *Speak, Silence* (2021:331), contends that "Kafka's problem with love was almost certainly different," though she does not elaborate.

K.: Pg. 115, This poem was written in 2011 after our stay at the Askanischer Hof Hotel at 53 Kurfürstendamm, when I was holding to the belief that I had perhaps sat at the desk Kafka had sat.

Mary Lou Paints the Little House on Her iPad: Pg. 126, "She gives it / a greyish roof, no windows. Bright leek-green front door." This piece was prompted by an iPad painting created on location by Women's Art Association of Canada studio artist, Mary Lou Payzant.

Franz Among the Animals: Pg. 139, "… even claiming mendaciously to Max that "his will is not directed to writing"; in a letter dated November 24, 1917.

Surfacing Behaviour: Pg. 145, "*Lay / naked by the pond, he wrote, rode his uncle's motorcycle, / herded cows and goats, played quoits; fell for a shortsighted / girl by way of her fat foreshortened legs, and went to temple*"; lines paraphrased from Franz's letter to Max, sent mid-August 1907 from Triesch (in *Letters to Friends, Family and Editors*).

M. and I were in Třešt on August 17, 2017, the same day we were in Siřem.

The Mammoth Village & Gmünd: Pg. 146, "… Collis's shimmery idea of picking up where Webb left off—to write his own Kropotkin poems "as a gift to the unwritten"; (Collis, 2018:50).

Pg. 146, "In March 2019, M., my (still sometimes) reluctant helpmate and I return to Vienna—the city Franz called 'that decaying mammoth village'"; written in a letter to Grete Bloch, April 8, 1914 (contained in *Letters to Felice*).

Pg. 148, "Franz Grillparzer was one of four authors Kafka named as his 'true blood-relations'. (Dostoevsky, Kleist and Flaubert were the others.)"; written in a letter to Felice, September 2, 1913.

Merano, 1920 / 2019: Pgs. 178-179, The italicized passages are paraphrased from Kafka's letters to Milena from Merano (in *Letters to Milena*).

Franz of the Magic: Pg. 191, "Both struggled with sexual ambivalence and guilt." Anthony Heilbut's groundbreaking 1996 biography, *Thomas Mann: Eros and Literature*, focuses on Mann's sexuality as reflected in his life and work. Homoerotic obsession is at the heart of his 1912 novella, *Death in Venice*, and thematic in *The Magic Mountain*. He explicitly recorded his personal obsessions in his diaries, which he was frantic to retrieve from Munich in wake of his exile in Switzerland in the early 1930s, lest the Nazis get hold of them and plot his ruin. First published in 1975, twenty years after his death, Mann's diaries are the primary source for revelations concerning the depth of his obsession with men, even with his own son, Klaus. Mann's marriage allowed him, with tacit understanding from his wife Katja, to preserve the guise of a bourgeois paterfamilias in the context of his ongoing homosexual preoccupations. It might be argued that Kafka, too, to the extent that he pursued marriage, sought its cover for bourgeois respectability; in his letters to Felice, her father Carl Bauer, Milena, and Max Brod, Kafka was open about his aversion to marital (and non-marital) sex. Indications of homoerotic attraction pepper his fiction as well. He, like Mann was often frantically guilt- and angst-ridden, though unlike Mann, was never explicit about the "deep-seated" root of his angst in his 'private' writing.

A Circle: Pg. 243, "Kafka lived in Berlin from September 1923 till March 1924 …" Kafka lived at three residences during his six months in Berlin: at 8 Miquelstrasse in the suburb of Steglitz; at 13 Grunewald, also in Steglitz, where he had two modest rooms in a villa that he nonetheless praised in letters to family and friends for exceptional beauty. This house is still standing, well-maintained, and Kafka's stay is commemorated with a bronze plaque at the entrance. In February 1924 Kafka (under a pseudonym) and Dora rented the ground floor in the house of poet Carl Busse's widow, Paula Busse, at 25-6 Heidestrasse in Zehlendorf. Heidestrasse was renamed Busseallee in honour of Carl Busse in 1931; https://en.wikipedia.org/wiki/Carl_Hermann_Busse "The story of Josephine features a female central character—one of only two Kafka stories to do so"; the other is "A Little Woman" ("Eine kleine Frau"), a short piece based on the landlady of the house on Miquelstrasse and published, together with "Josefine …" in the Easter supplement of Prager Tagblatt and included in *A Hunger Artist*.

Rereading "Conversation with the Supplicant" in the Pandemic: Pg. 251, "… a text I've found difficult, off-putting, and repeatedly set aside." After "Conversation with the Supplicant" and "Conversations with a Drunk," both extracted from *Description of a Struggle*, were published in *Hyperion* in 1909 with Max Brod's encouragement, Kafka expressed aversion for the pieces. In a letter to Brod, August 7, 1912, he wrote: "Is not going unpublished not far less bad than this damnable forcing oneself?" Almost always highly self-critical, Kafka maintained that what he had written so far was insufficient for a book, and even "bad."

On Translation: Pg. 256, "'Have you read Kafka?'" Milan Kundera asks Carlos Fuentes …" This conversation is paraphrased from the opening of Fuentes' entry on Kafka in *This I Believe: An A to Z of Life* (2005:155).

K. Under Erasure: Pg. 260, Informed by Kafka's 1920 short story "The Top" ("Der Kreisel").

Later: Pg. 261: "In his essay 'The Composite Artist,' Salman Rushdie writes …" in *Languages of Truth, Essays 2003-2020*, (2021:287). "*In the Penal Colony*, which he attempted to revise …" In *Kafka: A Writer's Life*, Joachim Unseld writes that in a non-extant letter from

October 1916 Kurt Wolff must have expressed his deep dislike for In the Penal Colony; his initial rejection of the novella, which he apparently clothed in the word "painful," was met with a forceful reply in a letter from Kafka: "Your criticism of the painful element accords completely with my opinion, but I feel the same way about almost everything I have written ... I need only add that the painfulness is not peculiar to [this story] alone but that our times in general and my own time as well have also been painful and continue to be ..." (1994:161). Kafka evidently also alienated the audience at the Hans Goltz Gallery in Munich where he read In the *Penal Colony* on November 10, 1916. One reviewer characterized Kafka as a "sensualist of terror"; Kafka himself considered the Munich appearance a complete failure and it remained his only public reading outside of Prague. Despite any initial misgivings, Wolff did, however, publish the novella, in November 1919.

"Dora Diamant had connections to a certain Maletz family at the kibbutz ..." This is related by Kathi Diamant, who visited the Maletz family and included a photograph of Kafka's hairbrush—evidently still in the Maletz family's possession—in her book, *Kafka's Last Love* (2003:183).

Pg. 262: "Art," after all, as critic James Woods puts it in *How Fiction Works*, "is close to life" (2018:xix).

On Falster: Pg. 264: "*Der Kampf* (*The Struggle*), first published in 1916 and retitled *Franziska* in 1919—a title that bears Kafka's stamp." Pushkin Press of London published an English translation by Anthea Bell in 2008.

Josef K.'s Mother Submits Her Report on the Trial: The italicized words in this piece are drawn from the main text of *The Trial*, particularly chapter six, "The Uncle, Leni," and from the fragments, "Journey to His Mother" and "Public Prosecutor"—not included in the body of the novel. The word "slander" at the end of the piece recalls the opening words of the novel: "Someone must have slandered Josef K. ..." This piece, what I would call an ekphrastic fiction, is a kind of 'picking up where the author left off—in the spirit of what Stephen

Collis refers to in his memoir of friendship with Phyllis Webb, *Almost Islands*. See "The Mammoth Village & Gmünd."

Concern for Soul Consumes Me: Italicized lines are from the posthumous collection, *Notes Without A Text*, by Roberto Bazlen (1902-1965); translation by Alex Andriesse; introduction by Roberto Calasso, Dublin: Dalkey Archive Press, 2019:164; 204. Bazlen published none of his own writings during his lifetime but was an advisor to Italian publishing houses, a translator of Freud and Jung, and a deep reader of Franz Kafka.

Key Dates and Events in Franz Kafka's Life

1883 – July 3: Franz Kafka is born in Prague, Kingdom of Bohemia, Austro-Hungarian Empire. First child of Hermann Kafka (1852 - 1931) and Julie Löwy Kafka (1856 - 1934). Two brothers, Georg (1885 - 1886) and Heinrich (1887 - 1888) die in infancy. Three sisters, Gabriele (Elli) (1889 - 1941), Valerie (Valli (1890 - 1942), and Ottilie (Ottla) (1892 - 1943) perish in the Nazi camps.

1889 - 1993 – Attends primary school at the German School for Boys (Deutsche Knabenschule) on Fleischmarktgasse (Masná 11/13).

1893 - 1897 – Attends grammar school at the elite German National Humanistic Gymnasium (Altstädter Deutsches Gymnasium) located in the Kinsky Palace, Old Town Square (Altstädter Ring).

1896 – June 13: Bar Mitzvah, Pinkassynagoge (Pinkas Synagogue), described as "Confirmation" in the family invitation.

1899 - 1903 – Early writings (destroyed).

1901 – June: Graduates from Gymnasium. Spends summer with maternal Uncle Siegfried at North Sea resorts on the German islands of Helgoland and Norderney. November: Begins studies at the German Karl Ferdinand University, Prague. Joins friend, Hugo Bergmann, at the Chemical Institute for two weeks before switching to Law.

1902 – October 23: Meets Max Brod, fellow law student at the Charles University Reading and Lecture Hall for German Students (Lese- und Redehalle der Deutschen Studenten). December: Earliest surviving work of fiction, "Shamefaced Lanky and Impure in Heart" ("Der Unredliche in seinem Herzen"), is included in a letter to school friend Oskar Pollak.

1903 – Summer: Begins his 'career' as a health enthusiast with a stay at Dr. Lahmann's Weisser Hirsch Sanatorium near Dresden.

1904 – Begins writing *Description of a Struggle* (*Beschreibung eines Kampfes*).

1905 – August 3-27: Vacations at Dr. Ludwig Schweinburg's sanatorium in Zuckmantel, Moravian Silesia; mysterious encounter with a person referred to only as 'B'. November 7: Takes first of three law exams, Austrian Civil and Criminal Law.

1906 – March 16: Takes second law exam, Constitutional and International Law. June 13: Takes third exam, Roman, German and canon law. June 18: Awarded doctor of laws degree. July 23 -August 29: Vacations at Zuckmantel; reunites with 'B'. September: Begins one-year mandatory clerking in provincial high court (Landesgericht) and criminal court (Strafgericht). Begins writing *Wedding Preparations in the Country (Hochzeitvorbereitungen auf dem Lande)*. Continues working on the manuscript intermittently until 1909.

1907 – August: Vacations in Triesch at the home of Uncle Siegfried. Meets nineteen-year-old Hedwig Weiler from Vienna; their correspondence continues for two years. October 1: Starts work at the Prague branch office of the privately owned Italian insurance company Assicurazioni Generali, headquartered in Trieste.

1908 – March: First publication of eight short prose pieces in bimonthly review *Hyperion*.

July 15: Quits Assicurazioni Generali. July 30: Joins semi-state-owned Workers' Accident Insurance Institute for the Kingdom of Bohemia in Prague (Arbeiter-Unfall-Versicherung-Anstalt für Königreich Böhmen in Prag) where he works (initially in the statistical and claims department) until retirement on June 30, 1922.

1909 – March: Two fragments from *Description of a Struggle* published in *Hyperion*: "Conversation with a Supplicant" ("Gespräch mit dem Beter") and "Conversation with a Drunk" ("Gespräch mit dem Betrunkenen"). September 4 -14: Travels with Max Brod and Brod's brother, Otto, to Riva on Lake Garda. Side-trip to Brescia. Writes "The Aeroplanes at Bresica" ("Die Aeroplane in Brescia"); published in daily paper *Bohemia*, September 29.

1910 – Begins keeping a diary in earnest: composite of dated entries, fragments, sketches for stories. May: Promoted to *Concipist* (junior legal adviser). October: Travels with Max and Otto Brod to Paris; an outbreak of boils forces him back to Prague after a week.

1911 – August: Travels with Max to Zürich, Lucerne, Lugano, Stresa. September: Travels on alone to Swiss sanatorium Erlenbach on Lake Zürich. September 30: Attends Yom Kippur service at Prague's Altneu Synagogue; first mention in letters and diaries of more than passing mention to his Jewish faith. October 11: Attendance at a performance of a Yiddish theatre troupe from Lemberg at Café Savoy, a revelation; friendship with leading actor, Yitzchak Löwy. 1911-1913: writes some thirty diary entries on aspects of Yiddish theatre; burgeoning interest in Judaism. Late in the year: Becomes a silent partner, with brother-in-law Karl Hermann, in the first asbestos factory in Prague-Žižkov (Prager Asbestwerke Hermann & Co.).

1912 – February 18: Organizes recitation by Yitzchak Löwy at Prague's Jewish Town Hall and delivers introductory address on the Yiddish language. Winter months: Works on first novel, *Der Verschollene / Amerika* (also translated as *The Man Who Disappeared; The Missing Person*). June: Travels with Max to Weimar, Dresden, Leipzig; meets publisher Ernst Rowohlt who offers to publish first collection of short prose pieces. July 8: Travels alone to Jungborn nature therapy resort in the Harz Mountains. August 13: Meets Felice Bauer at the Brod home in Prague. September 20: Writes first letter to Felice. September 22-23: overnight, writes breakthrough story "The Judgement" ("Das Urteil"), dedicated to "Miss F.B." October: Distressed over having to take charge at the Prague Asbestos Works Hermann & Co., in which he is co-proprietor; considers suicide. November 17- December 6: Interrupts work on novel (*Amerika*) to write *The Metamorphosis* (*Die Verwandlung*). Mid-December: Publication of first book, *Meditation* (*Betrachtung*) with Kurt Wolff at Rowohlt; collection of eighteen short prose pieces written between 1904 and 1912.

1913 – Extensive correspondence with Felice whom he visits three times in Berlin. Promoted to vice-secretary at the Insurance Institute. Publication of "The Stoker" ("Der Heizer"; first chapter of *Amerika*) with Kurt Wolff (who took over from Rowohlt). June: Publication of "The Judgement" in *Arkadia*; Max Brod, publisher. September: Travels to Vienna on business. Meets physician and novelist Ernst Weiss. Travels on alone to Trieste, Venice (sends break-up letter to Felice), Verona, Desenzano, Riva del Garda. October 30: Meets Grete Bloch, Felice's intermediary, in Prague; intense one-year correspondence with Grete ensues.

1914 – June 1: Official engagement to Felice in Berlin. July 11: Engagement is dissolved at Hotel Askanischer Hof, Berlin. July 12: Travels to Lübeck, then on to Marielyst on Falster Island, Denmark with Ernst Weiss and girlfriend Hanni Bleschke (later actress and writer, Rahel Sansara). August: Begins writing *The Trial* (*Der Prozess*). October-November: Writes *In the Penal Colony* (*In der Strafkolonie*). Continues working on *Amerika*.

1915 – January 23: Reunion with Felice at Bodenbach (Děčin). March: At age thirty-one moves to his own apartment at 22 Bilekgasse (Bilkova). March 25: Meets Georg Morchechai Langer. April: Travels with Elli to eastern Hungary to visit her husband Karl Hermann at the front. July: Vacations at Sanatorium Rumburg (Rumburk), north Bohemia. November: Publication of *The Metamorphosis* (*Die Verwandlung*) with Kurt Wolff.

1916 – July 3 -13: Vacations with Felice in Marienbad; July 13-26, stays on at Marienbad, meets up with Georg Langer. Republication of "The Judgement" ("Das Urteil") in Kurt Wolff's Young Writers' Series. From November writes by night on Alchemists' Lane (Alchemistengasse), stories to be collected in *A Country Doctor* (*Ein Landarzt*)). November 10: Travels to Munich; reads from *In the Penal Colony* at Galerie-Kunst Hans Goltz; Felice is present.

1917 – March: Rents a room at Schönborn Palace. Continues writing by night on Alchemists' Lane. July: Felice comes to Prague; second engagement. Travels with Felice to Budapest and Arad, Hungary; returns via Vienna alone. August 12-13: Pulmonary hemorrhage; start of tuberculosis. From September: In Zürau (Siřem) west Bohemia under Ottla's care. From October: Writes reflections; later named aphorisms. December: Second engagement to Felice formally dissolved in Prague. Application is made to liquidate Prague Asbestos Works Hermann & Co.

1918 – January-April in Zürau: Continues work on reflections / aphorisms. May: Returns to work at the Insurance Institute. November: Contracts Spanish flu. November 30 - December 24: Convalesces at Pension Stüdl in Schelesen (Želizy), central Bohemia.

1919 – January 22 - end of March: Convalesces at Pension Stüdl, Schelesen. Meets Julie Wohryzek. Spring and summer: Courts Julie in Prague. Summer engagement. November: Publication of *In the Penal Colony* with Kurt Wolff; marriage to Julie postponed; writes long indicting "Letter to His Father" at Pension Stüdl in Schelesen.

1920 – Promotion to institute secretary. April 3 - June 29: Convalesces in Merano, northern Italy. Intense correspondence with Czech translator, Milena Jesenská. May: Publication of *A Country Doctor*, dedicated "To My Father"; Kurt Wolff publisher. June 30 - July 4: Visits Milena in Vienna. July: Engagement to Julie Wohryzek dissolved. August 14: Reunites with Milena in Gmünd, Austrian / Czech bordertown. September - December: Writes several short stories in Prague; published posthumously. December 18: Begins convalescence at Matliary, Tatra Mountains, Slovakia.

1921 – January-August 20: Continues convalescing at Matliary; friendship with Robert Klopstock. October: Hands diaries over to Milena in Prague. (She already holds manuscripts of *Amerika* and "Letter to His Father.") Writes "First Sorrow" ("Erstes Leid"); one of four stories in *A Hunger Artist* (*Ein Hungerkünstler*), published by Die Schmiede, 1924.

1922 – January - February: Convalesces at Spindelmühle (Špindlerův Mlýn), east Bohemia; begins writing The Castle (Das Schloss). Continues work on *The Castle* in Prague; reads beginning section to Max Brod. Writes "A Hunger Artist" ("Ein Hungerkünstler"). June: Promoted to secretary general and retired with pension. June 23 - September 18: At Planá, south Bohemia with Ottla. End of August / beginning of September: Abandons work on *The Castle*.

1923 – July 10 - August 8: Vacations at Müritz (Graal-Müritz) on the Baltic Sea. Meets Dora Diamant. September 23 - March 17, 1924: Lives under Dora's care in inflation-ridden Berlin. Writes "A Little Woman" ("Eine kleine Frau") and "The Burrow" ("Der Bau"); other stories are destroyed or lost.

1924 – Health deteriorates. March: Returns to Prague with Max Brod. Writes last story: "Josephine the Singer, or the Mouse Folk" ("Josefine, die Sängerin oder Das Volk der Mäuse") at his parents' apartment, Oppelt-Haus, Old Town Square; published in Prague's *Prager Presse*, April 20, along with "A Little Woman"; both are included in *A Hunger Artist*. April 19: Transferred to Hoffmann Sanatorium in Kierling. June 3: Dies. June 11: Buried at the New Jewish Cemetery, Prague-Strašnice. June 6: Milena Jesenská's obituary appears in *Národní Listy*.

Acknowledgements

I extend my sincere thanks to the editors and publishers of the following publications in which pieces in *Faithfully Seeking Franz* first appeared, most in earlier iterations:

Before the Door: *Shape Taking*. Ekstasis Editions, 2021.

Kafka's Death House: *White Wall Review*, March 1, 2022: https://whitewallreview.com/kafkas-death-house/

At the Cemetery: *Cargo Literary*, July 18, 2018 under the title "Kafka at the Cemetery": https://cargoliterary.com/kafka-at-the-cemetery/. An earlier version was a finalist for *The Malahat Review, 2017 Constance Rooke Prize.*

Paging Kafka's Elegist: Winner of *The New Quarterly* Edna Staebler Personal Essay Contest; Issue 136, Fall 1915; republished in *Best Canadian Essays*, 2016, Tightrope Books.

Kafka-in-Between: *Wanderlust Journal*, March 8, 2018: https://wanderlust-journal.com/2018/03/08/kafka-in-between-by-elana-wolff/

Resurrecting Frank's Foot: *Humber Literary Review*, Vol. 4, Issue 2, Fall/Winter, 2017/18.

Two Short Talks: *Brick Books*, March 12, 2015 under the title "Two Short Talks by Anne Carson: An Appreciation," part of a commemorative project celebrating Brick Books 40th Anniversary: https://www.brickbooks.ca/week-11-anne-carson-and-short-talks-presented-by-elana-wolff/

At Weisser Hirsch: *Wanderlust Journal*, December 15, 2018 under the title "Kafka at Weisser Hirsch": https://wanderlust-journal.com/2018/12/15/kafka-at-weisser-hirsch-by-elana-wolff/

What More Is There to Say of Hearts: *Adelaide Literary Magazine*, May 19, 2019
http://adelaidemagazine.org/2019/05/19/calm-by-elana-wolff-2/; republished in *Swoon* (Guernica Editions, 2020.)

Back at the Office: *Wanderlust Journal*, April 11, 2019 under the title "Faithfully Seeking Franz: Revisiting the Office." An earlier version was published under the title "Faithfully Seeking Franz: The Office Stop" in *New Madrid, Journal of Contemporary Literature*, Summer 2017 and listed in *The Best American Essays*, 2018, Hilton Als, editor, among Notable Essays and Literary Nonfiction of 2017.

In Berlin: *Eclectica Magazine*, January 2020 under the title "After Kafka in Berlin": http://www.eclectica.org/v24n1/wolff.html

K.: *Shirim: A Jewish Poetry Journal, Canandian Jewish Poetry Issue*, Vol. XXIX, No. 11 (2011) & Vol. XXX, No. 1, 2012; republished in *Everything Reminds You of Something Else* (Guernica Editions, 2017).

At Marienbad: *The Nashwaak Review*, Volume 40/41, Number 1, Fall/Winter 2018/19 under the title "This Year in Marienbad: Tracking Kafka."

So Good at This: *Acta Victoriana*, 143.2, Spring 2019, republished in *Swoon* (Guernica Editions, 2020).

Franz Among the Animals: GRIFFEL 2, January 2020: https://www.griffel.no/article/franz-among-the-animals/

Ottla: *Literary Review of Canada*, Vol. 6, No. 4, May 2018 under the title "Ottla Kafka"; republished under the same title in *Swoon*. Guernica Editions, 2020.

Surfacing Behaviour: *Grain: the journal of eclectic writing*, Volume 45, No. 4, Summer 2018; republished in *Swoon*. Guernica Editions, 2020.

Concatentations: Hotel Gabrielli-Sandwirth, 1913 / 2019: *Sepia Journal*, January 15, 2021:
https://thesepia.org/blog/6brced5lcr1uccb1vznqtkujy9um6l

Tactitly / Translating: *Shape Taking*. Ekstasis Editions, 2021.

At Planá: *Eunoia Review*, May 18, 2020 under the title "Tracking Franz at Planá": https://eunoiareview.wordpress.com/2020/05/18/tracking-franz-at-plana

Graal-Müritz: *The Bangalore Review*, September 2019 under the title "Franz at Müritz": http://bangalorereview.com/2019/09/franz-at-muritz/

Trumpeldor Cemetery: *The Beauty of Being Elsewhere Anthology*. Hidden Brook Press, 2021.

Rereading "Conversation with the Supplicant" in the Pandemic: *Literature for the People*, Issue 2, April 2021.

Concern for Soul Consumes Me: *Literary Review of Canada*, Vol. 30, No. 9, November, 2022. Included in *Best Canadian Poetry 2024*. Editor, Bardia Sinaee. Biblioasis, 2023.

Gratitude to my colleagues in The Long Dash writing group: John Oughton, Mary Lou Soutar-Hynes, Sheila Stewart, Clara Blackwood, Brenda Clews, Merle Nudelman, and Kath MacLean. My writing life is immeasurably enriched by our exchanges and camaraderie over poetry.

Gratitude to Sandra Barry, Hanna Grünfeld, and Thor Polson for their valuable feedback on individual pieces in this collection.

Gratitude to Regine Kurek, founder and director of *Arscura: School for Living Art* for her gifts of creativity and exceptional mentoring at Arscura and beyond.

Gratitude to Conan Tobias, publisher and editor of *Taddle Creek* magazine for his longstanding support of my writing and for recommending me for an Ontario Arts Council grant, which contributed to defraying quest-costs to Denmark in 2022.

Gratitude to Elizabeth Greene, Carmelo Militano, B. W. Powe, and J. J. Steinfeld for reading a draft of this work and writing such perspicacious words in support.

Thanks to the jurors at Exile Editions for shortlisting my suite of poems, "After Kafka," for the *2021 Gwendolyn MacEwen Poetry Prize*. The following pieces from the suite are included in *Faithfully Seeking Franz*: "Before the Door," "Merano, 1920 / 2019," "Sanatorium Hartungen, *Riva del Garda*," "Mary Lou Paints the Little House on Her iPad," "Snapshots from Pension Stüdl, *Schelesen / Želízy, Central Bohemia*," "Tacitly / Translating," and "K. Under Erasure."

Special thanks to Guernica Editions publishers Connie McParland and Michael Mirolla and associate publisher Anna van Valkenburg for their continuing faith in my writing and tireless support of authors and literature in Canada and internationally. It is my pleasure and privilege to have my work on Guernica. Added thanks to Michael Mirolla for his kind professionalism and diligence in preparing the manuscript of *Faithfully Seeking Franz* for publication, inspirited in this case by a mutual appreciation for all things Kafka. Thanks to my colleague, Julie Roorda, for her fine editorial eye and supportive, insightful comments on the final draft of the manuscript. Thanks to designer Errol F. Richardson for his expertise and adroitness in bringing my vision for the cover and interior of this book into being.

Deep thanks to my dear family, most of all to my husband and life-partner-in-quest, Menachem Wolff.

Sources

Angier, Carole. 2021. *Speak, Silence: In Search of W.G. Sebald*. London: Bloomsbury Circus.

Bachelard, Gaston. 1994. *The Poetics of Space*, trans. Maria Jolas. New Foreword by John R. Stilgoe. Boston: Beacon Press.

Balint, Benjamin. 2018. *Kafka's Last Trial: The Case of a Literary Legacy*. New York: W. W. Norton.

Begley, Louis. 2008. *Franz Kafka: The Tremendous World I Have Inside My Head*. New York: Atlas & Co.

Brod, Max. 1995. *Franz Kafka: A Biography*, trans. G. Humphreys Roberts and Robert Winston. New York: Da Capo Press, Inc. in the name of Schocken Books. (Originally published in 1937.)

Brod, Max. 1955. *Ha-Tira / The Castle*, a dramatization of *Das Schloss / The Castle* by Franz Kafka. trans. A. D. Shapir. Tel Aviv: Schocken Publishing House.

Buber-Neumann, Margarete. 1988. *Milena*, trans. Ralph Manheim. New York: Arcade Publishing by arrangement with Sever Books.

Canetti, Elias. 1974. *Kafka's Other Trial: The Letters to Felice*, trans. Christopher Middleton. New York: Schocken Books.

—2005. *Party in the Blitz*, trans. Michael Hofmann. London: The Harvill Press, Random House.

Carson, Anne. 1992. *Short Talks*. Toronto: Brick Books.

Collis, Stephen. 2018. *Almost Islands: Phyllis Webb and the Pursuit of the Unwritten*. Vancouver: Talonbooks.

Corngold, Stanley, editor. 2009. *Franz Kafka: The Office Writings*. Princeton: Princeton University Press.

Costa, Margaret Jull. 2020, Summer. "The Art of Translation No. 7," *The Paris Review*, Issue 233:176-207.

Deleuze, Gilles and Guattari, Felix. 1986. *Kafka: Toward a Minor Literature*, trans. Dana Polan. Minneapolis: University of Minneapolis Press.

Downden, Stephen D. 1995. *Kafka's Castle and the Critical Imagination*. London: Camden House.

Dror, Miriam, editor. 1984. *Me'at Tsori: Asupat Ketavav / Collected*

Writings of Georg Mordechai Langer. Jerusalem: Hosta'at Agudat Ha-sofrim Ha-Ivriim Bi-medinat Israel.

Friedländer, Saul. 2013. *Franz Kafka: The Poet of Shame and Guilt*. New Haven, CT.: Yale University Press.

Gilman, Sander. 1995. *Franz Kafka: The Jewish Patient*. London: Routledge.

—2005. *Franz Kafka*. London: Reaktion Books Ltd.

Gray, Richard T, Ruth V. Gross, Rolf J. Goebel, and Clayton Koelb. 2005. *A Franz Kafka Encyclopedia*. Westport, Conneticut: Greenwood Press.

Grillparzer, Franz. 1967; 1848. *The Poor Fiddler*, trans. Alexander and Elizabeth Henderson. Introduction by Ivar Ivesk. New York: Frederick Ungar Publishing Co.

Heibut, Anthony. 1996. *Thomas Mann: Eros and Literature*. New York: Alfred A. Knopf.

Heller, Erich. 1974. *Franz Kafka*. Princeton: Princeton University Press.

Fuentes, Carlos. 2005. *This I Believe: An A to Z of a Life*, trans. Kristina Cordero. New York: Random House.

Halper, Shaun Jacob. 2011. "Coming out of the Hasidic Closet: Jiří Mordechai Langer (1894-1944) and the Fashioning of Homosexual-Jewish Identity." *The Jewish Quarterly*, Volume 101, Number (189-231).

Hockaday, Mary. 1995. *Kafka, Love and Courage: The Life of Milena Jensenská*. New York: The Overlook Press.

Janouch, Gustav. 1985. *Conversations with Kafka*, trans. Goronwy Rees. London, Melbourne and New York: Quartet Books.

Kafka, Franz. 1946. *Amerika*, trans. Willa and Edwin Muir. Preface by Klaus Mann. Afterword by Max Brod. New York: A New Directions Paperback by arrangements with Schocken Books.

—1946. *The Castle*, trans. Willa and Edwin Muir. Additional materials translated by Eithne Wilkins and Ernst Kaiser. With an homage by Thomas Mann. New York: Alfred A. Knopf.

—1960. *The Great Wall of China. Stories and Reflections*, trans. Willa and Edwin Muir. New York: Schocken Books.

—1961. *In the Penal Colony: Stories and Short Pieces*, trans. Willa and

Edwin Muir. New York: Schocken Books.

—1962. *Amerika*, trans. Willa and Edwin Muir. New York: Schocken Books.

—1964. *Ha-Mishpat* (Hebrew edition of *The Trial*), trans. Yeshurun Keshet. Tel Aviv: Schocken Publishing House.

—1972. *The Metamorphosis*, trans. Stanley Corngold. New York: Bantam Dell, A Division of Random House Inc.

—1973. *The Great Wall of China and Other Short Works*, trans. Malcolm Pasley. London: Penguin Books.

—1973; 2016. *Letters to Felice*, trans. James Stern and Elisabeth Duckworth. Introduction by Erich Heller. New York: Schocken Books.

—1974; 1982. *Letters to Ottla & the Family*, trans. Richard and Clara Winston. Edited by Nahum N. Glatzer. New York: Schocken Books.

—1975. *Kafka: Parables and Paradoxes*, Bilingual Edition, trans. Clement Greenberg, Ernst Kaiser and Eithne Wilkins, and Tania and James Stern. Selected and edited by Nahum N. Glatzer. New York: Schocken Books.

—1976. *Franz Kafka: Diaries 1910-1923*. Edited by Max Brod, trans. Joseph Kresh, Martin Greenberg and Hannah Arendt. New York: Schocken Books. (First published in two volumes, 1948 and 1949.)

—1976. *The Complete Stories*, trans. Willa and Edwin Muir and Tania and James Stern. New York: Schocken Books.

—1978. *Letters to Friends, Family and Editors*, trans. Richard and Clara Winston. London: John Calder.

—1983. *The Complete Stories*, trans. Willa and Edwin Muir and Tania and James Stern. Foreword by John Updike. New York: Schocken Books.

—1990. *Letters to Milena*, trans. Philip Boehm. New York: Schocken Books.

—1992. *Nachgelassene Schriften und Fragmente II*. Frankfurt am Main: S. Fischer Verlag.

—1994. *Ti-ur shel Ma-avak* (Hebrew edition of *Beschreibung eines Kampfes / Description of a Struggle*), trans. Avraham Carmel. Tel Aviv: Schocken Publishing House.

—1996. *The Metamorphosis*, trans. Stanley Corngold. New York:

Norton Critical Edition.

—1997. *Ha-Ne-edar* (Hebrew edition of *Der Verschollene / The Missing Person*), trans. Avraham Carmel. Tel Aviv: Schocken Publishing House.

—1998. *Machbarōt Ha-Octavo* (Hebrew edition of *The Octavo Notebooks*), trans. Ilana Hammerman. Tel Aviv: Am Oved Publishers Ltd.

—1998. *The Castle*, trans. Mark Harman. New York: Schocken Books.

—1998. *The Trial*, trans. Breon Mitchell. New York: Schocken Books.

—2000. *Rofeh Kafri* (Hebrew edition of *A County Doctor* and other pieces published in Kafka's lifetime), trans. Ilana Hammerman and Nili Mirsky. Tel Aviv: Am Oved Publishers Ltd.

—2002. *Amerika: The Man Who Disappeared*, trans. Michael Hofmann. New York: New Directions Books.

—2002. *Das Schloss*. Frankfurt am Main: S. Fischer Verlag.

—2006. *The Zürau Aphorisms of Franz Kafka*, trans. Michael Hofmann. Commentary by Roberto Calasso. New York: Schocken Books.

—2007. *Metamorphosis and Other Stories*, trans. Michael Hofmann. Introduction by Michael Hofmann. New York: Penguin Group.

—2007. *Ha-Yona sh'al Ha-Gag* (Hebrew edition of *Letter to His Father* and Selections from the Estate, II), trans. Ilana Hammerman. Tel Aviv: Am Oved Publishers Ltd.

—2008. *Amerika: The Missing Person*, trans. Mark Harman. New York: Schocken Books.

—2008. *Metamorphosis and Other Stories*, trans. Michael Hofmann. New York: Schocken Books.

—2009. *The Castle*, trans. Anthea Bell. Oxford: Oxford World Classics.

—2012. *A Hunger Artist and Other Stories*, trans. Joyce Crick. Oxford. Oxford World Classics.

—2015. (Second printing.) *A Hunger Artist and Other Stories*, trans. Thor Polson. Toronto: Guernica Editions, Inc. Title on added title page, inverted: *Poems and Songs of Love*. Langer, Georg Mordechai. Translated from the Hebrew by Elana and Menachem Wolff

—2020. *Ha-Tira* (Hebrew edition of *Das Schloss / The Castle*), trans. Nili Mirsky and Ran Ha-Cohen. Tel Aviv: Achuzat Bayit Publishing House.

—2020. *The Lost Writing*. Texts from Volume 2 of *Nachgelassene Schriften und Fragmenten*, trans. Michael Hofmann. Selection and afterword by Reiner Stach. New York: New Directions Books.

—2022. *The Aphorisms of Franz Kakfa*, trans. Shelley Frisch. Edited, introduced, and with commentary by Reiner Stach. Princeton and Oxford: Princeton University Press.

—2022. *Diaries*, trans. Ross Benjamin. New York: Schocken Books.

Karl, Frederick, R. 1991. *Franz Kafka: Representative Man*. Boston: Houghton Mifflin Company.

Langer, Georg Mordechai (Jiří). 1961. *Nine Gates*, trans. Stephen Jolly. Plymouth: James Clarke & Co. Ltd. Foreword by František Langer.

—2006. *Die Erotik der Kabbala*. Darmstadt, Germany: Melzer Verlag.

—2015 (Second printing). *Poems and Songs of Love / Piyyutim ve-Shirei Yedidōt* (Prague: Dr. Josef Fläsch, 1929). Translated from the Hebrew by Elana and Menachem Wolff. Toronto: Guernica Editions Inc. Title on added title page, inverted: Kafka, Franz. *A Hunger Artist and Other Stories*. Translated from the German by Thor Polson.

Koch, Hans-Gerd. 2008. *Kafka in Berlin*. Berlin: Verlag Klaus Wagenbach.

Kundera, Milan. 1996. *Testaments Betrayed: An Essays in Nine Parts*, trans. Linda Asher. London: Faber and Faber.

Mann, Thomas. 1975. *The Magic Mountain*, trans. H. T. Lowe-Porter. Middlesex, England: Penguin Books in Association with Martin Secker & Warburg.

—1996. *The Magic Mountain*, trans. John E. Woods. New York: Vintage International, A Division of Random House Inc.

—1999. *Death in Venice and Other Tales*, trans. Joachim Neugroschel. New York: Penguin Classics.

Miller, Elaine P. 2014. *Head Cases*. New York: Columbia University Press.

Murray, Nicholas. 2004. *Kafka*. London: Abacus.

Pawel, Ernst. 1984. *The Nightmare of Reason: A Life of Franz Kafka*. New York: Quality Paper Book Club.

Preece, Julian, editor. 2002. *The Cambridge Companion to Kafka*.

Cambridge: Cambridge University Press.

Rolleston, James, editor. 2006. *A Companion to the Works of Franz Kafka*. New York: Camden House.

Rushdie, Salman. 2021. *Language of Truth: Essays 2003-2020*. London: Jonathan Cape.

Salfellner, Harald. 2008. *Kafka's Prague*, trans. Anthony Northey. Prague: Vitalis.

Sebald, W. G. 1999. *Vertigo*, trans. Michael Hulse. New York: New Directions Books.

Smith, Zadie. 2009. *Changing My Mind: Occasional Essays*. London: Hamish Hamilton.

Sokel, Walter. 2002. *The Myth of Power and the Self: Essays on Franz Kafka*. Detroit: Wayne State University Press.

Stach, Reiner. 2005; 2013 in paperback. *Kafka: The Decisive Years*, trans. Shelley Frisch. Princeton: Princeton University Press.

—2013. *Kafka: The Years of Insight*, trans. Shelley Frisch. Princeton and Oxford: Princeton University Press.

—2016. *Is that Kafka? 99 Finds*, trans. Kurt Beals. New York: New Directions Books.

—2017. *Kafka: The Early Years*, trans. Shelley Frisch. Princeton and Oxford: Princeton University Press.

—2020. *The Lost Writings*, selected by Reiner Stach from volume two of *Nachgelassene Schriften und Fragmente*, trans. Michael Hofmann. New York: New Directions Books.

Tokarczuk, Olga. 2017. *Flights*, trans. Jennifer Croft. London: Fitzcarraldo Editions.

Unseld, Joachim. 1982. *Franz Kafka: A Writer's Life*, trans. Paul D. Dvořák. Riverside, California: Ariadne Press. .

Wagenbach, Klaus. 1964, 2002, 2003. *Kafka*, trans. Ewald Osers. Introduction by Ritchie Robertson. London: Haus Publishing.

—1968. *Franz Kafka 1883-1924*, Catalogue from an exhibition at the Goethe Institute, Munich. Berlin: Akademie der Künste.

—1984. *Franz Kafka: Pictures of a Life*, trans. Arthur S. Wensinger. New York: Pantheon Books.

—1996. *Kafka's Prague: A Travel Reader*, trans. Shaun Overside. New York: The Overlook Press.

—2003. *Kafka: A Life in Prague*, trans. Ewald Osers. Introduction by Ritchie Richardson. London: Armchair Traveller at the Book Haus.

Weiss, Ernst. 2008. *Franziska*, trans. Anthea Bell. London: Pushkin Press.

Woods, James. 2018. *How Fiction Works.* (Tenth anniversary edition.) New York: Farrar, Straus and Giroux.

Woods, Michelle. 2017. *Kafka Translated: How Translators have Shaped our Reading of Kafka.* New Delhi: Bloomsbury Publishing India.

Woolf, Virginia. 1992. *Mrs. Dalloway.* London: Penguin Books.

Yalom, Irvin D. 1992. *When Nietzsche Wept.* New York: Basic Books.

About the Author

Elana Wolff is the author of eight collections of poetry and a collection of short essays on poems. She has also co-authored, with the late Malca Litovitz, a collection of rengas; co-authored, with Susie Petersiel Berg, a limited-edition chapbook of poems; and co-translated, with Menachem Wolff, poems from the Hebrew by Georg Mordechai Langer—part of a joint Kafka-Langer flipside book (translations by Thor Polson of late stories by Franz Kafka). Elana's writing has been widely published in Canada and internationally and has garnered awards. She has taught English for Academic Purposes at York University in Toronto and at The Hebrew University in Jerusalem. She currently lives and works in Thornhill, Ontario.

Also by Elana Wolff

POETRY:

Birdheart
Mask
You Speak to Me in Trees, Winner of the F. G. Bressani Prize; short-listed for the Acorn-Plantos Award for People's Poetry
Startled Night, nominated for the ReLit Award
Helleborus & Alchémille (Bilingual editions of poems selected from *Birdheart, Mask, You Speak to Me in Trees* and *Startled Night*; French translation by Stéphanie Roesler), Awarded the John Glassco Prize in Literary Translation
Everything Reminds You of Something Else
Swoon, Winner of Canadian Jewish Literary Award for Poetry
Shape Taking

ESSAYS:

Implicate Me: Short Essays on Contemporary Poems, with an introduction by Ellen S. Jaffe

CO-AUTHORED:

Slow Dancing: Creativity and Illness (Rengas and Dulogue), with Malca Litovitz
You Will Still Have Birds: a conversation in poems, limited edition chapbook with Susie Petersiel Berg
Songs and Poems of Love by Georg Mordechai Langer, original translation from the Hebrew with Menachem Wolff; a flipside book including A *Hunger Artist & Other Stories* by Franz Kafka, translation by Thor Polson

CO-EDITED:

Poet to Poet: Poems written to poets and the stories than inspired them, with Julie Roorda

Printed by Imprimerie Gauvin
Gatineau, Québec